Far Above The World

PAUL MORLEY

Far Above The World

THE TIME AND SPACE OF
DAVID BOWIE

Copyright © Paul Morley 2025

The right of Paul Morley to be identified as the Author of
the Work has been asserted by him in accordance with the
Copyright, Designs and Patents Act 1988.

First published in 2025 by Headline Publishing Group Limited

1

Apart from any use permitted under UK copyright law,
this publication may only be reproduced, stored, or transmitted,
in any form, or by any means, with prior permission in writing
of the publishers or, in the case of reprographic production,
in accordance with the terms of licences issued by
the Copyright Licensing Agency.

Please refer to page 380 for picture credits.

Cataloguing in Publication Data is available from the British Library.

Hardback ISBN 9781472289476
Trade Paperback ISBN 9781472289469

Designed and typeset by EM&EN
Printed and bound in Great Britain by Clays Ltd, Elcograf S.p.A.

Headline's policy is to use papers that are natural, renewable and recyclable
products and made from wood grown in well-managed forests and other
controlled sources. The logging and manufacturing processes are expected
to conform to the environmental regulations of the country of origin.

Headline Publishing Group Limited
An Hachette UK Company
Carmelite House
50 Victoria Embankment
London EC4Y 0DZ

The authorised representative in the EEA is Hachette Ireland,
8 Castlecourt Centre, Dublin 15, D15 XTP3, Ireland (email: info@hbgi.ie)

www.headline.co.uk
www.hachette.co.uk

TO

e.s.p.

All I need is a sheet of paper and
something to write with, and then
I can turn the world upside down.
FRIEDRICH NIETZSCHE

Life is a blank canvas, and you need to
throw all the paint on it you can.
DANNY KAYE

CONTENTS

SEEING AND BELIEVING 1

GENTLENESS AND CLARITY 5

BE ALL AND END ALL 7

FANTASY AND REALITY 10

SURVIVAL AND EXISTENCE 13

PERSONAL AND IMPERSONAL 15

RULES AND ETHICS 20

SHOW AND BUSINESS 29

GLORIOUS AND INSANE 31

REAL AND UNREAL 34   CURIO AND CURIO 36

BLACK AND WHITE 44

ARRIVAL AND DEPARTURE 48

SMOKE AND MIRRORS 51

BEGINNING AND THEN 54

COMING AND GOING 61

EXPERIENCE AND KNOWLEDGE 70

TRIAL AND ERROR 73

STRANGE AND STRANGER 76

LOVE AND OBSESSION 87

BACK AND FORTH 94

AMBITION AND ARROGANCE 106

SHADOWS AND DUST 113

THOUGHTS AND PRAYERS 116

SOMETHING AND NOTHING 119

ETERNITY AND A DAY 124

LUCK AND TRAGEDY 133

HOPE AND VISION 137

PEOPLE AND PLACES 140

TOUCH AND GO 142

ONE AND THE SAME 144   MYSTERY AND ACTION 148

IDENTITY AND OPPOSITION 154

FANTASY AND ECSTASY 156

MAD AND BEAUTIFUL 159

FREAK AND SHOW 167

LIGHT AND DARK 172

FUNK AND FOREMOST 174

HEAT AND WONDER 179

HIRE AND HIGHER 187

JOHN AND DAVID 189

REACT AND REFINE 193

CHER AND ALIKE   198

SERIOUS AND IMMINENT   201

DISEASE AND SHADOWS   208

PAST AND PRESENT   212

ACTING AND BEING   218

EGO AND CONTROL   227

SHOW AND HIDE   229

SECRET AND CERTAIN   233

COSMIC AND EARTH   240

SENSE AND FORCE   245

DREAM AND LOGIC   248   FAST AND SLOW   251

SONG AND TRANCE   254

COULD AND SHOULD   259

FIXED AND FITTING   261

DIRECTION AND MISDIRECTION   266

ART AND COMMERCE   269

EAST AND WEST   275

CHANCE AND ORDER   280

THREE AND MORE   284

RISING AND FALLING   290

ART AND DEATH   295

CRASH AND BURN 298

BEAUTY AND BEAST 302

BOWIE AND BOWIE 306

STRANGE AND DANGER 311

PAGEANTRY AND OFFSPRING 314

FACE AND FACT 317

THEN AND NOW 321

DRUM AND DANCE 323

SUIT AND TIE 330

DOWN AND OUT 332

TENSION AND ATTENTION 335   IMAN AND DAVID 339

OLD AND NEW 344

HOME AND AWAY 348

RETREAT AND REMAKE 352

GHOSTS AND ANGELS 358

REALITY AND BEYOND 366

WHERE AND WHEN 371

EVER AND EVER 375

Thanks and Noted 379

Look and Now 381

Index 382

SEEING AND BELIEVING

Look into his eyes.

The eyes that are different. One seems mortal, the other not so much. Put them together and what do you get? Beauty and the beast. Past and future. Happy and sad. Chance and mystery. Human and machine. Sage and sceptic. Positive and negative. Back and forth. Questions and answers. Popular culture and serious art. Demon and angel.

The eyes he used to put you in a spin. The eyes that give away everything and give away nothing. The arch of his eyebrows. The quizzical look. The sheer amusement. A trace of impatience. Some surprise, some distant fear, a constant gazing scrutiny. A sense of wonder.

One eye sees, the other eye feels. The eyes without speaking confess the secrets of the heart.

The eyes of David Bowie, flashing his soul and something other, seeing so many things the rest of us miss. The eyes that say the past, present and future is all the same. The David Bowie who is in his songs, as himself, as versions of himself, the public and private always colliding and commingling as he hides himself and reveals himself, perpetually constructing himself, always becoming.

The David Bowie who always looked so good in photographs because he knew what he looked like from every angle.

The David Bowie who knew what had made great art and great music from the beginning of time: the mystery of being.

The David Bowie who proclaimed we live in the mind, in ideas, in fragments. Who left traces of his self and his thinking in other ways and other forms, as though preparing for a world where he could be found outside the songs.

The eyes of David Bowie were on the future, especially a media future. Always fastidious about his image, ideas, appearance, about the processes involved in becoming David Bowie, he patiently gathered a collection of physical, professional and personal paraphernalia as he created himself and transformed his preoccupations and inherited mannerisms into a personal style. An accumulation of personal and commercial material that would eventually become a comprehensive, world-travelling exhibition, *David Bowie Is*, and a vast, permanent collection of everything Bowie in the David Bowie Centre at the V&A East in Stratford, London, to some extent the final resting place of the restless, roaming David Bowie. He'd leave behind clues, hints and abandoned projects that would only be discovered after he'd died.

There was another place he ended up, always on the move in his mind and the minds of others. He also created a less formal and controllable but equally valuable collection when, for nearly half a century, he talked on radio and television about himself, his desire to make connections in a lonely world, and his relationship to music as an art and to other musical artists.

This was at a time when it didn't seem possible that those often unheralded, here-today-gone-tomorrow, pre-digital appearances, and ultimately performances, would one day be readily available to hear and watch on TV and film screens, but also computer, phone screens and other machines.

Bowie was mostly living through a period when time passed and disappeared behind you, and there seemed more future ahead of you to be filled in than history banking up behind you and blocking the light. The idea seemed fantasy-remote of an instantly connected worldwide library of entertainment, a widely accessible, cheap archive of events, appearances, insights and moments, and sometimes revelations.

Even when he wasn't in the mood, or wasn't, for various reasons, in the best physical and mental shape to be seen in any kind of public setting, he would keep up what became through resources such as YouTube a significant way of watching the life of an artist as he designed his life as an artist. Bowie gifted us a series of calm, nervy, sensational, polite, unadorned, watchful, arrogant, excitable, stoned, friendly, touchy, wise, distracted, edgy, jaunty, quick, powerful Bowies as a form of autobiography, left behind as fragments to be hunted down and put together in whatever order you fancy. It was another of the ways he fucked with the fabric of time.

He was constantly captured, officially and unofficially, where he could be seen and heard talking about himself and promoting himself, so that future audiences could keep track of his movements and ideas all through his performing life. You can see his work and you can also see him *at* work.

Any comprehensive 'playlist' of David Bowie doesn't simply include the songs and the albums. There are his appearances and collaborations – and the incidental contributions of collaborators and observers – on talk shows, radio shows, award shows; in press conferences, interviews, confessions, films, pop videos, photographs and documentaries. There are performances on TV shows with a variety of his bands and supporting casts that, as time goes by, become as significant as the more formally arranged singles and albums.

This collection is now out there, electronically anywhere and everywhere, a multitude of Bowies generated by and for Bowie in a time and space he learnt to manipulate as he was going along for a canvas that didn't yet exist.

He produced – or invented – an insight into his life, beliefs and obsessions, which covered the breadth of his interests and the extent of his emotional craving, his hunger for experience of every kind, as if he knew this media landscape would eventually happen, or perhaps just in case it did. With the mind of a journalist as well as a writer, singer and artist, he had an instinct these appearances were not going to be temporary. In the future, when record albums, pop singles and twentieth-century pop culture were things of the past, he could be known as much by this accidental series as by his music, by this abstract reportage of him growing, learning, changing, questioning, retreating, recovering, explaining, starring.

Somewhere between knowing and not so knowing, and with the assistance of anonymous, obsessive aides, he planted a selective, splintered fusion of biography and autobiography into YouTube. Thousands of fragments and found moments travelling through time, existing from his teenage years to his final days, as he ages backwards and forwards, young and old at the same time. It's a way of following some of the extraordinary encounters and transformations he had during his life.

He rarely seemed to be in any kind of hurry, even as things happened so fast, covering so much ground, as his life of self-fashioning and self-reflexivity continued. He was assembling ghosts of himself that would be around far longer than he would.

These fragments and moments can be combined in numerous ways to tell the story of who he was and what he was up to as artist and performer, as a unique chronicler of the chaotic times he inhabited that previewed and anticipated even more chaotic times, a world at risk both from the world outside and from within ourselves. He grew increasingly convinced there would be ways his voice could still be heard and his image seen even after his life was over, and not only through the songs. How we would experience and manipulate reality through access to new technology would inevitably change by the twenty-first century, disrupt and reshape our perception of the world – there were previews and guesses of what that world might be in many of his songs – but the words and music, his stories and singing of Bowie, his wonder at the world and the life he found himself living, would exist in some form.

GENTLENESS AND CLARITY

Look into his eyes and listen to him speak. He knew how to use his voice in all sorts of beguiling ways. A soft, seductive and confident voice that pulls you closer and closer, as if he's only speaking to you. He's not forcing anything; he knows his own mind. At the same time, he knows you can never fully know your own mind: consciousness is mindreading turned inwards.

Watch him walk into a room with a kind of chivalrous grace – or, at least, watch him walk into a television studio or onto a stage straight-backed, eyes straight ahead – and appreciate how there was something dangerous about his allure.

Hello, David Bowie. Which is where we begin. Click. The recording starts. The camera shoots. He's all dressed up and ready to go. He always is, as far as we can tell, even for a radio interview. If he isn't, there's usually a reason – he's making some kind of statement for some to decode at some later stage.

The ever-present cigarette is lit. The handsome, bewitching smile appears. The teeth, postwar before, the derelict, bad teeth of Orwell's England, the mature, post-fame after. Before: crooked and crowded, eventually smoke stained – but maybe sexier than after, when the gaps were sorted, the discolouration removed and the angles corrected. When it's time to grow up, some time in his forties, the fangs that once gave him a delightful, wicked edge sadly disappear.

The question is asked and he has the answer. He says what he means. He has this tendency to go the long way round but he gets there. Eventually.

He's talking about something mundane like his tour schedule and when his next record is out as though he alone knows the unbearable truth about existence.

He's explaining about the tangible drone of sorrow that constantly passes through his music, however packed it is with excitement.

He's giving the answer along the lines of how negative emotions like loneliness, envy and guilt have important roles to play in living a creative life, or just in living at all, bravely facing the unknown. They're signals that something needs to change. They help create the high jinks, but the high jinks are nothing without the mystical insinuation.

BE ALL AND END ALL

It didn't take long after David Bowie died for people to start saying, sadly, that everything fell apart after he died on a stunning blue Monday in early January 2016. His soul-shaking, time-stopping departure wreaked havoc on the Earth, as if he alone had been placating the malevolent forces that challenge the equilibrium.

It was a shock beyond it being a shock that a legendary, beloved pop star, someone a generation or two had grown up with, had died too early, even if by only a few years. Something did seem to go missing, as if there was now menace hanging in the sterile air, a threat to mind and limb, to dreams and hope, to what once was that he'd often written about.

The man who sang of changes – in life, in circumstances, in appearance – as a special and necessary form of creative energy, as nature's delight – had now made the biggest change of all. His fans were not ready for this ultimate change, this spectacular exit, but also the universe itself didn't seem ready. When David Bowie died, the universe itself groaned. It too needed time to mourn. It slumped, lost in thought.

While it did, the world as we thought we knew it fell off its hinges. It revealed a grim new dystopian face, rotten and corrupt to the core leading to increasing disorientating chaos and a succession of catastrophes: fierce, unsolvable wars, pandemics, lockdowns, disasters and deprivations, political earthquakes, gang violence. Strongmen posed as saviours as though brute force was enough to see us through the world's dangers, psychopaths with reality TV backgrounds accidentally, or not, given real power, wondering if it was time to nuke a city. Storms, floods and forest fires, random shootings, rattling election results allowed incongruous-seeming, mind-narrowing movements to take over reality as though protecting us from 'enemies within' only they could see. It was becoming a world of nearly constant surveillance. Humanity's traditional sources of meaning – work, community, family and identity – were severely compromised. It was a sequence of events and daily frivolities that seemed to wipe away idealism and shut down open minds and limit possibilities. We entered a new era of rearmament. America abandoned its 80-year-long role as leader of the West. In Britain, and elsewhere, relative decline headed for terminal decline.

By the second decade of the twenty-first century, let's say after January 2016, the widespread belief following the Second World War – especially in Britain, Europe and America – that explosive but manageable seeming technological advances were about to cause a tremendous leap in progress for humanity switched to a different kind of widespread belief, pulsating out from America and the countries that had relied on it since the war for leadership and balance. The world was coming to an end – through overpopulation, pollution, the unreason of the natural world, plague, nuclear holocaust, social media-induced societal madness, the emergence of artificial intelligence, the cooling or overheating of the planet, the collapse of the British Empire followed by the disintegration of the American empire, the collapse of any distinction between the real and the super-real, between fact and fiction, truth and lie.

Sentences that once seem consigned to the past or film or TV fizzed and slashed through our lives from the media, which were always catching up with abrupt changes in circumstances and adopting and often normalising a doomsday mentality.

The West as we knew it is dead

The fall of what we believe is democracy

Tearing apart your ideological enemy, accusing them of doing exactly what you do

Freedom of expression under mortal threat

The rule of law is under attack

An epic demolition of freedom

Warning signs everywhere

A President who believes he is Judge Dredd and thinks he is infallible and can do whatever he wants; he needs loyalty, he expects loyalty – or he's comedian John Mulaney's horse loose in a hospital who's just fired the horse catcher because it turns out he can

He's hitting the reverse gear after years of change

Intellectual vandalism as a deliberate ideological purge

Nothing is true everything is permitted like nothing you have ever seen before

People being snatched from the streets for writing editorials in student newspapers or protesting about job losses

America's dictator-in-chief, the insurrectionist-in-chief

Flooding the zone with shit

Following the classic authoritarian playbook

The ball of string is unravelling

We're at the point when the truth stops mattering

What's the plan and how worried should we be?

FANTASY AND REALITY

Ideas were replaced by slogans. Nuanced thinking was replaced by flat, abbreviated and often illogical content. Twitter and then X and Truth, crudely simplifying the English language, were increasingly the home of hourly hate campaigns generating a directionless, or strategically targeted, wind-up mess of anger, abuse and conflict, of false claims and conspiracy theories. Much of this happened automatically through bots set up using generative artificial intelligence to amplify and redirect hate speech. You were being told who to be and what to think and where to look.

A bombardment of online ugliness, misogyny and disinformation started to leak into what was once more clearly the real world, but which increasingly seemed like the secondary world, or the debased, neglected underworld. Tech engineers were now the disrupters of reality and assumed civil order, adopting revolutionary techniques of dissent and disguise to smooth the way towards organising a slippery, reined in 'reality', where there was no place for independent thinking and dishonest conjecture reigned.

TikTok enabled influencers to become media superstars through the constant repetition of glib ideas and basic, self-advertising silliness. The progressive intellectual life of moral critiques and ethical idealism that Bowie savoured, a romantic view of the world, turned to ash.

The kind of thoughtful, articulate and radical celebrity like Bowie started to seem as out of place as a silent movie star, as though ideas and complicated thinking were now as quaint as Chaplin and Keaton.

The sweet utopian dream of the internet as the planet's loving, nurturing brain was replaced with real signs of it being at the centre of a book-burning, mind-shrinking, technologically controlled, dystopian nightmare. It took a turn from appealing to those who thought it could enhance a spirit of communal discovery and progress to becoming the perfect machine to celebrate, marshal and unleash the deviant strains of our personalities. Our imaginations, experiences and sensations were simply fuel to keep it operating and tighten its grip on our hearts and minds. It was built to replicate pleasure and to warp our psychologies, to keep us all in line.

There was too much reality, too much fantasy, one becoming the other in a weird, disorientating new mutation. There were too many influencers, commentators, disruptors, podcasters and advisors, with too many opinions and recommendations, spouting too many contradictions, and fewer ways to make sense of it all as everything crashed around us.

Information, gossip and conspiracies slithered into our minds through screens and channels that seemed under our control, but which were diverting us into our own lonely, individual alcoves. Inside our specially designed spaces, shrines built from computers and electronics, tailored to satisfy and confirm our own carefully calculated interests and desires, it would become increasingly difficult to know who to trust, who was telling you the truth, what was happening in what was left of the real world. It was as though we were being forced to endure constant consciousness, or constant self-consciousness, and yet losing track of our own identity.

At times, it seemed the only response was to shut ourselves down and start again. It might be too late, but perhaps the best way to fight this pressure and peril is with the imagination, if we can just hold onto it.

Hadn't David Bowie been telling us about this impending doom as he sent his characters – the damaged loners, lost selves, deviant freaks, super creeps, time-travelling explorers, disturbed individuals, stricken lovers, ecstatic show-offs – and, of course, himself on a quest to find meaning in a world of pain, violence and ultimately very human motivations?

SURVIVAL AND EXISTENCE

As soon as news of his death spread, there was a sudden and substantial change in the collective lives of Bowie fans. Time passed more strangely, which seemed to foreshadow the impact of the 2020/21 pandemic. (Bowie, ahead of things as usual, had been writing since the late 1960s about the finite nature of this life, about a heightened sense of urgency, about time playing tricks.) The years of isolation and uncertainty led to the mourning of the world we once knew and a period of anxiety as we waited for a new world to kick in – a fear of and anxiety at the free-for-all that followed the pandemic.

Maybe it wasn't merely fans and all forms of media going over the top in the years that followed Bowie's death, where everything went wrong and the world turned increasingly unsettled and frightening. Perhaps he really was the glue, the cosmic force, that held everything and everyone together. Since his death, what once seemed coherent about a maintenance of truth and reality, about the weather, about the democratic process, had become distorted, interfered with, fundamentally transformed.

Alternatively, perhaps, he was no such metaphysical adhesive, but he had become a consistently present and visible living symbol of the progressive minded, democratic, reality-supplying stability that seemed to stumble and crumble after January 2016. The stability that had been taken for a permanent state of affairs by those thoroughly locked inside it, a stability apparently confirmed by the fall of the Berlin Wall – with Bowie himself given some of the credit as a megaphone for new found freedom and togetherness.

It was as if someone in control of the simulation we were all inside lost concentration or fancied a different, more dissonant direction. The world didn't take a turn for the worst because he died, but he represented a time when his kind of thinking and curiosity, his kind of art and music, seemed at the centre, holding reality together. For those born at a certain time, this was how things should be, and it would take unimaginable insanity to challenge its apparent certainties and destiny. It was how things should be for those living in certain parts of the world, as the world recovered and repaired itself from a devastating and exhausting world war, its suddenly liberated youth looking for freedoms and methods of resisting the threats and shadows of the Atomic Age.

There was nothing new in a world dealing with darkness and violence, repression and commercialised, even glamorised, authoritarian control, destitution and decay, but the years following Bowie's death seemed different – the darkness darker than before, the chaos more virulent, the emotional and ideological violence more wilful. Our awareness of it happening was more acute, because the entertainment landscape now included never-ending sensationalist news of a world turning as deranged and self-destructive, as fractured and unreal, as any science fiction prophet had forecast.

Of course, the idea that a world of empathy, ethics and moral certainty had collapsed because of the death of Bowie, one damned thing leading to another, was the unquiet hyperbole of his fans, of those who viewed the consolations and distractions of popular culture as central to their lives.

It had become central to their lives because of the actions and discoveries of personalities and performers like David Bowie, channelling the visions, themes and militancy of the counterculture and the experimental fearlessness of the avant-garde into the mainstream where it could take charge of truth and reality, taking it out of the hands of the mean spirited, self-serving and destructive.

PERSONAL AND IMPERSONAL

Look where he is now. He's being interviewed by the equally sensitive and thoughtful Japanese musician Ryuichi Sakamoto in 1979, who he later acted with in *Merry Christmas, Mr. Lawrence*, one of his more compelling movies, one which seemed part of his unfolding world rather than existing somewhere else, outside him.

Bowie had just completed the series of albums on which he had collaborated with the experimental pop art musician Brian Eno, who he described as a small mobile high intelligent unit. Someone who didn't call himself a musician even as he worked in music, but who was interested in concepts and methodologies, which excited Bowie, always part musician part conceptual artist, part unorthodox singer who sometimes couldn't help but croon his heart out, part enthusiastic painter who sometime regretted he couldn't make a living from fine art. His collaboration with Eno reflected how he had tended to make albums that were about things other than just the music.

They both essentially made music as artists, following and defying art history as much as absorbing and manipulating music history, as did Sakamoto. All of them were attracted to what the classically trained Sakamoto would express to Bowie as the modernity and futurism – and inchoate dynamism – embedded in rock.

They talked about their shared interest in the early 1970s radical German music that blended rock energy, jazz improvisation and electronically generated avant-garde classical sound – bands like Can, Faust, Neu!, Cluster, La Düsseldorf. Eventually, its presence was felt in the cultural mainstream, in all forms of popular music, through Kraftwerk, a kind of intellectual classical quartet inspired by pop music form and pop culture content exploring how technology is evidence of a collective dream, who ultimately helped reverse the post-war image of Germany itself. Sakamoto, also coming from a background of classical musical theory, was part of Yellow Magic Orchestra, a Japanese pop group inspired by the electronics of Kraftwerk whose take on popular culture was more buoyant and joyous than Kraftwerk's, a knowing satire on the superficial Western view of Japanese orientalism. YMO were deliberately upbeat and excitable where Kraftwerk were deliberately brutalist and placid.

YMO would help adjust the post-war image of Japan. Michael Jackson, who was once thinking of asking Kraftwerk to produce him, toyed with including Yellow Magic Orchestra's instrumental 'Behind the Mask' on his world conquering *Thriller* album after his producer Quincy Jones played it to him. Jackson added words but a royalty dispute meant it never made the album, and it eventually appeared on the first posthumous Jackson album, *Michael*.

As they talk, Bowie takes the lead, as though Sakamoto is his student, a junior member of the pop and rock scheme of things, YMO coming after *Low* and *Heroes*. He loved showing off his knowledge. Bowie takes his 'lecture' about how the more experimental rock music had taken direction from serious avant-garde music into a short, sweet history of twentieth-century classical music. He moves from the early atonal furies of Arnold Schoenberg to his disobedient mid-century pupil John Cage, who broke away from what Cage thought still sounded nineteenth-century about Schoenberg.

Cage found abstract methods to make music without using conventional musical instruments – or if he did use them, he manipulated them in various ways, and sometimes made unusual use of them. He applied to composing music various theories, concepts and systems borrowed from science, religion, Eastern music and conceptual art, and his spiritual rearrangement of musical possibilities influenced a diverse group of musicians forming a new instrumental genre, given the label minimalist: the label's fab four were La Monte Young, Terry Riley, Steve Reich and Philip Glass. On the surface of their music there was incredible repetition, but beneath the surface, there was constant variation.

In the early 1970s, Eno had used some of these techniques of manipulation, adding warped sonics to the surreal, transmogrified pop songs of Roxy Music, and made his own forms of instrumental electronic minimalism presented as though he were a pop musician. His instruments were the synthesiser, which he didn't play with his hands but with his mind, and the studio, which theoretically could take sound as far you wanted it to go, and help you put sounds together as if you were combining objects as well as feelings.

He helped Bowie understand how you could apply minimalist techniques, and the playful compositional processes of John Cage, to pop music. He made the making of music a playground where you could find happiness through discovery. It was a way of being rock and pop but always finding new music, which by then was Bowie's favourite thing – being pop but being anomalous, recreating how alien and energising the pop music of American rock and rollers and then the Beatles, the Who and the Kinks actually was when it first appeared.

There's always new music out there, he says, optimistically, at just the moment he was at his most inventive at being a pop musician by making what he did new, by cracking open new worlds, and, in particular, by finding and adding the intangible – some elements that weren't necessarily an obvious part of a pop song.

For Bowie, the most exciting thing about what he would always call, even when it was long out of date to do so, *rock'n'roll*, or sometimes, in a more polite, almost square-sounding way, 'the rock genre', was that it allowed you more than anything else to be eclectic. It permitted you to borrow from everywhere.

Or, at least, it gave permission to those who allowed themselves to be permitted.

Originality was undetected plagiarism. Eno was very good and cunning at this – not thinking too much about what he was doing because that interfered with his plagiarism, and his methods of taking existing ideas and improving them. He'd think about it before and perhaps a little after – not too much because there was nothing you could do then – but not really when he was in the middle of doing something.

His intention always seemed to be to bring you closer to the creative process, something secret and private that is in the end for everyone.

One artist or another – Paul Gauguin, or TS Eliot, or Frank Zappa – once said that art was either plagiarism or revolutionary. Eno thought not. It was both.

Bowie, always craving surprise and magical variety, was a similar thinker, which is why they worked well together, if only for periods at a time. Plagiarism, in the sense of taking something else, erasing it and replacing it with your own unique version, was an important component in progress. It took a while for him to get the hang of it because he needed other models to copy – in his early days, it just looked like stealing, like barefaced imitation, but he learnt to disguise his sources or ecstatically celebrate them, and his plagiarism became elegant and erudite. It wasn't where you took things from. It was where you took them.

It began to feel as though he wasn't slipping on someone else's skin, he was slipping on his own. He wasn't dreaming in others' sleep, he was dreaming in his own.

Sakamoto was also partial to combining rock and pop structures and energies with the artful, experimental repetitions and insistency of the minimalists, but he listens patiently as Bowie explains to him that what he loved about the minimalists was their subtlety. You had to take your time listening to the changes in the music.

Sakamoto tells Bowie that he didn't really respond to Bowie's music before the *Low* album because it didn't sound interesting to him, but that it now had a kind of depth he understood. It's a very peaceful album, says Bowie. Sakamoto disagrees – spiritually, it was anything but peaceful. It was almost maniacal. It was tumultuous. Up to then, the conversation had been mediated by a translator but here, Bowie says in his rudimentary Japanese that he understands what Sakamoto means and he gives him a playful wink. Language, he would say, is the most ambiguous form of communication. The meanings of his lyrics do not lie on the surface but are embedded within. You have to look beneath to uncover hidden messages.

Bowie was having this captivating, serious conversation about music with another complicated, ambitious musician, shy but very sure of himself. Both are intensely interested in each other's techniques, methods and motivations in ways you often don't hear about outside of one artist talking to another.

RULES AND ETHICS

In 2002, Bowie was interviewed by the influential Danish film maker Thomas Vinterberg – or Bowie interviewed him. Both were equally charmed by the other, used to charming people into liking them, steering them away from the darker, more absurdist or sombre parts of their work and interests. Both put a disarming smile on things, having developed their own ways of not looking too deeply into the abyss and the irresistible, dangerous pull there is at the bottom, which can easily attract the curious, those who tend to be seduced by the unknown.

As Vinterberg arrives on the set, the cameras and crew in view, an ostentatiously formal Bowie is cheerfully humming to himself, legs crossed at the knee, pouring a drink, in his own world, acting as though he's surprised when Vinterberg interrupts him, that he is in fact in a professional setting. It's all an act but effortlessly created.

Vinterberg was part of a collection of young Danish directors who founded the Dogme 95 avant-garde film group and he had written its manifesto with fellow conspirator Lars von Trier, which included the severe, uncompromising anti-commercial, rules-based 'Vows of Chastity'. Vinterberg claimed they came up with their list of rules in half an hour, which included shooting only using a handheld camera and that the director's name must not be credited. They were committed to remodelling what cinema could be after more or less a hundred years of film making, replacing the special effects and digital coldness with emphasis on storytelling and performance.

Some suggested the 'sweet' and 'innocent' Vinterberg with his boyish glamour was being manipulated by the more abrasive and devil-may-care von Trier. The first Dogme films, of the 31

Dogme productions amongst the purest reflection of the vows' spirit, were Vinterberg's searing tragedy *Festen* and cheerful enfant terrible von Trier bad-taste black comedy *The Idiots*.

The conversation followed its own rules. Bowie and Vinterberg had 25 minutes to talk. They had never met before. Bowie had just released *Heathen*, his twenty-third studio album, with one of those cover photographs that seems to set him in some film that was never made, where he might place various film genres and film stars in a time and space of his own choosing. (The cover for *The Next Day*, his black and white *Heroes* front cover image brutally wiped out with a white rectangle, was perhaps his closest to being Dogme 95. *Heathen* was future noir.)

Vinterberg was about to madly stray from the austere Dogme commandments with the big budget *It's All About Love*, an intensely personal fable set in the near future starring Sean Penn, Joaquin Phoenix and Claire Danes, which would seem to some as though he'd quickly crashed and burned, fame and notoriety coming too early, stuck with a label that was never meant to be a restriction but a liberation. It was about renewal, not about boxing himself in. Oddly enough, success can be bad for the self-esteem.

Bowie knew all about that. He had been through his own battles between following your artistic instincts and having to negotiate the bossy, turbulent demands of commerciality. He's sympathetic to Dogme's renegade, non-conformist ambitions, recognises a fellow ironist and over-sensitive, paranoid outsider looking in when he sees one. He's not sure, though, if Dogme 95 was a serious, idealistic, inevitably doomed attempt to radically strip back glossy, expensive modern cinema and recover its emotional roots, or simply a failed publicity stunt that quickly became exactly the kind of fashionable novelty they were trying to resist.

The conversation could be part of some film where the 55-year-old elder statesman, who's made a few musical masterpieces in his time and changed lives, and the respectful

32-year-old emotional radical determined to make a few film masterpieces try to see if a connection can be made.

Or maybe Bowie's interviewing a potential ghostwriter for his autobiography – quite an interesting choice – while not really convinced he needs a helper. He can do it himself. He doesn't need the fan, however smart and creative he's become – the fan who tells him he used to have him hanging on his bedroom wall when he was a teenager. A picture, not the real thing.

Bowie says he thought it must have been one of his drunken weekends when he was quite likely to have ended up hanging over someone's bed.

The songs you've written, says Vinterberg, so many since you were hanging on my bedroom wall, and so many more to come. They just seem to float out of you. Where do they come from, all these impressions, all these ideas and feelings?

Bowie admits that melodies and song structures do seem to just come from within. He can be with a piano or a guitar or some instrument and within half an hour, find that he's writing something new, whether he wanted to or not. It's inside him. It just seems to be there. The irony is it took him a long time to learn how to be a songwriter.

He had a voice. He could sing a bit, sometimes, it seemed, a little too powerfully, able to unleash a panoramic baritone that didn't suit small venues and obscurity. But none of the tools and techniques of being a songwriter came naturally. He worked really hard for ten years and made some ghastly mistakes – he gives a near evil little smile – which, alas, are still there, available – the smile becomes a cackle – because he had the stupidity to record them.

He wondered how others managed. It used to frustrate him. Maybe from here the drive came. He went through agony trying to come up with songs. Now, it's the reverse.

The lyrics come because he has a need to solve problems and worries within himself. If he wasn't such a prisoner of his anxieties, he would probably just write instrumentals. Writing lyrics gives him another way of accessing those things that bother him. And each time he writes some lyrics about the same thing, it helps if the view changes – a different window in the same house, preferably a different town, a different atmosphere, that pulls something out of him he never knew was there.

He talks about how in the seventies, starting when he was about 23, when he'd cracked the problem of how to write songs, he couldn't stop. He made so many records, for himself, with other artists, he couldn't stop himself. He didn't want to stop. If he stopped maybe he'd forget what he'd learnt.

There's something about youth you can't buy or replace. He had an uneasy sense that none of it was going to happen and he had to do it all *now*. Later on, when there is more time, or you make more time, you realise there's no rush but when you're young, you think that what you are saying is the most important thing in the world. You have to say it as quickly as you can and in as many different ways as you can dream up.

Even when he slammed into a period of chronic self-abuse, he still managed to keep the pace up. His reality was difficult to deal with, the sheer thrill of doing what he was doing had crashed into a maelstrom of pressure and panic, but the work became an alternative reality he could slip into. The work, the songs somehow continued at the same pace; an artistic focus took over and it gave him a purpose he lacked elsewhere. Even when everything had gone to hell, he was still connected to some kind of spiritual search. From the very beginning, almost as soon as he started having thoughts as a six-year-old about who and what he was, he felt some need to define his relationship with the universe, sensed something in the area of what could be called God. He was always trying to express a spiritual reality and sometimes that helped save him when he was losing his mind.

He never felt the need to define God – and in the end, he felt never feeling the need to define God was the definition. He didn't want to give anything a voice, a shape, a story, and that was the best place to work out what place we have in God's life and what place he has in ours.

Bowie doesn't seem like he's about to ride into the sunset to reminisce about battles fought, depressions outwitted and music made. Vinterberg is in the presence of someone content to know he has lived long enough to learn some of life's lessons and is ready to apply the knowledge.

The inquisitive Bowie is in action very quickly. Within minutes, Bowie relaxes into this being a moderately serious interchange of ideas and is asking Vinterberg about the structure that Dogme went out of their way to apply to making films, which to some extent looked counterintuitive, as though it was reducing their freedom, not liberating them. Why do we have structures as artists, he wonders. Is it to fill in for something we think is lacking in the reality we experience, a way of symbolising how there need to be rules? We create synthetic structure to make sense of the chaos of everything. Or do rules and models destroy art?

To take away options, perhaps, says Vinterberg, because there are now too many choices you can make.

Bowie agrees and nimbly brings the conversation back to the record he is promoting at the time, *Heathen*. Working on it with his long time producer Tony Visconti, he realised that what made life more bearable for the music they were making was to take away options. He's seen so many people make enormous mistakes, himself included, when they are given enormous budgets and had 'everything at their command'.

Established or establishment? Bowie asks about Dogme, now it is five years old. Establishment, admits Vinterberg. Dogme 95 had become a brand in Denmark, standing for something that is naked, not decorated. It had been appropriated to mean anything that apparently had integrity. There is even Dogme 95 furniture. The rebellion only lasts so long and then there has to be a new rebellion, which will last even less time, and so on. Anyway, a good manifesto, a good set of rules, is there to be broken immediately. Dogme's were just a different set of rules, to show there could be different rules to the rules that we thought were ruining cinema. We made them up, he says, to show we were playing by different rules, and then we could bend them and then contradict them. First you observe the rules and then you violate them.

Bowie smiles knowingly. Eno liked to make up rules and follow them maybe once, and then try some new ones, even if the old ones tended to stick a little. Or the same rule can mean different things in different circumstances.

Vinterberg asks him a question about the way he keeps changing what he does so that he doesn't repeat himself. By 2002, Bowie has been making music for over 35 years, and the changes are more superficial than he would have thought ten or twenty years before.

He simply always tries to find a newer way of approaching the same questions. The subject matter has never really changed. There are common themes that run through everything he has done. It's all rooted in isolation and then it moves out from there. 'Quite drearily,' he grins, in case he's straying into areas that might seem too personal or could begin to give the game away. He doesn't yet want to reveal that he's already on a line that would take him towards the next few albums, and ultimately to his final album. It's as though, from this point on, he approached each of his albums as though they might be the final one.

The changes are more to do with how he creeps up on those same themes from different places, how he can re-pose those questions because, he now realises, sadly and hopefully, 'I'll be writing about the same thing until my dying days,' forever chasing the one good idea he'd had.

The subject matter will always be fairly dark, and it will be about spiritual abandonment, loneliness, ageing, loss, grief, fears 'and all those things', he sighs. The uncertainty at the core of the human experience.

Vinterberg gently nods, as if to say, of course.

The form around it changes, so the changes are only partial. The changes represent getting into the same areas with a new approach, to find different answers. His favourite musicians, writers, painters do the same thing – they develop and make changes but they return to the same concerns and interests. As you get old, it becomes clearer what you are writing or singing about or painting. When you're younger, you don't fully understand what you are working on. Towards the end, you do get a picture of what it is you have been doing and that's the time to go, oh my god! What a mess. Or, yes, that was worth doing. 'I'm not at that point yet, so don't ask me.'

The conversation becomes one about the desire to learn, to know where you are, why you're there, what's happening around you. The need to find other artists and thinkers who can help you know more and feel more.

Bowie complains that knowledge and curiosity is seen by more and more in America, where he lives, where his immediate experience now is, as something elitist and negative. Learning is seen as nothing to aspire to and the message from the mainstream media, unlike in the sixties, is increasingly that it is cool to be dumb.

The dumbing down seems to come from the sheer amount of information that there is now, as if it is just too much to bear, when the idea of some kind of expert, some kind of guide to helping you work out how to assess and select the right information is becoming suspect. Experts seem like self-satisfied show-offs. They seem like know-it-all snobs, looking down on the rest of humanity from some self-awarded height. The expert is distrusted, or their view is seen as having no more weight than the opinions of those who simply follow their instinct. There's no difference between the knowledgeable ones and the ignorant ones, and the ignorant ones become more trusted because they don't make things complicated, and they trust the con men and the conspiracy theorists more, who comfort them with the pretence.

When there's an overload of information, there is a tendency to want to withdraw from it. Withdraw from the lessons of the past, withdraw from having to work hard to decipher everything and put it into some kind of order. The tendency is to turn away into the wilderness to find truth, which sometimes can be an answer, but not if it also comes with a kind of wilful numbness, a general lack of curiosity.

In a way, Bowie is bringing attention back to *Heathen*, an album he said was about the unilluminated mind, a sense of what twenty-first century humanity might become, promoting the record in the most oblique way by talking about things that were clearly on his mind at the time.

He wonders if that means he's becoming the grumpy old guy bemoaning that things ain't what they used to be, but decides no, because when he was 20, 21, he wanted to know more about more things, about new things, new ways of thinking and being and understanding other people. Being alive meant knowing things, and knowing things led to opportunity and a wider sense of the astonishment of being alive, and to an even greater need to know and understand things. We only know the miracle of life fully when we allow the unexpected to happen.

The dumbness that is being pushed in America is incredibly dangerous, he says. How is it to live there? Well, he doesn't live in America. He lives in New York. Cheeky smile. It's another country. It had a kind of cosmopolitanism you don't find in many other places in America. Even then, it can be very insular. The great danger of America is that it's essentially America First. In everything it does.

There's virtually no interest in the ambitions, or the interests, or the needs and sensitivities of any other nation. That's scary and it's one of the things that makes us resent America so much. It always feels that everything they do is only about America. And you're being reminded of it constantly. They need to understand that people in other countries are their neighbours and in the end, just like them, they have the same problems, the same worries, the same questions. Otherwise, you lose contact with reality.

Art and culture actually bring you closer to reality. Art and culture are about sharing things, ideas, opinions, thoughts, which is part of the human condition. He fears the boredom that comes with not learning and not taking chances.

He's not Americanised, he says. He's still very much European. He lives there, but he very quietly tries to tell people they're wrong. You have to be fairly discreet about it. It's become a war over what the truth is. It won't end well. Resigned smile.

SHOW AND BUSINESS

Bowie, unlike Sakamoto and Vinterberg – and Eno – is also in showbusiness and knows it, and loves it, and a couple of years later, there he is, jaunty in floppy middle-aged fringe laid-back New York zip-up hoodie and baggy cargo pants, still somehow impeccably dressed, appearing on one-time national treasure Ellen DeGeneres' happy-go-lucky afternoon chat show. He makes his entrance, goofily dancing to a song he'd written 30 years before, 'Rebel Rebel', because to a daytime American audience, who probably know very little about him and are familiar with maybe a handful of his songs, that is what he is. You can't tell if he's a boy or a girl, even, really, when you can, just as you actually know what species he is. It's fun to imagine though.

He's with Ellen, half all-American, half slightly off-beat comedian, tottering on the edge of the transgressive, so he easily adopts a friendly, stand-up comedian energy. They're in a contained setting like a play, both playing a role, which involves playing themselves to some extent.

Something real happens, as artificial as the whole set-up is, and sometimes it approaches the sublime; in the years to come, once the context and the triviality of the situation have fallen away, it will seem a strange, wonderful encounter between the smiling man in the hoodie who seems to possess some extraordinary power and the jumpy, excitable woman who's aware of his power but tries to act like he's someone who lives next door.

Bowie is mocking up a conversation he's had with his daughter, doing her voice when she says she's four and he patiently explains to her that she's only three and three quarters.

His time as a mime artist is brought up and he says he realised at 17 that he was a man trapped in a mime's body. You mustn't mention being a mime in America because in the land of Stephen King, clowns kill people. He explains how he was in a revolutionary mime company – revolutionary because they spoke. That's not mime, Ellen says. That's why they were revolutionary, he replies. There's so much laughter from Ellen's audience of women, who've made the decision – or had it forced upon them – to believe in what they're experiencing, that you'd swear it was canned.

Ellen grins. And then in the late sixties you studied to be a monk? Yes, he realised when he was 18 that he was a monk trapped in a mime's body. He's doing the light, nicely accessible version of his life story, which for this occasion, he had compressed to: he was young, fancy free, and Tibetan Buddhism appealed to him at that time, and he thought, there's salvation. It didn't really work and he went through Nietzsche, Satanism, Christianity and pottery, and then he ended up singing. It's been a long road. He gives the audience the gift of a smile they'll never forget. They don't quite know why but it makes life more beautiful.

From his little daughter Lexi to Satanism in a couple of minutes. He's adorable but don't forget what lurks deep down – the rebel rebel. He's in touch with the momentary and the permanent. The momentary is on the surface of things. The permanent is connected to the mysterious and consecutive life that constantly flows beneath the surface of things. There's goodness in love and flowers, in song and dance, but another force – wild pain, anxiety and decay, anarchy, rejection and heartbreak – accompanies everything.

GLORIOUS AND INSANE

The momentary and permanent, the surface and the depth, the charmer and the prophet of doom; it was all there in his music and there were times when a collision with another artist or entertainer on a television show would produce an intense, isolated version of Bowie in full flight. The sighting would be outside the usual single to single, album to album, character to character, tour to tour, film to film, record sleeve to record sleeve ways that were once how the shape of Bowie was reliably assembled.

Sometimes, on a random promotional appearance, there would be Bowie, a fine mess of chaos and clarity, mutating from one state into another, as if what we were watching was some part of his thought process, some fractured evidence of where he was at the time as an artist, and someone getting used to where he was in whatever his life had become. The appearance would have passed in a flash, become a rumour – what the hell was *that* about? – and only in a later time, a different world, would it become fixed and a part of the persona he was always in the process of creating, whether with some deliberate intention or accidentally, as he deals with circumstances beyond his control.

It's now available for everyone to see, where once it was only seen by its immediate audience, which started spreading the word – who thought of *that*? – and then it was gone, lost in time, for a while.

Look into his eyes. He's talking about the importance of noticing the world around him, of attending to what he is thinking and feeling at a given time. A great deal of discipline is required to 'just notice'. He's communicating his self-awareness and a spellbinding eye for detail, gently moving our focus back and forth between the familiar and the unfamiliar, between nothing in particular and everything that we are.

It was remarkable that someone so mysterious could speak so openly about his doubts and convictions, his wants and needs, his successes and failures, his enthusiasms and artistic game plans. But maybe that was part of the mystery.

He's also promoting his latest record/film/tour/production because, as well as knowing that the self is beyond knowledge, he's a hardworking, beguiling professional entertainer introducing and selling himself and making friends wherever he goes.

He had a weird sense of responsibility, always determined to avoid self-congratulation. Everything seemed to fascinate him; he needed to find out everything, even if that meant taking a detour into the obvious. Even the dumbest question was worth considering because he knew it was up to him to make the answer sound like it was a response to a great question. He didn't want to waste a word, as though he knew that eventually it was as much these words as his songs that would last forever. These awkward, sometimes fluent, always quick encounters, leading to anecdotes, confessions, occasional lofty thoughts, odd indiscretions, where he was doing his duty, or maybe doing some form of psychotherapy.

Hear him asked about what drives him and reply (more or less): *One of the forces that has always driven me both as an artist and as a private person has been the search for a reason – a rational, comprehensible reason for my existence. That is an intensely deep type of quest that forcibly leads one into a religious-spiritual examination of oneself.*

He has one life which is nowhere to be seen – a deeply private one, maybe glimpsed or guessed at or stitched together in biographies from scattered clues and accumulated second-hand impressions – and one where he is sublime at pretending to be what people want him to be.

He's selling his wares and selling his ideas. Selling the idea that ideas are the best thing in the world. Everything happens because of an idea. He was hungry for experience, addicted to ideas, to finding things he was interested in and waiting for his next fix in a world forsaken by a non-existent God. He found ways to make a life without purpose become a reason to exist. He was always driving towards the ultimate, knowing it's unreachable. Sooner or later some purpose would reveal itself, without having to be forced. Meanwhile, he focused on the things he loved.

He's in control and sometimes out of control of his image and his story, where his ideas take flight. He loves the authority and power he has and treats it with respect. He also doesn't take it too seriously, but it gives him the freedom to roam the world and organise his mind. He doesn't want to end up feeling he simply visited the world and kept it all to himself. He doesn't want to die without any scars. He's always up to something. Sharing impressions. Moving on.

Look how humble and self-effacing he is, or how effortlessly he can play humble and self-effacing – remember how long he had to rehearse and how many auditions it took before he got the part? Is it for real? It is and it isn't. Everything to him is and isn't. Here and not really here.

REAL AND UNREAL

Sometimes he had to behave in public. Sometimes he disappeared from view, where his scandalous misbehaviour, black-outs and strung out, drugged misadventures with what he blamed on occult forces became the stuff of legend.

He's too famous for his own good, but it's everything he ever wanted, so he deals with it. He'll take the space his fame creates for him, even if sometimes it puts him in a corner, forces him to repeat himself, answer the dumb questions or ones that get a little too close to the bone.

Sometimes in his fame, it seems that he's everywhere and sometimes it allows him to stay in the shadows. He needs time to himself. Some things he doesn't want to feel he has to explain.

A question is asked. A thought occurs. It always does, as far as he ever lets on. He's in a playful mood. Exuberant, mischievous and tender, he was always good with the chirpy patter, as though some early tutors were London bus conductors of the 1950s and chattering, bantering barrow boys promising a bargain.

There was a cheeky chappie side to him rooted in music hall variety acts of his 1950s childhood that he never lost, even as he developed a fascination with altering and enhancing reality and exploring areas of concern and curiosity that opened up in the Space Age; even when he was dabbling in any number of occult obsessions and self-imposed intellectual obligations, from Egyptian mysticism to libertine Aleister Crowley's esoteric pathways to personal freedom and self-discovery.

Even if he took a little too seriously the idea he was on a mission to liberate people, or got caught up at his loneliest and lost in the transatlantic cult of Crowley, the wickedest man alive, he was likely to pull a silly face and prick his own pomposity. Even when he was at rock bottom, he could still force himself to sound as though he was on top of the world. He would look a little dead around the eyes, cheeks sinking into his skull, body withering away from lack of nutrition, mind bending from lack of sleep, but the cheeky boy in Bowie hung on, the disintegrating remains of his wit and wonder the last thing to go.

He liked to spin a yarn. It was one way to get his bearings, part of how he created imaginary worlds where he could live and perform.

A question is asked and the answer can be anything, but it often comes down to another question.

Where are we now?

CURIO AND CURIO

Watch him over decades always being David Bowie. Perfectly being David Bowie, even when he seemed to be losing track of the idea of David Bowie. Sometimes, when he's lost control, teetering on the edge of disaster, stranded above the abyss, trapped inside a fatalistic drive, just about managing to crawl from the wreckage, he can seem the most David Bowie he's ever been, physically revealing the otherness within, experiencing a darkness he'll never forget.

He'll make some kind of miraculous recovery and recover his lightheaded, deep-thinking version of showbusiness. All the better, he says, for having flown so close to the sun, for having sunk so low. Not that he'd recommend such an adventure to anyone, but in his case, he lived a little shamefully to tell the tale, or what he could remember of it.

Perhaps he was always, whatever state he was in – wretched addict, celebrity bohemian, arch, civic national treasure – pretending to be David Bowie, which turned out to be his life's work since he decided to use the name, covering up for most people the David Jones he had been born as.

Born and raised in the south of England to a mother, Margaret/Peggy, whose parents were Irish immigrants in Manchester, and a father, Haywood, born in Doncaster, roots either side of the English Pennines. So David was already a provisional shape shifter as soon as he was breathing. His boyhood was spent as a Jones. As a Bowie, he becomes the performer Davy Jones had been dreaming of, able to become whatever he decided, one way or another. A living experiment, a flawed experiment, but always needing to be continued because it was flawed.

It took a while to find his feet. The boy Jones stumbled through the early 1960s towards a vitality that was perhaps beyond him. Any future as a pop singer seemed snuffed out before it began by the sudden brilliance of the Beatles, the Kinks, the Small Faces, the Rolling Stones and the Pretty Things, already a few steps, a few great records and haircuts ahead of him. Eventually, with further study and various revisions, and the atypical eyes of Bowie materialising after a fight with a schoolfriend over a girl, he cracked it.

Listen to a famous musician, say, Elvis Costello, pay tribute to Bowie's singing and songwriting, and perhaps sum him up best when he says he only met him once or twice, by chance, on the road, in some TV station or hotel, and he was 'splendid company'. Being splendid company was one of Bowie's favourite roles, one of the disguises he liked wearing the most.

Watch him sat around a table in 1972 with Lou Reed and Iggy Pop, each of them self-consciously sizing each other up, none of them ready yet to speak to each other, needing to keep their cool, their misfit aura, engaged in some battle of the egos, working out their place in history. They don't want to reveal to the others what they have up their sleeve – not yet, anyway.

Watch him sat in a busy bar in limbo with Bono and BB King, as though he'd specifically bought a ticket for this particular ride, this particular combination of myth and coincidence, and he's enjoying every single moment, knowing that he's David Bowie and the people around him will adjust their behaviour accordingly. He has a great way of pretending everything he experiences is totally natural and at the same time, nothing of the sort.

See him across time, talking as a gawky 17-year-old about the importance of long hair on a man, talking to a children's television presenter in the 1970s, to a Japanese interviewer translating him as he calmly, very reasonably, talks about the line between life and death, to an MTV interviewer in 1983 about his disgust with the channel's racism and their flimsy excuses, to a political journalist in 1999 about being a recovering addict for whom one lapse would kill him, to a fan about his old home town he's not been to for years, to a musician collaborator about a carefully considered drop in a song's rhythm.

Hear him explain that in his songs he's always dealt with isolation, using himself as a canvas. Thinking about isolation, his own, others he imagines, leads to better songs and greater emotions.

See him appear, for many out of nowhere, with the three musicians that would end up being called the Spiders from Mars in early February 1972 on the BBC television show *The Old Grey Whistle Test*. This was the serious minded, late night rock show showcasing more grown-up, rock performers, ostensibly playing live, certainly pretending they were live, and mostly singing live. It was unlike the more commercial, early evening BBC pop show *Top of the Pops* that concentrated on the addictive randomness of the charts, and the bestselling hit singles of the week, many of them here today, gone tomorrow.

Top of the Pops was, in effect, a weekly parade of performers obviously miming, holding instruments and lip syncing the words with as much intent or indifference as they fancied. At this time, Bowie was still more an underground artist, known to a few early outliers, with no particular sense that might change, and certainly not as suddenly as it did – he seemed more *OGWT* than *TOTP*, at a time when there was a big division between the two, and few crossed over from one to the other. Certainly no-one whose songs seemed so filled with ideas and allusions summoned up thick and fast.

It was about eight weeks after his *Hunky Dory* album had been released a few days before Christmas 1971, which for all its glittering flourish had yielded no hit singles, and four months before *The Rise and Fall of Ziggy Stardust and the Spiders from Mars* album came out in June 1972. The fourth track,

'Starman', a song about the magic of a hit single, announced his arrival as a pop star with a new voice by, slowly, taking shape as a hit single. Which would lead to the lit up, dancing fun and games of *Top of the Pops*, where pop stars were confirmed, even crowned. Bowie's debut *Top of the Pops* appearance was quite a coronation.

On *The Old Grey Whistle Test* a few weeks earlier, in what turned out to be a revelatory theatrical build-up before the fame to come, in a grand, undaunted dress rehearsal, Bowie and the Spiders from Mars performed three tracks – 'Oh You Pretty Things' and 'Queen Bitch' from *Hunky Dory*, two songs celebrating the effervescent brightness and spectacular vanity and nerve of the young, and the moody, mesmerising opening track from the *Rise and Fall of Ziggy Stardust*, 'Five Years', which wondered how we would face up to the end of the world. How would we keep each other alive when everything is falling apart?

The song steadily accumulates small, powerful details as it dawns on humanity that they are faced with unavoidable global catastrophe. Human beings have five years to live, extinction is coming, and the countdown starts now. When the world ends, if there are survivors, what do we become? What part of humanity survives? Bowie's vocals were live and radiant, and he sang this riveting song of despair like everyone should pay attention; this was a real warning. He seemed to be breaking under the burden of some recently acquired knowledge, and was urging people to think about what makes us human.

On *The Old Grey Whistle Test*, Bowie was clearly a deep thinking, observant introvert with serious things on his mind, acutely attuned to cultural forces, presenting his songs with the ostentatious self-assurance of an irresistible entertainer. He was transforming into the luminous, idealised Ziggy Stardust, changing in front of our eyes, deeply at ease in his newly formed alien/human skin, already glowing like the Starman. He lived a version of life like no-one else, and was fully committed to showing us how.

He knew full well this was going to be the first time many in the audience were going to be looking into his eyes and beginning to see what he saw and felt what he felt. Fifty years after it was first shown – and then for years there were no more showings, maybe an occasional repeat, a dream-like flashback of scintillating weirdness – it still looks as though Bowie has beamed back from some time in the future, casually bringing greatness with him. You can see it whenever you want now, something powerfully new always coming to life.

Hear him respond to a question a little later in the 1970s about the power he has as a rock star to influence others, to live as a kind of God, to do what he wants, sometimes to extremes. Does he feel he has power? 'Lord no,' he laughs, the 'lord' giving away his genial Englishness, as if to emphasise how down to earth he is, or wants you to believe he is. He doesn't think about that at all. The only power he thinks about is the strange power of art and of the song.

All he is, he says, is a fairly good social observer with an ability to capture the times he's living in. He may seem creatively active and with a considerable influence on his fans, but that's nothing to do with him; it wasn't what he set out to achieve. He believed almost instinctively in the human value of creativity as a mode of truth-telling, self-expression and homage to the twin miracles of creation and consciousness. He wasn't trying to change the world, that's really difficult, maybe just keep an essential margin of non-conformity alive.

See him explain that he made so many records in the seventies, as himself, with others, and toured so many times, enjoying the first ten or so shows and then having to grit his teeth to make it through the rest because he was always so anxious about what he was going to do next.

He wanted to do so much in a week, move things along, in case it all stopped. He was living in a time of swift and tremendous change, and felt a responsibility to keep up and even keep ahead, just to see if it was possible.

Playing his big shows, he would have an anxiety attack every night because he was worried that something would fall down or someone would forget to do something important or he would forget the words to one of his hits. As soon as a tour was over, he'd say *never again*. And then he'd worry that he was being forgotten or he'd need the money, and another tour would be set up.

Hear him tell a radio host looking for nice, light answers to harmless questions that his three ideal TV show guests if he was the host would be Maxim Gorky, Christopher Isherwood and Marc Bolan. They're doing the interview on a train travelling to London in 1976 and he explains that he loves travelling by train. If you travel everywhere by plane, you leave countries behind; at best, you glimpse them on the way to and from an airport. He likes to make an effort when he's travelling, see and feel where he is as he passes through, observe the changes on the journey, feel them change him.

Hear him talking almost to himself as he cheerfully wanders around the streets of Madrid in 1987 looking for a beer, somewhere between an ordinary tourist and a one-of-a-kind pop star loving to be in the thick of things. He's followed by an MTV camera crew and a polite posse of stunned autograph hunters. He occasionally wonders 'where are we now?' as he ponders two or three different directions he could choose next.

Then he's talking about how in the late 1960s, in return for writing some music for a production, he studied mime with one of his great mentors Lindsay Kemp and his theatre company. They were reinventing traditional and classical mime, like scientists who happened to be poets. Studying and working with Kemp first as an apprentice and increasingly as a master, Bowie learnt to make an exotic impression on stage without using props, just the movement of the body – and the eyes – which he continued to do for the rest of his life. He used what he'd discovered with Kemp on TV, during a show in front of thousands, or when he was simply talking, about his latest record, or now and then about the evolution of humanity, weaving a spell with every gesture and every word.

Hear him on one of his last radio interviews, on the BBC Radio 2's *Jazz Crusade* show in 2005, presented by the British saxophonist Courtney Pine. It was a year after he had suffered from a heart attack, and begun a decade where he seemed to be getting quieter and quieter, a kind of retirement from regular appearances – a guest appearance here and there, a surprise role as himself in the Ricky Gervais *Extras* comedy, as though that might be the last we ever see of him, happily playing the fool. He's calling Courtney from New York. When he's asked how he is, he says: getting there, doing some workouts, on the right track.

It's an interview about Bowie's long-lasting love of jazz, from the first jazz albums he heard, introduced to him by his older half-brother Terry, who listened to jazz to get through painful nights. There was a 1956 album by the Modern Jazz Quartet, *Fontessa*, and a 1953 cool West Coast jazz album by Bob Gordon, *Moods in Jazz*.

'Beautiful album,' he sighs, his mind floating back fifty years to the relaxed, but strange, comforting sounds entering his unsettling London life, never really leaving his imagination, deeply influencing the complexity of his songs. *Fontessa* includes a languid, timeless version of the 1939 Harold Arlen and Yip Harburg song of hope and home 'Over the Rainbow' made famous in *The Wizard of Oz* by Judy Garland, with the heady, spell-casting one-octave leap between 'some' and 'where' that Bowie used between 'star' and 'man' in 'Starman', the song that made him a star.

Harburg would talk of how he wanted their songs to create a better world – a rainbow world. His generation, he knew, didn't create that rainbow world and couldn't hand it to the next generation. But, in times of confusion, when all the world is a hopeless jumble, they could still hand down their songs. There were others here before you and they were there to help.

The latest album Bowie has bought, and he's still as excited as a kid with anything new to him, is a live album only discovered in 2004 of perhaps the very first appearance by the Dizzy Gillespie Quintet, in 1945, when Dizzy was discovering bebop, with Charlie 'Bird' Parker, Max Roach on drums, Curley Russell on bass, Al Haig on piano. Bird, Dizzy would say, is the other half of my heartbeat. Bowie's bowled over by it.

'Isn't that amazing? It's spectacular.' He's also been listening to the fractured funk of pianist Matthew Shipp, and Courtney plays the blissfully eclectic New York chaos of 'Rocket Shipp' from his 2002 *Nu Bop* album.

Bowie talks about meeting one of his favourite musicians, an original member of the Modern Jazz Quartet, the vibraphonist Milt Jackson, at the Montreux Jazz Festival in the mid-1980s. He had dinner with Jackson and the jazz musician and producer, composer and arranger Quincy Jones – who'd worked with everyone from Ray Charles and Little Richard to Michael Jackson – and he said he just sat back and listened as they talked and talked through the entire history of jazz.

Would he ever make a jazz album, asks Courtney? Bowie laughs. 'It's a good idea, but I don't think so . . . but what a good idea.'

He leaves the thought hanging. It does sound like he's thinking . . . *you never know.*

BLACK AND WHITE

Listen to his speaking voice.

Talking to an interviewer on daytime television about the small universes that can be created in the mind. Talking about his apparent fascination with aliens actually being a metaphor for alienation. About discovering Little Richard as an already self-aware eight-year-old, enthusiastically responding to this unprecedented, transcendent American outrageousness from inside grey and limited mid-1950s England, which gave him an early destination, which led him to John Lee Hooker and Robert Johnson, 'et al', as he liked to say, flamboyantly drawing out the two little syllables, smirking at his own pretentiousness, referring to the blues singers he eventually preferred to think of as Afro-American modernists, primal rather than primitive. The madcap raucousness and dressed-up glee of Little Richard's rock and roll on vinyl records wrapped in torn paper seemed rare and mystical, exactly what he needed at the age of eight. A ruinous, dispiriting war, Britain's darkest days, still lingered in the blackened London air. The British Empire, clearly and dimly, was coming to an end.

For Bowie, Little Richard led on to further musical destinations and detours. These would include Elgar and Vaughan Williams and the Yardbirds and the Velvet Underground and Scott Walker and Philip Glass and Stravinsky and the Pixies – complicated, outsider worlds filtered through the mind of someone who grew up during the fag end of vaudeville, at a time when records could seem revolutionary and world changing, oceans of possibility, portals into alluring world-transporting states of mind. Television was in black and white then, and reception was sketchy and ghostly; radio was not so much where you'd find music other than from the old days, and maybe some Boy's Own storytelling adventure, and stuffy voices issuing vague instructions and droning sermons. It was decades before mixtapes and playlists were everyday ways of sharing the same feelings and memories before being quickly replaced with another readily available set of ordered songs and routines.

By the time streaming took greater control of music distribution, what was once new and transformative had become nothing new and conformist – a commentary on the idea of being new and transformative rather than actual radical action. Possibility is controlled elsewhere and music is controlled by the forces now controlling possibility, which is what many of David Bowie's songs were about: he thought nothing of writing a song urging you to madly shake a jive-cat tail feather combined with some subtle or not-so-subtle observation about how civilisation was breaking down.

'I just love music,' he would say, as if there was nothing else to say. Well, there was because nothing is quite so simple it can't be expanded upon. 'I like complications' and 'I'm an eclectic creature' and 'I never wanted to be bored' and 'I'm an actor and entertainer.' Most of all, he used music to tell stories. He took contemporary events and viewed them through the lens of fantasy to see what they meant in mythic terms. Because of music, which put him in the limelight, he could tell stories in interviews and at press conferences, the curse and blessing of being a star. He could place himself at the centre of his own fantasy.

He gets calmer and more measured as he grows older, marries into calmness, leaving the twentieth century and drifting into the twenty-first, receding into the future. He's still driven to distraction, but more resigned to his quirks and more at ease with himself and his lifelong uncertainties, his volatile artistic positions. Each interaction with the outside world on record or screen, in magazine or newspaper, gives you an oblique insight not only into his approach to life, art and self-promotion, but into his mysterious, enchanting sense of timing.

And, of course, his charisma.

Stare into his charisma, which can take you wherever you wish to go.

And, of course, there's his smile, which swings from shy to thoughtful, mocking to seductive, and often materialises when you least expect it, but always when it should, lightly expressing his enjoyment of the world, its never-ending unlikely combinations and where at that moment he finds himself in relation to it. He's always in the moment but at the same time somewhere far away, observing, analysing, opening himself up but keeping himself to himself, perfecting to the very end the art of touching others with his mind.

The man with the cigarette in his hand who described himself as a collector: collecting impressions, expressions, sounds, emotions, attitudes, alter-egos, styles, voices and outlooks, meticulously piecing himself together, juxtaposing perspectives, copying the world around him and making up his own. He restructured experience as he went along because, he found, he could. A private, sensitive man who to enable his travels, often found himself performing in public, as if testing himself out, clarifying his findings, evading being pinned down. He preferred to be lost in a hall of mirrors solving various puzzles.

Hear David Bowie explain his thinking, being serious about himself and lightly flippant somehow at the same time. Hear him fly ecstatically high and find time for the downbeat and sceptical. Hear him sing a song he wrote and recorded in 1967, or 1977, or 1987, or 1997, leading his voice on or letting his voice lead him on. Hear him sing a song he wrote in 1970, ten, fifteen, twenty, thirty years later.

Read all about his 1970s, where he seemed to do and try everything as one character spun into another and one song and musical style led to a different one, tumbling through a hot-house nexus of highs and lows, withdrawals and understandings, routines and revelations, paradoxical states and sensations, coming one after the other, before he settled down into a whole different way of finding out what's what until he ran out of time.

Even at his most riotously alive, extraordinary in his exuberance, he both craved solitude and worried about being lonely – especially in those frantic, famous 1970s, as he sped from his wide-eyed twenties into his wounded thirties, when he was crashing and burning, confessing and bending backwards for the sake of a stardom he demanded if only to experiment with it. He loved being part of a community, often creating one himself, but was reluctant to commit himself to a group. He was moving around from place to place to change his life, revitalise it or restore it, but he seemed to be already shadowed by the loneliness of old age. Sometimes it seemed all he ever wanted was to ensure he gave himself the time and space to read, think and write.

In his final few months, over 30 years later, as he stealthily used up his last remnants of energy and lust for life, refusing to stop being musical, dashing against darkness, he seemed as young and fiercely ambitious as he ever was. He was finding ways to say goodbye, good night, I'll be gone for a while, but still able to say hello, good day, here I am. Who'd have thought it.

ARRIVAL AND DEPARTURE

Listen to the man who once described himself as simply a traveller, quietly trying to settle the matter on his own terms about what and who he was, while faced with others continually calling him for the sake of convenience rock star, pop idol, glam hero, cosmic dancer, chameleon, changeling, prophet, alien, freak, superstar, icon, innovator. Yes, all of that, and all those other labels and descriptions, all coming about because of his nomadic disposition, his interest in the power of images and the various ways that they function, and his skill in controlling how photography and imaginative self-management combine to create multiple identities.

To some he will always be Ziggy Stardust, or Aladdin Sane, or the Thin White Duke, or the man who fell to Earth, or Halloween Jack, or the Pierrot, or the Goblin King, or Button Eyes, permanently wondering in so many words is there life on Mars, singing about astronauts, kooks, changes, romance, genies, legends, heroes, lone wolves, love interests, grand delusions, daydreams, fashion, fame, god-given ass, strange happenings, dancing, young Americans, homo superior, scary monsters, golden years and the erotic, mercurial, televised Star Man, always coming to meet you.

It was all part of his travels. Loves, ideas, mysteries, insights, rhythms and moods he picked up as he went along. He moved beyond his more popular characters, his most loved songs, to new places and phases, new eras and dark corners, new interzones containing enigmatic and restless souls like himself that he'd met or knew and put into words and into his worlds.

He had to keep moving. It knocked his thoughts into shape. Because travel made him think, he never stopped travelling, until the very end, when there were other things that made him think and the journeys got shorter. He loved to go astray, wandering the world from city din to the vertigo of the desert, from hotel room into the wilderness. Looking for ways to open up the imagination and keep on being an outsider, a stranger in a strange land, as much as is possible when your face is so known and your songs and images so familiar, and your world changes because you become wealthy, and know the wealthy.

Sometimes he passed the characters and songs on in various ways, coming across them by surprise, taking some of them with him wherever he went but making sure they didn't weigh him down. He liked to travel light, was never a fan of baggage, emotional or otherwise.

He intermittently checked in on his songs, adding to the stories, singing some in new ways, making connections between old and new songs, but never staying for as long as some would have liked within the glowing realm of his greatest hits and his most striking characters. After the early splashes, the spectacular visitations, the most dramatic transformations, he tended to travel a little incognito.

He could have been born a few centuries before and he would still have been a traveller, an explorer, some kind of savant, passing the time, having a ball, looking for the source of his own being, on the hunt for invisible splendours and imperceptible delights.

He was lusting for things that bewitched and inspired him, which he could then use to bewitch and inspire others. Sometimes, he'd have no fixed plans, seeing what he saw in no particular order and particularly not caring if he ever arrived anywhere. He'd travel for its own sake and let it make sense later. He liked the sense of never feeling at home, the first few days when you find yourself in a new city, like you are falling in love.

Being born when he was, overlapping the lives of those born in the nineteenth century, helped him become a certain sort of late twentieth-century traveller, finding a multitude of ways to get his bearings and see more of the world than most, responding intensely to its peculiarity, perversions and power, a disorientating future world always moving into place.

He also described himself as a closet shaman or a closet holy man – a statement he followed with one of his heartier winning laughs, or maybe one of his hollower cackles, because he was not being serious or he was being entirely serious. An entire biography of David Bowie could be written, or an aural one compiled, based on his laughter, which was sometimes so joyous it was oddly jolly. The laugh of an earnest, otherworldly gentleman who cultivated a deliciously precise ultimately placeless English accent and who also took a delight in disorder. Sometimes his laughter seemed like a form of dancing, to a piece of music only he could hear. One thing was for sure: he was enjoying himself, being out and about, completing all sorts of tasks, from the mundane to the enjoyable, always reacting to his surroundings and always in the process of forming his consciousness.

SMOKE AND MIRRORS

Hear him laugh at a question he's being asked for the first or hundredth time and then laugh at the answer he gives, or one he didn't actually give and kept to himself. He was also a master at laughing at himself and the absurdity of his position, where he found himself, known to millions but also completely unknown. He was also, he admitted, a great liar, something he wished he could give up, like his relentless smoking, the brutal habit forged in the smoking 1950s and '60s that hastened his demise.

When he started smoking, the majority of adults smoked and it seemed natural to kids growing up that it was what adults did. People smoked indoors and outdoors, on trains and buses, in cinemas and theatres, in doctors' waiting rooms, at home and at work. Teachers smoked at school, passing the smell over to books and classrooms. Television presenters smoked on television while interviewing politicians.

For those growing up in the fifties and sixties, it seemed a conventional rite of passage, a basic part of being young and human, of belonging, of tasting pleasure and sampling sophistication. It was a post-war sign of freedom and optimism, of time to plan a new world, as if the smoke charged up the intellect.

They were cheap, alluring sticks of exotica you could pick up at the shop nearest your house that also sold sweets and daily newspapers – for those strapped for cash you could buy them individually, with a couple of matches for each cigarette. Pink-tipped candy cigarettes for children were sold in boxes branded with cheery cartoon characters like Popeye the Sailor Man. You could pretend to smoke along with your parents and grandparents, preparing for the moment you smoked the real thing.

After regular British brands like Player's Weights, Senior Service and Woodbines, Bowie moved up a level or two and started smoking the strong, acrid Gauloises, not for the faint hearted, cool as you like, in their glamorous Matisse blue packaging with its always modern-looking winged military helmet logo. Gauloises or Gitanes were ever-present between the fingers or dangling from the lips of French Resistance fighters, of French writers and thinkers, Cocteau, Malraux, Gide, Bardot, Gainsbourg, Sartre, Camus and Barthes, never without one in publicity photographs. George Orwell mentions 'squandering two francs fifty' on a pack in his 1933 book *Down and Out in Paris and London*. The tobacco smoke curled and swirled between Nazi-occupied Vichy France in the 1940s and the revolution on the streets in Paris, 1968.

Intellectuals, rebels and rock stars, the seductive chic of European cinema, the bliss of reading Jean Genet and sinking into reverie surrounded by a ghostly shroud of smoke. The smoke linking Ravel and Jim Morrison and John Lennon, the smoke associated with ideas, sex and resistance; how could Bowie, a poseur from his early teens, resist? It represented the world of bohemian haunts, hazy dives and jazz clubs he hankered for, linking the intellectual nobility with artists with celebrities with film noir and popular music.

Eventually, Bowie switched to the lighter, sweeter Marlboros, as if they were cleaner and less fatally rough on the lungs, unable to ditch the prop which was, through all the changes in his life and appearance, a central part of his identity. He was a part of the gang he so much wanted to be part of. He knew all along he was dicing with death but it was a way of life, a way of dealing with anxiety, tension and panic and then somehow turning it into creative action. Superstitiously, he believed that if he stopped smoking, his singing, his writing, his art, all his magic powers, would disappear in a puff of smoke

By the end of his life – the murderous smoke catching him out from the inside – cigarettes had become culturally exiled, hidden, expensive, replaced by some ugly, soulless simulation: the vape, the e-cigarette. Yes, cigarettes, for the committed smoker had soul, as though you were communing with another being, even if they could take yours away. For some, working out in the gym, working on muscles rather than the mind, was sexier than the smell, the cough, the decaying insides, but the gym didn't lead to ideas, to thinking, to an invigorated mind.

He could stop for a few days when he really forced himself to but he never really stopped, smoking, or lying, both a smokescreen, a crutch, a deep comfort, an escape from various predicaments.

BEGINNING AND THEN

Up to and immediately after his death, the story, the order, the what-happened-next of David Bowie had settled down into a recognisable, increasingly conventional pattern, however you came to it. Slowly, as time passes, as the distance between it actually happening and becoming history, it gets broken up, but a central structure remains.

It began in Brixton, London, in 1947, a year and a half after the end of the Second World War, and ended in SoHo, New York, in 2016, the year that seemed for many to be when the world fell apart, as if there was a World War III already going on, but we didn't call it war. It was just the news.

Thinking about music and what it could do to a young mind and body, it all started with Little Richard, smashing out of nowhere for the living hell of it into the slow, densely packed streets of Bromley, on the Kent border with London, where his family had moved from Brixton in 1953.

West Indian migration and a new multi-cultural society were just beginning, and the Brixton markets and Electric Avenue would be filled with market stalls selling new kinds of fruit, vegetables, meat and fish with their competing, shouting traders. Mouthy, cocky barrow boys lured in new local residents wearing brightly coloured clothes and a variety of buskers – acrobats, jugglers, singers and sword swallowers – used the pavement as their stage. Images stick in the mind while his mum buys some fruit. A tumbling clown, a lone singer unsteady on his feet singing something melodramatic with a faraway look in his eyes, a sad-looking magician making passers-by laugh with what he finds in his hat.

All kinds of weird pills and potions promising miracle cures were being sold; there were stalls piled high with mounds of loose toffee, boiled sweets, liquorice and broken chocolate, and out front, the big, jocular, slightly sinister sweet man filling bags with all this spectacular transformed sugar. Just as young David is forming memories of this haywire cosmopolitan commotion happening above and around him, he's pulled away by his parents needing to find a more permanent home. The less frantic Bromley road they eventually settled in a few miles south-east of Brixton was mainly Jamaican and Irish, bringing their own rituals and liveliness into their homes.

First memories are of quiet, strangely atmospheric Sundays, when the stress of a week of school and work and the tension between past and present were relieved by music on the radio, even if the arguments between his parents didn't stop. The arguments were about things he didn't yet understand, but seeing them adopt positions as they battled for homeland superiority supplied early hints about the art of deception.

The town had been a constant target of German incendiaries and V1 rockets during the Blitz in 1940 and 1941, with its indiscriminate destruction designed to bomb Britain into submission, causing extensive damage to churches, houses, pubs and shops. In 1944, a V2 rocket fired from the Hook of Holland hit the area surrounding the Crooked Billet pub after a six-minute journey, devastating a 300-yard radius, killing 27 people and seriously wounding dozens of others.

The effects of the war, on buildings and community spirit, hung over Bromley throughout the 1950s. Kids continued to play on bomb sites, a reminder even into the sixties of the continuing legacy of the war. Children playing on the ruins were in their own way building a new order, using this temporary freedom where they would step outside the confines of family and school to get themselves ready for when there were new tools to foster a sense of renewal and future possibility.

Young David was never taken by traditional children's things. He was particularly allergic to Disney characters like

Donald Duck – who he would say taught him how to hate – and Mickey Mouse. Even as a seven-year-old, it was music and entertainers that were getting inside his head, with an insistence that he would struggle to shake off for years, if he actually ever did.

He was entranced by the tongue-twisting so-called patter songs of the all-round American actor, comic entertainer and mimic Danny Kaye, Brooklyn-raised son of Ukrainian immigrants. Playing Hans Christian Andersen, the dreamer of dreams, in the 1952 film of the same name, he sang 'Inchworm', which stayed with Bowie for the rest of his life. Written by Frank Loesser, who also wrote the *Guys and Doll* musical, including 'Luck Be a Lady Tonight' and 'Sit Down You're Rockin' the Boat', it was a first exposure to the power of song that could influence personal reality. For Bowie, it became a kind of wellspring – the memory of when he would feel happy and sad at the same time, and eventually try to understand and explain that feeling as a five-year-old boy, when he felt as lost and abandoned in his twenties.

Over time, it became clear that 'Inchworm' was an original imaginative source of the melancholy that would exist in many of his songs, often taking charge. The song itself, with Danny Kaye's world weary delivery, is a kind of haunting incongrous masterpiece. The film it came from was essentially about being the odd one out, a feeling that would also linger through Bowie's life, the original spark of his endless curiosity as he searched for ways to fit in, to belong and, you never know, stand out.

He would admit that 'Inchworm' spun off into many of his songs – his surreal later minor-key lullabies as well as the obvious, musical theatre-styled ones he wrote in the mid-1960s that sometimes seem to have the Danny Kaye of *Hans Christian Andersen* looking over his shoulder – the singer of the fairy tales turned into perky, storytelling songs, 'Ugly Duckling' and 'Thumbelina'. It helps explain why as a teenager, Bowie would be so besotted with the idea of writing a Broadway musical without really knowing what one was. 'Inchworm' would bring back memories that would almost hurt. It drifted into 'Ashes to Ashes' in 1980, which he acknowledged owed a considerable debt to its bewitching, bittersweet mood. He would be haunted by the use of numbers as backing vocals, recited in a melancholy way.

At first, he couldn't imagine music beyond Danny Kaye, but it turned out there was. When David was eight, his often silent and brooding father came home from work one day with a rare surprise: a bundle of rock and roll records in multicoloured paper sleeves.

The phrase rock and roll had come from songs in the 1920s and '30s, tangling up sex and dancing, rooted in the rocking and rolling sailors used in the seventeenth century to describe the motion of a ship at sea. (Bowie's internet alias in the late 1990s was 'Sailor'.) It was popularised in the 1950s when the New York based DJ Alan Freed was looking for a way of describing a new stirred up hybrid of country and western, blues and gospel that was all of that but something else.

By the time rock and roll was in the bag David's dad had brought home, it had lost the more blatant traces of original sexual connotation, otherwise the bag wouldn't have been allowed in the house. It was just music now, its name still strange on the tongue, like all American slang, the absolute latest thing when latest things for teenagers were beginning to take over the world.

The rock and roll records his dad brought home out of the blue were something else altogether. They looked like magical artifacts. They were all the small seven-inch, 45rpm singles first produced by RCA Victor in 1949, which had been replacing the clumsier, stiffer-looking shellac ten-inch, 78rpm singles. Those were more likely to break and even melt – one of the first records Bowie owned was a Fats Domino 78, which melted in the sun when his cousin Kristina left it on a windowsill. He cheekily confiscated her 78rpm copy of Elvis Presley's 'Heartbreak Hotel' as repayment. The coming replacement for 78s was more durable, and there were even claims that these new discs were indestructible.

Rock and roll sounded better and clearer in the smaller, modern and sexy-looking 45rpm format, making the 78s seem an old-fashioned format for old-fashioned music. The rise of the less expensive, highly portable seven-inch single coincided with the rise of rock and roll and a newly named 'teenage demographic', and the singers like Elvis Presley, Fats Domino, the Platters and Little Richard his dad had introduced into their dreary, stifling, post-war home lodged in a faded part of the world.

It was an early sighting of what would soon be the singles revolution – Britain was slower to get to the 45 because of wartime rationing, and this collection of singles his dad gave him was like something from the future. And the most astonishingly future-sounding of them all was one called 'Tutti Frutti' by Little Richard, who had a sound and a voice that seemed to break open the world, bringing an unbelievable, organised aggression into life that wasn't violent or destructive, but somehow a way of venting frustration without causing physical damage.

The loud, sudden first sounds of Richard's furious made-up curse 'a wop bop a loo bop a wop bam boom' instantly introduced a mutant new language. You could only imagine what someone who sounded like that actually looked like. He must have the hair, the eyes, the movement, the clothing of something from another planet. Colours flooded into a black and white world.

The colours took some getting used to in grey Bromley, where what colour there was tended to be absorbed by the weather and atmosphere. Along with the colours Little Richard was putting into music, you could hear thoughts and noise never heard before.

In David's mixed up eight-year-old mind, presumably missing the sexual excitement and libidinal chaos but sensing something irresistible dirty and undone, the rampant, gloriously nonsensical sound launched into his world was inextricably linked with the otherworldly seven-inch disc it somehow came on. The seven-inch single had magical properties. It could take you anywhere. He made his mind up to become a rock and roll star, like Little Richard or Elvis Presley, whose birthday he shared to his absolute delight.

Being like them meant he wouldn't have to live at home anymore, tangled up in a fractious, nerve-jangling world he didn't understand, where his mother seemed to resent her husband and his father felt irritated and trapped by his spirited, independently minded wife. His dad, something of a heavy drinker, was a classic fifties character, expecting domestic and social deference with everyone knowing their place. David loved his parents but there were all sorts of resentments spinning around the house as a typical post-war English family learnt, or never did, how to communicate and relate to others.

Bowie did credit his dad with creating an openness he had about religion. As a child, being in a brooding church, hearing prayers, listening to the unworldly choir seemed completely separate from the weight he eventually realised it all carried, which would be either suffocating or inspirational. His father, unlike many of his friends' parents, had a wider understanding of religions other than the standard, dour and austere, very masculine English Protestantism, that was increasingly becoming, because of its inflexibility, a stepping stone towards an inevitable secularism and the major tipping point there was in the sixties and seventies. As pop music joined cinema, theatre and television, absorbing its power and adding its own, British churchgoing seemed to represent a respectability that was making less sense amidst new complexity and the new distractions that came with it.

David seemed to be the annoying, troubled thing that kept his parents together, so if he left, they would be free to be what the other stopped them from being. The tension would chase him into his bedroom, where his record collection was. All that freedom in their bewitching protective paper bags, and his books, all those words making up a truth cutting through the Bromley apathy as he made his first tentative steps into the wider social world outside their house.

The records he began buying, with their yearning and subversive rawness, soon dragged him from his stubborn young love for lightly cheering, old-fashioned PG Wodehouse to the energy, rantings and freewheeling rhapsodies of Jack Kerouac and Allen Ginsberg and the poet and painter ee cummings, with their wonderful, unceasing ideas about language, structure and the mind, about what drives things forward. It takes courage, wrote ee cummings, to grow up and become who you really are. We can never be born enough, he said.

The music and book recommendations came from his wayward, spontaneous half-brother Terry who didn't mind admitting that existence was tricky. Terry was what the young David imagined a beatnik was like and instrumental in his early reading, making him understand how he could choose the books he wanted to read. He didn't have to follow any particular curriculum or head down the same old beaten paths, doing what he was told by grown-ups who didn't seem to have his best interests at heart. One book would lead to another, telling him about the wonderful new universes that were just next door. Let's go, Terry kept saying. Fill in the void of what you are not taught with acts of your own creation.

COMING AND GOING

If music was something he could call his own, started for real with surreal trouper and soul shouter Little Richard, that soon led to Medhursts, a high-end department store in an Art Deco building in Bromley now occupied by a branch of Primark. Medhursts had started as a single shop in the late 1860s, its owners buying up those around it, slowly expanding along the High Street near the market square.

One of those shops they took over included an unsuccessful business selling china, glassware and crockery next door to the butchers, owned by prescient proto-science fiction writer HG Wells' father, Joseph. This was where Wells, born in 1866, grew up, later reacting in his writing to the massive social changes and suburbanisation that reached even an out-of-the-way place like Bromley, which he described as a 'morbid sprawl of population, a multitude of uncoordinated false starts'.

Wells was in Bromley in the years after the railways came bringing noise and smoke; when he was in his thirties and forties, motor vehicles started to replace horse drawn vehicles. His books and stories emerged from the dismay of locals losing control of their world as a fast, noxious future seemed to be swallowing them up. The future made life easier and it made it harder, and once there was machinery, reality would be constantly under threat.

In *The Time Machine* and *The War of the Worlds*, Wells imagined the planes, wars, tanks, motorways, class war, space travel, high-rise flat, atomic bombs, genetic engineering, virtual assistants and distance-abolishing internet to come, filling the quiet, undistinguished flatness of places like Bromley with visions of a future. A blue plaque for HG Wells is situated on a wall of Primark in Bromley's market square.

In the early 1960s, Medhursts had a surprisingly good record department stocked by a gay couple, Jimmy and Charles, with a modest but engrossing selection of rhythm and blues and jazz records. Some were by those who Little Richard instantly fired up, including James Brown and Otis Redding, who began as Little Richard impersonators.

Little Richard opened the road to the blues musicians like Elmore James, Albert King, John Lee Hooker, Robert Johnson it seemed all young, white teenagers in the early sixties were fixated by, especially those studying art. David was studying art earlier than most, in particular at his school, Bromley Technical High School for Boys, which taught modern art years before other schools.

School was mostly an unhappy time, made particularly difficult when as a left hander he was encouraged to write with his right hand. There was an attitude even in the 1950s that left handedness was a precursor to later problems with mental illness, rooted in centuries-old superstitions that being left handed was a mark of the devil. It was the attempt to retrain children to write with their right hand that actually led to conditions such as stuttering, difficulty concentrating and dyslexia.

There was none of this pressure in the forward thinking art classes that were part of the curriculum at his school. David attended an open-minded art and graphic design class available from the age of 12, taught by Owen Frampton, the father of his friend, Peter. As Bowie wryly recalled, the late fifties, early sixties teenagers who would form bands like the Beatles, the Who, the Kinks and the Rolling Stones went to the more formal art schools to learn to play the blues on guitar as much as to learn how to paint.

The art schools were also unusual institutions where you could learn how to think for yourself, even articulate rebellion, particularly valuable qualities at the time, almost new forms of practical qualifications. Owen Frampton enjoyed passing on this kind of information to younger teens, so they could use symbols to smuggle subversion into their immediate surroundings.

Studying art in his early teens with the generous Frampton, with its access to other worlds, showed up even more that nothing much happened in Bromley for a teenager looking for thrills, for what art, and music, made you feel. You were taught how to go looking for it, and because of the Medhursts record department, where you could get hold of illusions and even real magic, there was always something happening. It was right there in a building where H. G. Wells began to imagine the future.

Over the road from Medhursts was a new Wimpy bar with colourful style, fast food, Formica tables, zingy branding imported from Chicago and a name taken from the Popeye cartoon. There were two Wimpys at either end of the High Street, and they quickly became a teenage, even first-date hangout for those with precious little to do, an anomalous pocket of diffused American glamour – with lingering traditional British café table service and cutlery – popping up in ageing, gloomy high streets throughout Britain. It was as if the initially American pop single had to come connected to necessary accessories: burgers, Coke and a knickerbocker glory.

Medhursts was where David would buy as many records as he could afford, darting in on his way home from school to listen to records in the listening booth until they closed at 5.30. At 14, he would be treated as a star customer by Jane, the 17-year-old shop assistant, who let him linger in the booth building a useful education, developing the taste for the invigorating vitality and verve of Black music that would later make so much sense. The information-seeking, acutely observant journalist side already forming inside him was gathering material for later songs about songs and their important place in life like 'Absolute Beginners'.

Jane took a fancy to him, drawn to a swagger and a hunger

below the surface of his shyness, and a sense of humour that made him seem older than he was. She let him have records from Little Richard to Eddie Cochran at a 'huge discount'. His collection was growing. One record, one astounding display of imagination, led to another.

A school friend, Geoff McCormack, came round to David's house one day clutching the *Live at the Apollo* album James Brown had financed himself because his label, Kink Records, didn't think it would be a success. Live albums were then mostly an unknown quality, but Brown correctly guessed that the way to break through to a wider, white audience was to capture the extreme excitement of his live performances, which he had honed by playing hundreds of shows a year for years.

The world was facing imminent destruction the night it was recorded. James Brown and a packed, worked-up audience of 1,500 were concerned with nothing other than what James Brown could make an audience feel, at more or less the exact moment President Kennedy and Chairman Khrushchev were triggering the Cuban Missile Crisis, a major, dangerous confrontation between the United States and the Soviet Union that brought the two superpowers as close as they had ever been to all-out nuclear war. The Soviets reacted to America's military presence on their borders in Europe with a plan to use Cuba, off the coast of Florida, as a strategic base for their own missile site, an explicit threat to American security. The world would live in the shadow of the Cuban Crisis for 60 years, until other, deeper shadows and other unimaginable, increasingly stranger dangers started to materialise.

Astonishingly, the rest of the world was mostly carrying on with their lives as President Kennedy and his cabinet were playing nerve-shredding end-of-the-world poker with their Soviet equivalents. Over an exhilarating, non-stop half an hour, the ten songs and associated atmosphere revealed Brown's power as showman and dramatist better than his studio albums. David and Geoff felt they were there inside the

Apollo, screaming along with those in the audience captured on the recording.

David raced straight around to Medhursts for a discounted copy. He represented the kids around Britain isolated in their own enclaves, who at the time could see ahead into a future where the *Live at the Apollo* album was acknowledged as one of the greatest albums ever made, and the live album that helped launch all live albums. These kids had a new kind of expansive insider knowledge about a new kind of world, and even in cut-off places, from their bedrooms, separated from the established centres of the world, they were helping to construct new realities. McCormack passing this valuable information on to David, who would pass it on to others, was an example of the word of mouth that meant the album sold millions, hurling James Brown into the mainstream, where he made more sense as a king of soul, a living legend, American Black energy that couldn't be kept in the margins, that could see a way out and describe a better world.

Ten years later, when David Bowie was thinking of the climactic song he needed for *The Rise and Fall of Ziggy Stardust and the Spiders From Mars* album that rapidly dragged him from off-world cult status onto the gaudy front pages of tabloid newspapers, he knew exactly where to look for inspiration – the focal point of the Apollo show, the imploring, demanding, shape shifting, time stopping ten minutes of 'Lost Someone', Brown squeezing out every last drop of emotion. He reaches into the audience and gets them to reach out to him, giving everything so they would give everything back. If the world's about to end – and on that night, nuclear Armageddon was as close as it ever got – you might as well go out having the time of your life. David Bowie transplanted the elation, desperation and stage craft into the world of Ziggy Stardust.

Another record discounted by Jane was drummer Bobby Gregg and His Friends' 1962 instrumental 'The Jam', with radical blues guitar stylist Roy Buchanan as one of the crazy noise friends. Gregg would later be the drummer on the electric side of Bob Dylan's *Bringing It All Back Home* and provided the startling snare shot at the beginning of 'Like a Rolling Stone' – a shot heard around the world, said those acclaiming the song as moving rock forward into a new dimension.

'The Jam' had Buchanan's hand-crafted wah-wah guitar that would soon rip through British blues and into heavy metal, but it was also driven hard by saxophones. And the tenor sax had become David's instrument.

David, too white and kept in check by shabby Bromley realism and his natural, gawky reserve, decided he might not have the courage and commitment, the sheer nerve, to become a rock and roll frontman. He'd seen the photographic evidence that the grandstanding, gender ambivalent and riotous exhibitionist Little Richard looked even more outrageous and unhinged than he sounded.

In 1963, he saw Little Richard at the Lewisham Odeon on Halloween night topping a bill with the Everly Brothers, Bo Diddley and local special guests opening the show, the Rolling Stones. Wild-eyed Richard in the best, loosest, loudest suit David had ever seen bursting out of years of exultantly singing in church, strip joints and drag shows was pure pleasure and pure freedom. A man hitting 30 was showing teenagers the way, and showing up the Cliff Richards, Tommy Steeles even Billy Furys-tempered Brit reaction to the all-or-nothing conviction of American rock and roll.

There was a sign though of an emergent and distinctive British edge. David was as enthralled by Sounds Incorporated, the saxophone-dominated Dartford band known as 'the Kentish Wall of Sound' backing Little Richard, savvy and snappy enough to keep up with his rip-roaring call-and-response speed of thought. They came from David's neighbourhood and showed him there was a way into the wider world from the far reaches of London where it petered out and became Kent. Later to tour with the Beatles as part of their manager Brian

Epstein's roster of acts, opening for the Beatles at their Shea Stadium concert, they made the sax seem sexy.

Also from close to home was Mick Jagger of the Rolling Stones, already picking up theatrical tips from watching closely how Little Richard whipped up a crowd with almost comic, somehow sincere exaggeration. Here was cocky, boy-next-door London rebellion and Bowie would remember, or maybe he dreamt it, how Jagger responded to a heckler mocking his long hair by replying, with louche south London contempt, what, and look like you?

The lippy, prancing Jagger seemed as beyond David's immediate ambitions as Little Richard; it was the Sounds Incorporated saxophonists, Alan 'Boots' Holmes, 'Major' Griff West and Barrie Cameron that he had his eye on. (Drummer Tony Newman would later appear on *Diamond Dogs* and join the album's 1974 North American tour, which captured the careering new vulnerability of a now famous and psychically overloaded Bowie that was recorded for the *David Live* album.)

David felt it was more realistic to aspire to become one of the saxophonists in Little Richard's backing band, still a central role, but leaving the born showman to get on with all the extreme, conformity-challenging hijinks. It was the quick-witted, no nonsense sax players, Lee Allen and Alvin Tyler, said New Orleans swamp-blues guru Dr John, who knew about these things, who put the growling, soulful sound around Little Richard and also gave the quieter innovator Fats Domino his force and grace and sonic weight. Allen played the solos, helping define the power of early rock and roll. Even in 1961, when 'The Jam' got David's attention, the saxophone was still a key part of the rock and roll sound, filling out the space that the coming noisier, nastier guitars would move into with more volume and intent.

Fourteen-year-old David was so keen on the collateral power of his favourite saxophonists that at the end of 1961, his father bought him a milky white Grafton plastic acrylic alto saxophone with flash gold keys on hire purchase from a shop on Tottenham Court Road in central London. He took lessons with Ronnie Ross, a highly experienced professional jazz man, one of the great British baritone saxophonists. He lived a couple of miles away and David had seen him play at a jazz club held at the Bromley Court Hotel.

For David, the venue was as a cool as the recently opened, then more international Ronnie Scott's in central London's more cosmopolitan Soho, and quickly increased his education in impressive, world-class British jazz musicians. They were playing right on his doorstep, reflecting a thriving British jazz scene and shaping his musical taste as much as anything American. He was already in hot pursuit of mentors.

As well as Ronnie Ross, inspired by one of Bowie's American heroes Gerry Mulligan, he would see the British-Jamaican tenor saxophone innovator Joe Harriott, who was already exploring a uniquely non-American free jazz in the early 1960s on a couple of audacious masterpieces, 1961's *Free Form* and 1963's *Abstract*; the dynamic, fearless tenor Tubby Hayes, whose 1960 album *Tubby's Groove* with his quartet was rated by the very selective Miles Davis; and the adventurous soprano Dick Heckstall-Smith, who in the early sixties was pumping jazz into the blues groups of early British blues musicians, led by magnetic mentor Alexis Korner directing the way forward towards rock. There were Jack Bruce and Ginger Baker later of Cream, Charlie Watts later of the Rolling Stones, and Graham Bond, fusing his blues with cavalier Mingus-style swagger.

David found Ross's number in the phone book and cheekily called him to say he'd heard his band and he'd really like to get some saxophone lessons. The gruff response was that he didn't give lessons – he didn't need any more saxophone players competing with him, British jazz was a small world – but on hearing the young kid's earnestness, he had a change of heart. He asked David how serious he was and seemed satisfied enough with the answer to have him come over one

Saturday morning and for a further five lessons, which he didn't charge for.

He asked his young student what kind of music he wanted to play and when David said music like Little Richard, Ross decided after the six lessons, well I think you've learnt enough to play rock and roll. Ten years or so later, Ronnie played the brief, sublime sax solo that elegantly wraps up and ushers to a fade Lou Reed's love song to downtown New York and its Warhol superstar creatures of the night 'Walk on the Wild Side' from the Bowie- and Ronson-produced album *Transformer*. Ronnie received for that a standard £10 session fee. The solo will last forever, though, or as long as the contemporary pop music of the twentieth century is listened to.

EXPERIENCE AND KNOWLEDGE

David's Grafton sax wasn't a toy, as plastic as it was. When he was a young, up and coming poll winning saxophonist in the 1950s, eventual rare British jazz star Johnny Dankworth gave the manufacturer some expert suggestions about its design and tone.

Charlie Parker had played one after he'd pawned his own for drug money at a legendary concert in New York in 1953 performed by the five central originators of bebop: Parker with Charles Mingus, Dizzy Gillespie, Max Roach and Bud Powell. Ornette Coleman was sometimes known as the man with the plastic horn because he replaced his broken tenor with one precisely because it was cheap.

After a few weeks of enthusiastic blowing, David's shiny Grafton did break like a toy, so he persuaded his father to help him replace it with a more solid tenor, part 1961 Christmas present, partly from a loan paid back doing odd jobs as a delivery boy for local shops. This one was bought from AT Furlong & Sons, a music instrument, radio, TV and record shop near Bromley South station. As a record shop, it was more obviously a music-mad mecca for connoisseur jazz, blues and R&B fans than Medhursts department store, although it didn't have an 'older woman' to introduce him to some of the arts of listening to music.

With experience and knowledge learnt at Medhursts, David charmed his way to a Saturday job, which he admitted boosted his local street credibility. It also helped with the girls, who saw working in Furlong's as a kind of show business activity, like he was performing, and with the boys, in front of whom he could act like a kind of superior hipster guide to the best latest releases, ushering them in to the new world of 45s.

He easily absorbed the integrity of the shop and its serious, New Orleans jazz-loving, pipe-smoking owner, Vic, an early example of a collaborative ability to identify useful energy and add it to his own.

Entering the dark shop interior was like entering a theatre, with its own mood and a sense your life might be changed by what you experienced inside. In his part-time role, David played a character, the recommender, proving his worth as tastemaker with inside knowledge on the latest trends. He'd whip his fair hair into a serviceable quiff to look the part, practising the genial, articulate chat-up lines that could make anyone feel he was focusing completely on them and their needs. The persuasive, larky patter would last him a lifetime and even survive the worst years of character-distorting repetition of endless interviews and living for years in New York.

Serving at Furlong's, he could see close up how records could make such a difference to people's behaviour. A new seven-inch single or cool-looking jazz album could make someone's day, and he loved to pass on details about the latest Muddy Waters, Ray Charles or Charles Mingus, whose kinky, modernist *Oh Yeah* album was recommended to him in 1961 by Jimmy at Medhursts, which also took David to the nicely dangerous-to-know Roland Kirk.

I am he who quotes, Bowie would say, with nothing to hide. I am the sponge that absorbs. And David gratefully nicked a Mingus *Oh Yeah* song title, 'Wham Bam Thank You Ma'am', to give further appropriated hipster heat and cocksure sleaze to the *Ziggy* album track 'Suffragette City'. It was his friend and creator of the mismatched eyes George Underwood who suddenly chanted it when he was listening to a demo of the song, and Bowie, never afraid of taking a good idea from anywhere, made it work in the finished version.

Perhaps he wanted to add a little bit of Detroit debauchery to Ziggy's fantasy city, as MC5's 'Rocket Reducer No.62' from their 1969 live *Kick Out the Jams* album also grabs hold of the

Mingus title for some extra kick. Or, as an old mod, Bowie was nodding acknowledgement to the use the Small Faces had made of it as the title of the B-side of their 1969 single 'Afterglow of Your Love'. As the self-confessed sponge that absorbs, the sweet man amassing a stall full of goodies, he could have been referring to all three.

Mingus said it was piece of slang he heard Buddy Rich use, about making an exit from a particularly tricky situation or failed encounter, and the track itself riffed on the chords of the Cole Porter standard 'What Is This Thing Called Love?', as a lot of jazzmen did in the mid-twentieth century. Like any good jazz thinker, by 1962, David's teenaged Bromley head was spinning with sounds and styles and titles, along with the words of writers that had the rhythm of jazz, blues, rock and roll. It made sense to make his first proper move into making music. He had to put all this information somewhere.

It was time to see if he could get close to making one of those seven-inch singles that were beginning to change the world by changing the world of people like David Jones in the quiet, solid, but intangible British suburbs where they lived and where counterintuitive little scenes were forming – teenagers swapping records, forming groups at school, chasing sensation, as though there was no option. The pop sixties of history were coming fast.

TRIAL AND ERROR

After leaving school at 16, David tried night classes at Croydon School of Art for a brief time. He quickly found he hated Croydon, a few miles down the road from Bromley. Croydon seemed trapped between times and was being turned into a trap; decaying Victorian grandeur was becoming hastily modernised, a would-be utopia being indiscriminately filled with anonymous civic spaces, concrete battlements and office blocks. He felt haunted by signs of a failed future.

Even more than Bromley, Croydon made it urgent that he had to find a way out of the suburbs, which seemed made for adults. He headed into central London, specifically multicultural, subcultural Soho, 25 minutes by train from the nearest station to his house, where he presumed the action was waiting to welcome him.

He wanted to be a painter but there was no way to make that work. A job as a Junior Visualiser in a London advertising agency, Nevin D. Hurst, was his immediate destination, his first experience of the media helped by his one O level in art, thanks to Mr Frampton. It was another short stay, not even making six months, disappointed by the fact he couldn't develop any of his own ideas and had to work on those of others. None of them inspired him. There was no room for his painting, for a teenage artist with dreams and ambitions. He hated it as much as Croydon, especially the English executives who were adopting awkward American accents, as if this proved their bona fide Madison Avenue integrity.

His time was mostly spent daydreaming as he methodically cut and pasted images into place for cigarette, furniture and chocolate advertising campaigns, one or two of which would give him ideas for certain strategies of persuasion and ways of advertising himself. Sometimes his boss would send him out to a local record shop, where he would spend hours getting the records on his boss's list and hearing others that added to his education.

Over 20 years later, he used the experience when playing the slick, obnoxious ad man Vendice Partners in Julien Temple's film musical adaptation of the Colin MacInnes' impressionist novel *Absolute Beginners*, about the London-based birth of the teenage revolution tangled up with early sixties racial tension. Bowie played Partners with relish, loving doing it because 'he was such a bastard'. As well as an ad conman, the character is the kind of property developer who'd turned Croydon into a concrete jungle. In Bowie's attempt to capture the vain, slippery businessman, he also used his ad agency bosses' slide between American and London accents, which added to all the confusion amidst the disaster the film became.

An incongruously lush musical spectacle released in the middle of Margaret Thatcher's society-trashing 1980s with a stream of camp cameos and star guests, from askew light entertainment dancer Lionel Blair to chic act of the moment Sade, the film, a series of over-excited but attractive set pieces, was over budget, over-hyped and critically undervalued. The kind of ripe, high sheen 1950s musicals it paid homage to and affectionately parodied were near-dead art forms, and its messy, heartfelt ambitions were mocked with fast-developing 1980s cynicism rather than praised.

The dead on, joyous jazz score by Gil Evans was trampled in the almost hysterical rush to effectively erase the film from history. Three songs supplied by Bowie included the rhapsodic title song, a work of art about teenage romance and one of his greatest love songs, at a time when his albums were slipping away from his control, as though he was being organised by outside forces. Bowie's 'Absolute Beginners' possessed an ethereal, timeless class that showed up the amateur earnestness of the film itself, and its beauty somehow worked against the film.

There were other individual songs he wrote for films at the time, separate from his albums and his self-consciousness about what he was beginning to think of as a career, even a business, against his instincts. When he started out, he had a different kind of self-consciousness, different things to think about.

There is always one moment in childhood when a door opens and lets the future in.

STRANGE AND STRANGER

Look into his eyes when they still seemed the same colour. David is ten years old and even at that age, he can't wait to get started. He forms a band, George and the Dragons, with his future friend, and temporary nemesis, George Underwood.

In 1958, he makes his first public appearance at the annual Bromley Summer Scout Camp on the Isle of Wight, playing ukulele and a single-string bass made from a broom handle and old tea chest, with George singing two Lonnie Donegan skiffle songs, 'Gamblin' Man' and 'Putting on the Style'.

At the time, this primitive, upbeat British version of blues and folk, with a little rock and roll, was the music being made by kids and teenagers, including the Beatles before they became the Beatles, as the Quarrymen, a few years before they flew beyond village green skiffle and made Donegan seem very twee and square.

After a few sax lessons, and trips to Medhursts and Furlong's, and developing musical good taste, David, as vain, earnest young mod, joined his first group, the Konrads, temporarily with George.

It was that awkward British early sixties limbo between Donegan's boisterous, homespun folk and the Beatles. The only British acts David had a liking for at the time were the genteel Shadows and the anomalous no frills, proto-power trio Johnny Kidd and the Pirates, with singer Kidd happy not to adopt an American accent like other early British rock acts, mocking it up as if rock and roll needed it to be authentic. David noticed that, and the costumes Johnny liked to wear, including an eye patch, and the group's gloomy, wistful lyrics and fondness for minor chords. Sixties beat music started with Kidd and his Pirates in the way they wrote their own songs, including an early rock and roll classic with one of the classic rock riffs 'Shakin' All Over', and played with a new kind of blistering English energy that would lead to the Who, the Kinks and the Small Faces.

Within a year, after a few shows in small local venues and at weddings and birthday parties, 17-year-old David – trying out Jay as a surname, after sax-heavy Peter Jay and the Jaywalkers – and the Konrads were recording a demo for Decca. He didn't enjoy the Konrads, especially the clothing: they wore brown corduroy suits and ridiculous black ties, which he changed to brown ties, to try to look like they had some flair. David soon left, wanting to play something noisier and bluesier than the pop songs the others preferred.

He started to experiment with his voice in his bedroom, using a tape recorder made by the Elizabethan company with a separate one he borrowed from a friend, so he could try to make something with a better, fuller sound. He was being driven by pure instinct and would build up – superimpose, as Elizabethan described it in their manual – acoustic guitar and vocals, back and forward between the machines, until he was left with nothing but a lot of tape hiss and, somewhere in the background, his voice and early attempts at melody, which he knew was the key to becoming a songwriter.

He would become, he said, the first person to be hooked on his voice. He didn't exactly like his singing voice – he would admit he hated it; singing didn't come naturally to him – but he decided if he wanted to be a songwriter, someone was going to have to sing his songs and when no one else wanted to sing them, it had to be him.

For a time, he would remember, he seemed to change bands every week, or was playing sax and singing in the same band that changed their name every week. The Hooker Brothers, with a nod to John Lee Hooker, sometime Dave's Reds and Blues – a sax, guitar and drums trio with trusty George – became in 1964 Davie Jones and the King Bees. Lasting a few weeks, with a hustling manager, ex-comedian, song plugger and talent scout Leslie Conn – 'Conn's the name, Conn's the game' – they got as far as making a record for an obscure budget subsidiary of Decca, Vocalion: an old blues folk song previously given a twist by Nina Simone, 'Liza Jane'. It was a David Jones single but it is counted as the first Bowie seven-inch record.

The record went nowhere fast and David made more money painting the walls of Conn's Tin Pan Alley offices than from any of the gigs that didn't come fast. He met another Conn client, Marc Bolan – maybe model, maybe man about town and maybe singer Mark Feld – who was even more full of himself, putting on a necessary front as he chased attention and any love he could find. Together, flashing their smiles and their energy, they brought to life the F Scott Fitzgerald observation that 'everyone's youth is a dream, a form of chemical madness.'

Meeting Feld did wonders for David's dress style. Marc knew all the bins around Carnaby Street, London's thriving fashion district, where at the end of the day, the boutiques would throw away any clothes with minor flaws, missing buttons or with tears. They'd go dustbin shopping together, raiding the bins at ten o'clock at night, sorting out their raffish mod boy wardrobes. Poor, but making space for themselves on the London streets that Bowie would turn into songs because there was plenty to notice.

Conn was always busy badgering and boasting, with a reputation for persistence and yet never following through with his promises. To the naïve if resourceful Bolan and Bowie, he was on the inside track. They should be so lucky. After getting the Shadows their first deal, Conn had looked after the UK interests of Doris Day, spotted and recommended to various labels Adam Faith and Georgie Fame, done PR for Petula Clark and Frankie Vaughan, and briefly managed Manfred Mann.

Conn was one of the first industry figures to be as convinced by the teenaged Bowie's talents as David himself was and persuaded David's parents to let him sign David to a five-year contract with an option for five more years.

In July 1964, the name of David's band was now the Manish Boys, a band based in Kent named after a Muddy Waters song. Conn had teamed them up with his new protégé believing it would benefit both sides. Conn's contacts led to a single on Parlophone, with a B-side, 'Take My Tip', written by David, his first recorded song, and produced by American record producer Shel Talmy.

Talmy was on a short visit to London in the summer of 1962 and, a master hustler, tricked his way into Decca Records by boosting his credentials, deciding to extend his stay. He became an independent house producer, noticing there was about to be what he called an explosion of British rock and roll bands. Back in Los Angeles, he told various labels about the Beatles and the Rolling Stones, possibly available for a few hundred dollars, but they couldn't imagine rock and roll coming from foggy old London town, unimpressed by the names that then meant nothing.

Talmy brought the latest American studio knowledge to new British bands, putting a dozen microphones on the drums compared with the more sensible but insipid-sounding British three or four. More intricate recording detail led to more dynamic force, and the British guitar bands he was working with had a particular power and determination the early American ones didn't. The British bands wanted to make statements with their sound, their look, their hair and with the songs they wrote, which took blues and soul and imagined a more playful world, with an occasional added measure of 'fuck you'.

Talmy had taken the Kinks to the Pye record label – another bunch of feisty, in-fighting kids who'd grown up on American rock and roll and played it with unexpected panache. The clamorous, coercive third single he produced for them, 'You Really Got Me', helped make British rock sound raw and dirty to match the defiance and desperation of the words and street image. He worked with the Kinks until 1967, which meant a run of singles up to 'Waterloo Sunset', including 'All Day and All Night' and 'Dedicated Follower of Fashion'.

The noise and fury, the sulky, world-building, post-war bad mood and bad attitude of 'You Really Got Me' was the destructive sound erudite art student Pete Townshend wanted for his group, the Who. Talmy was persuaded to produce their debut single 'I Can't Explain', the answer to the dumb question 'what does your music sound like?', and 'My Generation', the definitive example of how early British bands used their first, impulsive songs as art manifestos and calls to action

These youthful, ambitious new musicians had studied at art school and been taught that without a manifesto, you cannot conceive the future. Their bolshy braininess got tangled up with the innovative technical skills of a new breed of producer, and the chaotic, near free-for-all of a rapidly forming new British music industry catering to the unpredictable whims and desires of a different kind of modern consumer.

The originality of early British rock and pop couldn't have happened without the producer, inventing technique and systems as they went along. Talmy was also gathering the best session players he could find, especially the best guitarists, who were becoming the core of a new British sound – he used the versatile Big Jim Sullivan and gave another art student, the 21-year-old Jimmy Page, some of his first sessions, including a record Talmy made for the Manish Boys, one of about 200 bands who by the mid-sixties, had followed those early manifestos, punkish sermons and public declarations like 'My Generation' and 'You Really Got Me' – and once the Rolling Stones started writing their own songs in 1965, 'Satisfaction'.

Page gave the Manish Boys' cover of Bobby Bland's 'I Pity the Fool' a riotous solo using a fuzz box he'd just bought, which sliced into the otherwise prosaic version from another time and space, from his own personal manifesto, which set out his intentions to remake the world by remaking music. He enjoyed being with David and gifted him a riff he'd been playing around with that David would make good use of later on. He then wandered off – ending up in Led Zeppelin via the Yardbirds – knowing the song he had just played on was definitely not going to be a hit.

Talmy sensed that David was something different, had some indefinable magnetism, even that he was destined for fame. He was bright, brash, smart. Perhaps too smart for his own good. He knew what he wanted but the songs he was writing – which Talmy tried to fit into the times – were weird. But that's because they were original and the world wasn't ready for them yet. They didn't have a snowball's chance in hell, Talmy felt, but sometimes miracles, or lucky breaks, or just the inexorable force of unshakeable self-belief happens.

David was worth working with and seemed to belong in the company of Ray Davies and Pete Townshend, but he hadn't yet reached the stage of writing his great single-minded manifesto. When he did, it wasn't directly urging the world to play loud, think fast, turn on, fight dreariness, smash routine; it was one at an oblique angle to the world, one that proposed a stepping into the unknown, that grappled with the perils of self-doubt, fear, inner criticism, second guessing, procrastination, ennui and even resignation. He could get worked up, he could stand up for freedom, he wasn't averse to anthems and noise, but his first musical manifestos were based in a more personal sphere – I create with music, I choose to continue to learn new things, mistakes are part of the process, I keep my mind and spirit alive and open.

I will turn away from fear and doubt.
I will find my space.
One day I will get it, I will know what I have to do, but it might not happen until I am 70. I might spend my life almost getting it.
I will find my time.

The timing wasn't right with the Manish Boys, with David and this particular genius of a producer, who believed in him but not the band: they weren't one in a million, despite all their efforts and doggedness.

The timing wasn't right when the name of his band by April 1965 was David Jones and the Lower Third – another hard-working, anonymous Kent group with a forgettable name David had been grafted onto, now officially as the lead singer, falling backwards into the role, adopting a clipped, stern mod look to suit the music this particular group played, with terrible timing, late to the party. In Bromley, he'd been a trend-setter, boys copied him and girls liked his difference; here, he was a follower, jumping from group to group trying to recapture that feeling that he was the leader of the pack. That there was no one like him.

He grew his hair, longer than even the Rolling Stones, appearing on television in 1964 when such an act was still notorious, protesting on behalf of a made-up campaign for the protection of long-haired boys. A first glimpse of fame, a first sighting of a manipulation of the media world around him, utilising the kind of gimmick Conn would be pleased with, but it didn't help the Manish Boys single he was meant to be promoting.

The timing got a little better when in early 1965, Conn ran out of steam, having proved himself a good star spotter but a terrible star maker, and a new manager materialised, with slightly stronger opinions and insights than Conn. Unspectacular, out-of-his-depth booking agent Ralph Horton took over and thought the name David Jones was too common; there was already a famous Davy Jones in the Monkees, so even his name was a copy of something else.

In September 1965, David Jones changed his name to David Bowie, a name that had been tugging at his imagination for a couple of years – a friend of his father, who worked for the Dr Barnado's charity, was called Bowie. The name for what to some extent was his first performing character was chosen without much thought. It didn't seem an incredibly important decision at the time, just something to satisfy his manager, a name forced on him.

The eventual explanation for the name would need something a little more romantic and a little sharper, and he began to think it was a good name, with a few attractive connotations. There was the knife made famous by the American frontiersman, Battle of the Alamo veteran and adventurer Jim Bowie, with its sharp, cutting edges allegedly designed by his brother Rezin and a name with Scottish origins derived from the Gaelic nickname *buidhe*, meaning yellow, or light haired.

Bowie was getting used to the idea of making changes, to adapting to a world that was changing so fast. These changes were what he wanted to reflect in his songs. Changing his name was a big step but it was the change that made a difference, and it would lead to all the other changes he would make to keep up, to get ahead, to stay sane, to leave traces.

The Lower Third became David Bowie & the Buzz for most of 1966, often with the group not even getting a credit on posters and records, as though they were flickering in and out of history. They often had trouble dealing with the maddening idiosyncrasy of Bowie's chords as he searched for something that would make a difference to how they sounded.

The Buzz didn't think that complicated chords and Bowie's intense mood swings were the way forward, his sharp new name didn't seem to help, and the group dissolved. Bowie was now on his own, taking with him the repertoire of songs he had been agonising over.

At the end of 1965, Horton lost the vague early trust of Bowie and in desperation asked for help from London publicist Ken Pitt – more refined, strategic and cultured. Pitt had represented Sinatra, Duke Ellington and Jerry Lee Lewis in the fifties, and as Manfred Mann's manager, persuaded them to record their first hit, 'Do Wah Diddy Diddy'.

Within a few months, Pitt the proper became Bowie's sole manager, the latest music business professional to see something in this madcap, self-styling know-it-all, the first to see how to collaborate with the design of a new kind of persona.

Bowie, still only 20 years old, after trying with so many different groups, excited that he has a proper album being released on the same label as Cat Stevens, seemed doomed before he's even begun. Pitt picked him up and took him on as an exciting newcomer, convinced that he's a promising songwriter if nothing else.

Pitt was the first manager Bowie had who fully understood what a naïvely optimistic and sometimes depressive and troubled auto-didact Bowie was; how he felt his way forward and pieced together a world of sensation and self-protection from a wide array of influences. Pitt became a calm, well-spoken and sophisticated guide to new culture and influence as much as an organiser, arranger and persuader.

Pitt built a certain part of Bowie in his image as an older man with old-fashioned taste, bringing a pre-rock and roll showbusiness with him – he saw the actor, composer and comedian Anthony Newley as successful all-round entertainer; Bowie saw him as anarchic dreamer, a riotous fantasist, and it wasn't so much his songs that he was drawn to but an attitude. There was something about him, behind the carefully calibrated extrovert, that screamed loneliness, a sense of solitude, of being adrift, which Bowie could empathise with. He could see how that could become a kind of force he could use, an energy in his writing that would make it different from all the others taking from the blues and desperately trying to find something of their own.

You couldn't classify Newley's creativity, which interested Bowie. He was a misfit who made it work for him. It's what Bowie wanted for himself. He also knew he didn't feel like a rock and roller, like the Jaggers, Marriotts and Daltreys, leaping around stages, mouths open, trousers bulging, baring their chests, metaphorically and actually.

He loved rock and roll, he wanted to be involved and he could see a way of using it as part of what he wanted to do, as a texture, an element, an angle of approach. He could see himself wearing the tight trousers, letting it all hang out, but he was never going to be a testosterone-filled, fist-in-the-air rocker, even when he was singing rock songs in his early groups.

You couldn't pin Newley down. He wasn't a crooner. He wasn't a pop singer really. He certainly wasn't a rock and roller. He was effectively an idiosyncratic actor who wrote very melodic and melancholy, quite mysterious and often paranoid, anxious songs.

The deeper, darker Newley was more of an influence on later Bowie, who wrote songs that slipped outside and through genre, than the young Bowie, just beginning to record songs. It was the lighter, larkier Newley that was splashed all over the *David Bowie* debut, as though he's already well known enough to confidently self-title his record, destined to live through a time when to some extent everyone would know his name.

The early, restive Bowie, just out of his teens, tried to decipher what it was about Newley that made him so desperately appealing by copying his melodramatic and sentimental vocal mannerisms, not quite yet inheriting or even understanding the tragic air that he brought with it.

David Bowie was a skewed, scatterbrained first (near)sighting of eventual full-blown esoteric Bowie-isms, a concealing of his ferocious ambition behind faintly unsettling cuteness. Only the photo on the cover – the dreamy hair and stare of a pop star, he's already prepared for the story pictures will tell – and the album's artwork and lettering give you a direct clue it is the 1967 of *Sgt. Pepper* – it's released the same day, asking for trouble – Floyd, the Who and Hendrix.

Then again, if this was the only thing he ever did, it would now be a cherished lost gem full of twisted nursery rhymes, twee love songs and deviant cautionary tales by a kinky, enigmatic king of experimental novelty, a dashing, playful and squandered suggestion of a non-existent, fascinating career that could have changed absolutely everything.

LOVE AND OBSESSION

Ken Pitt also knew to feed Bowie's hunger for the new, the unfiltered, the avant-garde. Bowie, for all his peculiar teenage allegiance to Danny Kaye and Anthony Newley, also wanted to be the most modern because tomorrow belongs to those who can hear it coming.

In late 1966, Pitt brought back from a visit to New York a test pressing of the debut album by the Velvet Underground and Nico, signed by their manager, producer – in the theatrical sense – exploiter and early artistic sponsor, Andy Warhol, who had been using them as part of his multi-sensory productions, including the 'Exploding Plastic Inevitable'. Pitt had met up with Warhol, hoping to promote the Velvet Underground in the UK.

Warhol had paid for the group's first studio session, which freed them from commercial record company interference, allowing them to experiment with the sound and content of rock and approach it from the literary, cinematic and musical avant-garde as much as the blues and early sixties pop.

Ken Pitt thought the album was actually by Andy Warhol and when he handed it to Bowie in the central London flat they were now sharing said, I don't know why he's making music if it's as bad as his paintings. Bowie knew at that moment he was going to like it. Ken was lovely but oddly square, and the modern world, and the modern art that came with it, was outside his sphere of interest.

The first track glided by and didn't immediately register. Then there was the opening, languid, sourceless bass and guitar of 'I'm Waiting for the Man', and everything fell into place and his mind immediately reacted. The music was savagely indifferent to his feelings. It didn't care if he liked it or not.

It couldn't give a fuck. It was completely preoccupied with a world he had never come across before. It made him realise how up to then, pop and rock writers were only writing about a tiny part of the human experience, and there was so much more out there.

There wasn't one blues reference in the music. The group actually had a rule that if one of them succumbed to playing something bluesy they would be fined.

Bowie had never heard anything quite like it. It was a revelation, lifting rock above the mod sound, the almost instantly nostalgic British beat sound that freely borrowed from the blues, English song, the Dylan folk surrealism, the utopian psychedelia. The Velvet Underground's weirdly tuned guitars, metronome beat and tense viola scrapes made the so-called far-out music of the time seem extremely ordinary and unglamorous.

Bowie was doing a version of 'I'm Waiting for the Man', languid, unapologetic, sung from the point of view of a disenfranchised junkie, before the Velvets themselves had been heard in Britain. So quick was his need to explore this ravishing new area, even take it for his own, in his last ever concert with the Buzz, in December 1966, Bowie signed off by singing the evocative, unapologetic 'I'm Waiting for the Man' as one of the encores, feeling his way into how singer Lou Reed delivered a song, on edge and off hand, in a different realm to Anthony Newley. He would claim that it was the first ever cover of a Velvet Underground song anywhere in the world.

This was Bowie's idea of glamour: a radiant, realistically degenerate and soulful fusing of art and music, of introspection and technology, of desire and terror. It was literary, dark and beautiful. The songs' subjects were sex, drugs, desolation and death, sung with deadpan dryness, written about and for misunderstood outcasts, the subdued but pop melodies clashing with dissonant, minimalist, deforming sounds. The precarious German-born actress and singer Nico, introduced into the group by Warhol to add his version of alien superstar quality, was an intoxicating, violating ghost of the then classic, decorative female lead singer, an ethereal, achingly lonely part of the independent reality the record created.

Bowie studied the record intensely like it was course work. There was nowhere it fitted in the rock music world as it was then that Bowie could immediately identify. American publicity for the record, desperately searching for a label, call it 'folk rock'. It wasn't made to fit anywhere; it wasn't even particularly concerned about making a world where it did fit. It didn't sound like it was made to be compared to anything. It didn't seem made by people who cared whether it was understood or not. It sounded like something that simply had to be made. It wasn't newness for the sake of it.

You can imagine Bowie writing an essay about its impact on his mind and its larger meaning. Abstractly, it was to influence what he was going to do for the next few years, spiritually and conceptually as much as musically.

He wasn't going to become a Velvets clone but Lou Reed as a lyric writer, an acutely observant storyteller, made a lot of sense to him, and also the use of cacophony as background noise. He would be more baroque than Lou but, then, as he admitted with a smile, he was British.

The fan, the student, with his constant crushes on the next Little Richard, the next Anthony Newley, becomes the artist: inspired not to copy or recreate except as part of a knowing celebration, but to combine a newfound approach and attitude with his own experience.

He noticed Lou Reed's writing influences: the city dwelling, low-life post-war poetry and prose of Hubert Selby, William Burroughs, Allen Ginsberg, and most of all the tortured, rueful Delmore Schwartz. Dylan had gone so far and then Dylan fan Reed wandered off Highway 61 and took it further, into the depths and dangers of New York, with roots in Baudelaire and Rimbaud – the God of puberty – and other poets more obscure at the time than they would soon become.

It was the New York Bowie wanted to know and hear about – underground, hidden, glimpsed in photos, poems, songs, album covers, films. The city with James Dean, or Bob Dylan, or Tony Curtis walking up the middle of the street on the way to adventure, the one with the Fugs and Ornette Coleman turning New York into noise, the intellectual bohemian extravaganza he'd dreamed of growing up in the south London suburbs. It was an invented, imagined, authentic New York where people like him wanted to be, far more than the West Coast, all that sun and softness.

It was as though Reed issued a challenge to songwriters like Bowie on the hunt for the next day – *this is where I have gone as a lyricist, take it or leave it, and if you want to, go where you will and where you can*. It all begins with a few chords, a deadpan, driving rhythm, a story that needs telling and a real-life setting.

A song like 'Heroin' was about feeling self-destructive and dark inside but it also seemed a way of exorcising those feelings. The song comes at you slowly at first, and then harder and faster, and it keeps on coming – it's a drug, it creeps up on you, and then it has you under control. You're addicted, you want more, you need more, you can't live without more, it takes over your mind, but it's a good takeover, it's about spiritual growth and transcendence. You can get all that and more from a song.

Reed and the music, twisted around the discordant, insomniac and perilous minimalism of John Cale and his viola, the androgynous voices of Nico and Reed spinning a web between art and life, taking things seriously, took over every aspect of his mind, body and soul. They brought to life the enraptured ecstasy of falling in love with a person, a place, a drug, a sensation, a memory. Bowie wanted to write songs like that: beautiful and truthful, grave, euphoric pieces of theatre that might be autobiographical and abstract and implied, but more importantly, create mind-altering new worlds. It made a lot of the pop and rock music he had been listening to seem like light-hearted romps – though he didn't necessarily include Anthony Newley in that, as he could see a direct line between the Velvet Underground's fallen sense of the uncanny and Newley's themes of disillusionment and existential despair. Reed and Newley both wrote lyrics featuring intricate character portrayals, and knew despondency inside out.

It helped set Bowie off into a somewhere that didn't sound like something that had just been done that he was simply following. He had known what he wanted his music to be like: music you could make like a painting, combining colours, moods, shadows, textures, atmosphere. And now he had found out there were others doing it. You didn't need to copy the sound or write songs about the same things, but you could follow the confessional, subversive and dreaming spirit; you could write a song piling up heaps of tremendous, seductive images that underneath have hidden undertones that are sort of disturbing and depressing.

After hearing the Velvet Underground, he started singing more obviously about himself, his own quests and cravings, moving away from the oddballs and the London characters he'd been writing about after he'd finally broken free of the sequence of hard-working but ordinary bands with their clichéd songs going nowhere fast. He brought things down to earth, where there was all this space to think, following Lou Reed, and yet giving his songs more depth and detail, not concerned if they were confusing, or longer than three minutes, or used oblique chord changes.

After all those groups he had been in before he heard the Velvet Underground, trying to find himself, with all their names, there was one last group Bowie was part of. Turquoise, who quickly became known as Feathers, was an abstract, multi-media link between those early, mod-fixated groups and the later, more fluid, multi-faceted, Velvets-shaped Bowie, between the immaturity and whimsy of his debut album and the tormented intimacy of 'Space Oddity', his majestic take-off song. It was a way of getting as far from the failure of his debut album as he could, which would make him wince for years, if not decades, and align with the anarchic, underground scene where you could be more artist than third-rate rock star flailing in empty venues and feel free of commercial bondage, if poor.

He'd formed the trio with one of the members of the Buzz, John 'Hutch' Hutchinson, and another mime artist, his then girlfriend Hermione Farthingale, bringing in an English sense of Nico enigma, all of them bonding in a different way from when he was in the groups. Bowie, said Hermione, looked about eight. They'd earn a few pounds mixing up some of the more ambiguous songs from Bowie's debut with Beatles and Jacques Brel covers, poetry and mime.

He was painting, working in the theatre as a mime artist, flirting with becoming a Buddhist, busying himself in the incestuous London arts underground, putting on extended theatrical performances, playing for an audience mostly made up of friends, other musicians, artists and actors, and the music became part of that, not all that he was.

When he split from Hermione, anguish reverberating throughout occasional songs over the next few months, Feathers shrank to a duo. Of course, eventually, he would be alone again, ready to start again, again.

He was learning to be a performer, which made a difference to his music, as he started to write songs imagining them as performances. His music wasn't trying to fit in anymore, to belong with other musicians with the same haircuts and tailored suits sweating their way either to the rocky top or the very sad bottom. It was still folk, even still coming out of the blues, but the folk was uncannier, the blues were more cutting and philosophical, not just copying the obvious patterns and passions. You could write about grief, about emotional turmoil, grievances, about life and death as one thread, and death itself as a kind of awakening.

BACK AND FORTH

Look into his eyes. He always knew one day he would have to make one final change of costume and come back as one final character, beyond himself, outside his own history, leaving his life, his confounding absence, in the memory of the living.

Perhaps he'd planned it all along, living and performing in hope of becoming a memory. Surviving in the hearts of the living. He'd turned his thoughts and discoveries into popular songs, into unforgettable artifacts, with all the modern fuss and paraphernalia that came with them, deciding that was the best way to preserve his imagination.

Death had always been on his mind and in his songs. Death as the great perhaps, a place in his heart he knew would never be filled. He was always fascinated by the idea that the spiritual realm ran parallel to the physical realm. He was searching, in life, and then in his art and music, which became part of his life, for what he called the God beyond God – an unnameable, unknowable incomprehensible realm not human made, an idea of God, which you pray to and please or displease, but beyond the boundaries of language and thoughts.

Look into his eyes and follow his line of thought if you can, as he politely, even shyly, perhaps just a shade irritated, answers another question he doesn't want to be asked twenty years after the fact, about Ziggy Stardust or the Thin White Duke. A question asked by someone who could not see the Bowies beyond the Bowie. He realises he is about to stray into territory not expected from a mere celebrity – however cerebral – temporarily engaged in a spot of publicity-seeking light relief. He wryly, self-mockingly chuckles at where his mind is taking him, towards pondering a mystery greater than our comprehension, but he can't help it.

It's part of what made his pop songs much more than pop songs. Even in his most glamorous, best-known songs, the ones that most gave him a reputation as glam rock star, as the ultimate pop star, he would be surrendering to the unknown, knowing that the true meaning of life is that it stops. Before you fully realise that, the meaning of life is sometimes thinking that it never stops.

He used pop songs as a way of perceiving and representing all movement and activity as he came across it in the universe, in his mind, and from an early age, he became a specialist, a custodian and archivist of its traditions, as untested as they were. Eventually, he would pioneer his own traditions. In the reality that was structured around him, his songs, haunted by humanity, were incantations, hymns, dramas, confessions, arias, lullabies and mysteries, lifted above the ordinary by sheer willpower, committed to what TS Eliot would say is more than enough for one person to do in their life: do the useful thing, say the courageous thing and contemplate the beautiful thing.

On *Blackstar*, his grand finale, a last-minute command performance, he showed that a pop song could carry the weight of the world as well as light up the world, as he had been doing since he was barely out of his teens, when to some he was closer to the wayward singer of sly comedy songs and infectious ditties than a composer of requiems and anthems that inspired the world and led to such grief when he left it.

It wasn't meant to end this way. The show wasn't supposed to stop, and certainly not stop with what seemed designed as a ceremonial event, a scheduled announcement. There wasn't meant to be a last note, a last sound, a last word, as carefully prepared as they were – nothing rushed here, no actual sense of a deadline, everything carried out as though he had all the time in the world.

Blackstar was produced by the producer most associated with David Bowie, Tony Visconti, who had worked with him as close friend and collaborator since 1967 and then in every decade until the end. When they met for the first time, Visconti was a couple of years older than the 21-year-old Bowie and at times, they were as close as brothers. They fell out like brothers as well.

They had years when they weren't talking, as Bowie entered different circles and had different needs, prone to reshuffling his musical, advisory and technical personnel after a certain project or album series was finished. At the end, Visconti was still there, part of Bowie's most intimate creative inner circle.

The American Visconti had travelled to London from Brooklyn in 1968, where he'd started working in studios because the sound quality of his demos was apparently better than the songs he was writing and recording, some for a hopeful Sonny and Cher duo he'd formed with his wife, Siegrid. He had also been a member of a later line-up of the white vocal group the Crew-Cuts, who'd had a hit with 'Sh-Boom' in the fifties. He realised his best performances were in the studio, learning the technical, emotional and psychological – and coaching – skills to become a record producer. Even in the late 1960s, after Phil Spector and George Martin, the role was still a mystery. What did they actually do?

Visconti started assisting the producer Denny Cordell, who had just produced with some self-confidence and flamboyance Procol Harum's wildly melodramatic hit 'A Whiter Shade of Pale' – he'd played it to Visconti in America as an example of his style, weeks before it was a hit. Visconti was impressed by one of the first British records that showed how London studios were beginning to catch up with the more modern American ones and even get better equipment.

The song made Visconti long to live in London, where music like that, which seemed to belong to no known genre, was somehow allowed to happen. The music from England sounded like there was a constant party going on and he wanted to see it for himself.

Visconti helped out on a Cordell-produced New York session for British jazz-pop Georgie Fame using some of the best local jazz musicians, including one of Visconti's favourites Clark Terry, the influential master trumpeter who'd worked with both the Count Basie and Duke Ellington orchestras and recorded with Charles Mingus and Thelonious Monk. When Visconti discovered that Cordell was innocently about to start the session with razor-sharp musicians without any music scores to read from, he hurriedly put one together for all eight musicians, saving the day.

As a non-musician, Cordell happened to need a production assistant to help liaise with musicians in the studio and work on charts and arrangements. His original vain hope that he could persuade Phil Spector or Artie Butler, who'd arranged the Monkees' 'I'm a Believer', to come over and work in London with him was quickly dashed, and he turned to the broke, keen Visconti, who, after struggling in New York, was beginning to believe his musical future lay in playing endless weddings and bar mitzvahs.

Visconti found himself in a London bustling with constantly emerging pop life three months before the release of the Beatles' *Sgt. Pepper*, of which Cordell had an early pressing. Visconti heard it on his first night in London. He had left Brooklyn obscurity and found himself at the centre of the pop world, where there *was* a constant party going on, where you might even spot a Beatle or a Rolling Stone hatching a plan or two, and he was amongst the very first to hear the latest, astounding Beatle experiments with pop.

The early white label test pressing of *Sgt. Pepper* was advanced news about how far rock had come in England in a few quick years. How the songs were made was of particular interest to musical fanatics and equipment addicts like Visconti. He was spending most of the time working out how to make records and keep up to speed with the sounds and effects coming out of EMI Studios on Abbey Road, north London, under the fastidious supervision of George Martin. It was a time when the crazier your sounds were, the more inventive in the studio, the more likely you were to get the attention of radio stations and record buyers. There were tidy, formulaic pop and groomed middle-of-the-road singers like Engelbert Humperdinck at the top of the charts at the same time as there were elaborate songs, newer, wilder fashions and turbulent, psychedelic sounds.

Cordell was part of a stable of producers in a company run by the German-born music publisher David Platz, who had started Essex Music in 1955. Commercially shrewd but with an instinct for discovering unlikely new talent in a rapidly changing world, he helped design the modern form of song publishing. He changed the image of the music publisher from brash and overbearing hustler to something more sensitive and creatively encouraging. He was dragging sluggish, old-time music publishing up to sixties speed and anticipating trends and new styles, as smart young musicians wrote their own increasingly complex but often still commercial songs, and needed deals that were more artist friendly and not so tailored to the previous generation of jobbing writers. Buddy Holly, Chuck Berry and Eddie Cochran, and then Bob Dylan and Lennon and McCartney, contributed to the emergence of teenagers forming bands and wanting to write their own songs.

In the 1950s, Platz's most American-style artist was the jovial, unsexy acoustic skiffle singer Lonnie Donegan, his bare-bones bluesy folk the closest Britain got for a while to rock and roll, triggering a craze for this jaunty home-grown version. By the electrified 1965, keeping up with creative and industry trends, Platz was signing the Rolling Stones' publishing, which made him the place the best new young writers wanted to be. His interests ranged across folk, jazz, pop and rock, and he soon represented the Who, the Moody Blues, Joe Cocker, the Move, Ralph McTell and Bowie's enterprising friend Mark Feld, now Marc Bolan, of underground cunning folk duo Tyrannosaurus Rex.

Platz was also working with Bowie's early vocal, musical theatre and entertainment idol Anthony Newley, marketing him as a sort of British Danny Kaye, helping to put together the musicals Newley wrote with his partner Leslie Bricusse, *Stop the World – I Want to Get Off* and *The Roar of the Greasepaint – The Smell of the Crowd* – the latter with its hit song, the ironic, elemental 'Feeling Good', given proper menace in Nina Simone's version – which would leave their fingerprints all over early Bowie songs.

Platz couldn't resist the energy and determination, and delightful company, of the 20-year-old Bowie, who sometimes seemed he might be a new Ray Davies or a new Pete Townshend, and other times like an efficient clone of Newley or lovable nephew of Danny Kaye. He signed the publishing of the eager, knowledgeable pop music fanatic, who obviously knew how to put together what ended up sounding like a song, but didn't necessarily know what kind of songs he wanted to write, and whether he wanted to just write for others, like Newley and Lionel Bart of the musical version of Charles Dickens' *Oliver Twist*, or become a romantically inclined, performing singer-songwriter like Cat Stevens. They were both on Deram Records, both with an infatuation with Broadway musicals as though they were the future, pop maybe a passing phase, but Cat seemed less distracted and skittish than Bowie.

It could seem as though Bowie was trying to please his publisher by covering all Platz's wide publishing interests – he could conjure up pop songs, folk songs, Dylan impersonations, blues rock songs, musical songs, show tunes, any kind of novelty song and even children's songs. He was a one-man song machine, desperate to prove his versatility and cleverness.

Outside of music, he was also experimenting with painting, poetry, Buddhism, mime, acting, performance art, and any one of those could have become a main pursuit.

He was overwhelmed by outside influences and stimuli, a fast, efficient and imaginative copier of the latest styles and sounds, having moved into the entertainment vortex that central London had become from the pokier suburban outskirts. He plunged into a constant upheaval of musicians, artists, entrepreneurs, publicists, actors, dancers, chancers, hustlers, never finding the centre, increasingly seeming to be one of those talented misfits destined always to miss the boat. For a while, it seemed his face, and his frisky mind, didn't fit.

By the time the idea of a Swinging Sixties fully made itself felt outside an intensely incestuous central London, in the early 1970s, Bowie, chasing and hassling from the very beginning, learning from the best at close quarters, would be a world-leading expert in its transgressive, transformative energies. In the late sixties, he tended to tumble down the wrong rabbit holes.

Platz was always on the side of the artist when it came to supporting their writing, but he still needed to know what kind of box his writers could be put in. The impulsive, impressionable Bowie never stopped leaping from box to box. Platz needed a solution.

He saw that Visconti had managed to get a coherent, distinctive sound out of one of his more idiosyncratic acts, a wild-haired, hyper-hippie acoustic duo, the penniless summer of love casualties Tyrannosaurus Rex, singing like mystic kooks of elves, wizards, unicorns and centaurs. They didn't write sure-fire hit singles but they were building a devoted following. They weren't necessarily a pop act and performed in a cloud of incense sat cross-legged on a tiny piece of carpet – which they'd also auditioned on when Visconti had them play for Cordell as something he wanted to produce. You never knew what was going to work in a world where 'A Whiter Shade of

Pale' rose to the top in all its stoical, baroque splendour. There were no rules yet, no particular fixed strategies or predictable business patterns. Teenage fans were a law unto themselves, so Platz had a feeling Tyrannosaurus Rex might yet be one of these freaky acts that would surprise him.

Visconti had set out looking for acts he could produce and Platz could sign, innocently hoping to find the next Beatles and instead found impish, insatiable Marc Bolan, who was living at home with his mum and dad after his recent, more conventional attempt at singing in a rock group, John's Children, had crashed and burned, and a chance to record with folk-rock producer catalyst of the time Joe Boyd, nurturing John Martyn and Fairport Convention, had come to nothing.

Tyrannosaurus Rex used acoustic guitars, bongos, finger cymbals, a Chinese gong and a toy xylophone mainly because it was all they could afford, but still managed to mesmerise audiences, and had the loving, committed support of trusted DJ to the gentle and weird ones, John Peel, who would read ornate poems and stories for the group.

Once Visconti had shown interest after seeing them in concert lifting a small but transfixed audience into another world, an initially cool-seeming and studiedly blasé Marc was on the phone first thing the next day. He was calling from a phone box over the road from the Platz empire office – him and 18-year-old rootless sidekick Steven Peregrine Took, named after a hobbit from the hippie bible *Lord of the Rings*, stuffed into the box with their guitar and bongos, excitedly thinking maybe their struggles were over.

Within minutes, Bolan and Took were sat on the office floor, singing, chanting and mumbling their arcane free-folk fairy tales, hypnotising Cordell into offering them a small deal. Cordell had decided that the label the Platz company was running for EMI, Regal Zonophone, needed a token underground act. Tyrannosaurus Rex looked and sounded the part like no one else.

Bolan attached himself to Visconti with no intention of letting go. To his surprise, whilst under Bolan's soft-spoken spell, Visconti found himself recruited to help Bolan find the fame he knew, against all apparent evidence, was written in the stars. The first album Visconti produced by Tyrannosaurus Rex had a title that took its time to tell you what it sounded like – *My People Were Fair and had Sky in Their Hair, But Now They're Content to Wear Stars on Their Brow* – and a cover illustration by George Underwood of Marc plunging, with mythical figures in his hair, into a densely detailed phantasmagorical forest, inspired by nineteenth-century French illustrator Gustave Doré's engravings for Milton's *Paradise Lost* and Dante's *Inferno*.

Underwood was the artist who, to put it mildly, changed the colour of David Jones's eyes when the two friends, who first met as nine-year-olds enrolling for the Bromley 18th Cubs and Scouts, had a fist fight over a girl when they were 15. Hearing David had been after the same girl who he thought was interested in him, Underwood punched him in the eye, a ring he was wearing doing most of the damage and paralysing one of David's pupils, leaving the permanent illusion that his eyes were different colours.

Usually, they would be after different girls, pretending they were backing singers for the Everly Brothers to impress them, which had middling success. Chasing the same girl was a rare problem but led to something that helped change the world.

Underwood would go on to create many small fantastical masterpieces, portraits, painting and drawings for Bolan and Bowie albums – including tinting the black and white cover photos of *Hunky Dory* and *The Rise and Fall of Ziggy Stardust* to hyperreal, timeless effect – as well as for groups such as Mott the Hoople and Gentle Giant, but the teenage fist fight and the consequences was perhaps his greatest artwork.

Bowie and Underwood soon became friends again, renewing their larky, girl-chasing, music-driven double act, calling each other by their middle names – David was Robert and

George was Michael. When Bowie was on his 1972 American tour and he could feel a fierce fame start to interfere with his sense of self, tipping into a new kind of danger as strangers surrounded him looking for reflected fame, glamour and precious parts of his psyche, he called on George to join him. He reached out to his old friend, art college and sparring partner for moral support and some necessary familiarity.

For the Tyrannosaurus Rex debut, Cordell gave Visconti enough money for two days' recording and two days' mixing, but by recording at Advision Studios, Visconti beat the Beatles and George Martin to having access to one of the first eight-track recorders – for records up to *Sgt. Pepper*, they would use pairs of four-track machines and didn't get to eight-track recording until the *White Album* in late 1968.

Equipment-mad Visconti was naturally one of the first to try out this new eight-track machine, using Tyrannosaurus Rex as his unlikely guinea pigs. *My People Were Fair* . . . , an album of weirdly tuned cosmically medieval miniatures made mostly using acoustic instruments, recorded in a hurry, was the first album in Britain to be made on an eight-track machine. Visconti fastidiously built up Bolan's mad hatter falsetto, the delicate instruments and erratic percussion of Tyrannosaurus Rex into an exotic small-scale wall of sound. Love it or hate it, it was a considerable piece of modern music recording.

Platz thought, if Visconti can make sense of lovable but infuriating and unplaceable Marc, then maybe he can do something with his other whimsical but undeniably fascinating problem, Marc's freaky, ultra-self-conscious friend, David Bowie.

Visconti could see what Platz meant when he listened to Bowie's debut Deram album, *David Bowie*. He thought the songs were all over the place. Here in one place was a sweetheart pop singer, a make-believe rock and roll star closer to Tommy Steele than Mick Jagger, a dreamy blue-eyed soul singer, a Broadway actor, a children's entertainer, an amiable storyteller, a vaudevillian trouper, a rambling folky, a tortured balladeer. Eventually, Bowie would integrate all the disparate parts and find myriad uses for his encyclopaedic musical knowledge, resonant imagery, feverish intelligence, vast influences and off-beat insights, but for an unknown 20-year-old solo artist looking for a break, needing to stand out in a crowded business but with no clear image, it was a mess.

But a marvellous mess. Bowie didn't know how to write a conventional pop song but there were bits of great songs happening all the time, sung with total, sometimes spooky, conviction or goofy gorgeousness. Even when it was at its most frivolous, there was a sense something profound might be going on. What was most noticeable was that amidst the lovely mess, erratic technique and good-hearted attempts to write catchy songs, Bowie had an immaculate sense of timing. He had to stop trying so hard to do things. He simply had to find a way to trust his instincts.

When Visconti didn't immediately dismiss the idea of working with Bowie, Platz said, if you'd like to meet him, he's in the next room. Here, he said to Visconti, you're an expert working with weirdos, meaning it as a compliment, let's go and meet David. Help me get him under control.

It was a set-up. Suddenly, Visconti was talking to a nervy but voluble Bowie, who attached himself to the producer not unlike the way Bolan had.

Both already knew the importance of the record producer in making a song, or even just an idea for a song, sound like a record, in turning ideas and concepts into dramatic sonic coherence. And Tony was American, which was a bonus to both Bowie and Bolan, with their idealised dreams of glamorous American rock and roll and the characters that came with it. Plus he had assisted Denny Cordell in the making of the first record to be played on Radio 1 when the station was launched in September 1967, catching up with the pirate radio stations Caroline and London playing non-stop pop music.

The Move's euphoric 'Flowers in the Rain' was too poppy for the group themselves, having just toured Britain with Jimi Hendrix as his support act. They liked to think of themselves as a heavier, cleverer group than the light-hearted pop act Cordell had turned them into, using them as a test case for new production techniques and for allowing Visconti to try out some of his more unusual musical ideas.

The earnest, ambitious Visconti was already wondering how to outdo the sound and instrumental innovations of the Beatles and their world-shaking *Sgt. Pepper*. He livened up the straightforward, featureless Move track with a wind quartet, giving perfect of-the-times flower-power friskiness – oboe, flute, clarinet and French horn – which George Martin hadn't considered for the Beatles. Visconti's deft arrangement showed how much he knew his Mendelssohn and Dvořák. Manipulating the sound, he seemed to slow down and simultaneously speed up the quartet in the middle eight to cover a mistake, creating a hook out of nowhere, proving quickly that one of the biggest influences on pop music in the late sixties was as much the arch, yearning Englishness of the fictional Lonely Hearts Club Band as it was the actual Beatles.

AMBITION AND ARROGANCE

Visconti had been in London for a few months, and had adjusted to the sarcasm and often spiky, defensive wit of British musicians, becoming a little anglicised. Spending time with Bolan especially, with his big ideas and often preposterous plans for what he was going to achieve, had been good practice for meeting Bowie. The pair seemed to infect each other with their ambition and, sometimes, breathtaking arrogance.

Within minutes of meeting, Visconti and Bowie had bonded over talk of anarchic American outsiders like Frank Zappa and the Fugs, and Visconti having worked with Clark Terry and his favourite bass player being Charles Mingus's and Bill Evans' young, virtuoso double bassist Scott LaFaro didn't hurt. They talked for hours, taking to the streets around Denmark Street – the British Tin Pan Alley filled with publishers, music shops and recording studios – after the Platz office was shut, discovering more things they had in common. They shared the same Buddhist beliefs and the same Tibetan Buddhist teacher, Lama Chime Rinpoche, and there was a kindliness and gentleness Visconti could identify with, the other side of the protective bantering and competitiveness.

They wandered around Soho in winding circles bonding by talking music. The talking led to Visconti producing Bowie's second album, which was also to be called *David Bowie*, as though he wanted another go at making a self-titled debut album. A record that still shot off in numerous different directions, but maybe one where not every song headed in a different direction.

They first tried a few tracks for Deram after they'd met in September 1967, Visconti pulling Bowie towards what he was seeing as an American outsider as exciting, but still eclectic, British rock and pop. He was essentially trying to stop Bowie sounding at times more middle-aged and oddly dated than the fresh faced, flash-thinking 20-year-old in front of him, who seemed more aware of the range of pop music than anyone he knew, from the fashion-forward, art-angled chart radicals like the Small Faces, the Kinks and the Who to American underground radicals like Iggy and the Stooges, the Fugs and Love. Bowie also talked about the Velvet Underground, wanting to achieve an atmosphere, a distinct, elusive multidimensional world like they did, without copying their sound, as if the songs themselves generated the appropriate mood and tension.

On their first collaboration, Visconti got to work immediately, stripping Bowie of anything baroque or twee for 'Let Me Sleep Beside You', a love song to lovers, a song about needing to grow up. They also recorded 'Karma Man', a song about Tibetan Buddhism as a process of reincarnation, but also about slowing down.

Visconti put David inside a hired rock band, the kind that played on the majority of pop records made by solo vocalists you'd hear at the time. This meant that the Bowie list of distinctive, exploratory guitarists that he would use throughout his music begins in the shadows with two of the three great British session players, along with Jimmy Page.

Visconti used John McLaughlin on electric guitar, who would soon leave soul-destroying session playing behind and find elegant, influential ways to fuse jazz and rock, eventually contributing to Miles Davis's electric early 1970s albums, leaving when Miles said he should form his own group,

For the acoustic guitar, Visconti used Shel Talmy regular Big Jim Sullivan, who'd played sitar on Bowie's debut album, because it was the sixties, and who was the guitarist on numerous number one records, including Cilla Black's 'Anyone Who Had a Heart', Georgie Fame's 'Yeh Yeh', the Walkers Brothers' 'Make It Easy on Yourself' and 'The Sun Ain't Gonna Shine

Anymore', and Chris Farlowe's 'Out of Time', and also played on Donovan's 'Catch the Wind' and 'Colours'.

Still high on the wind instruments he'd added to the Move's number two single 'I Can Hear the Flowers Grow', Visconti added some cello he arranged himself, and the song had the swagger and woozy sixties excitability of a hit. Deram, fast losing patience with the strung-out Bowie, thought the title 'Let Me Sleep Beside You' and chorus too risqué, and asked for more tracks before they decided about any new album.

Bowie kept writing, including some songs maybe destined for others to sing and others where he was still struggling to work out what David Bowie should sound like. But by early 1968, Deram had decided they only needed one singer songwriter with a confusing musical theatre infatuation, and they kept Cat Stevens and let Bowie go.

By the time Cat Stevens shook off his infatuation, or affliction, he had signed to Island Records and was going through a parallel transformation to Bowie, from planning ambitious, incongruous musicals about Rasputin without any real experience to refining a performing persona and concentrating on standalone spiritual songs.

Bowie without the safety of a record deal could have disappeared into obscurity, or into a monastery, or into the lost land of mime. Those who believed in Bowie didn't lose their belief, though. His committed manager Ken Pitt had worked on getting a deal with Mercury Records in America, Philips in the UK and he had a new label by the end of 1968, to go along with the new producer.

Platz was always asking Visconti from his practical publisher's point of view to get Bowie to commit to one style, something that a wider audience could relate to. Bowie, from the wound-up, serious artist perspective, wanted a challenging pop sound that was extreme and accessible, which hadn't worked out on the first *David Bowie* album – the intensity got in the way of the theatricality, and vice versa.

Visconti went to see him play at the Sunday night Folk Club that Bowie was running with journalist friend Mary Finnigan in the summer of 1969 at the Three Tuns pub in Beckenham, where Bowie was living. He'd drifted back to the London suburbs after failing to discover the secret password that would give him access to the ultimate London inside track. In Beckenham, he tried to make his own creative scene, determined to bring the hipsters and freaks 20 minutes by train out of town, so he could try again, this time with more of a name, to join in where the action was back in London's music industry headquarters.

He would transform the scruffy pub stage into something fit to host experimental ideas and kaleidoscopic post-Dylan folk music, nicking ideas from the psychedelic central London clubs with their trippy light projections, putting candles on tables and lighting joss sticks. The underground always needed a touch of knocked-together showbusiness. A stark, dowdy back room in a south London pub became a psychedelic playground.

Later, following the Drury Lane Arts Club with its counterculture happenings and social activism where David would rehearse his mime performances, the Folk Club became an Arts Lab. A network of Arts Labs opened around the country following the original radical Arts Lab manifesto, which set out the space as a non-institutional energy centre where anything could happen depending on the surroundings and a fluid setting for a variety of life as art and art as political purposes, where no one was paid, and people could bring their own paintings, poetry, stories, craft, food, kids, instruments – all experimental ideas welcome.

A few friends would turn up, and Bowie would sing his raw, romantic-sounding new songs using his latest precious 12-string Hagstrom guitar. He loved it for the way it created a lusher, fuller sound, so that when he was writing a song, it was as if he was playing two or three instruments at once. When he played his early shows, often supporting Tyrannosaurus Rex with their particular acoustic chamber sound, he called his 12-string guitar his orchestra. He would drive himself to gigs up and down the newish motorways that were a boon to travelling musicians, with the speakers he used to amplify his guitar strapped to the roof of his Fiat 400. The mime he would also add to his act didn't need any luggage space, just a straight face.

He didn't think of himself as a guitarist. It had just become a way to write songs, which inevitably seemed folk because one person expressing themselves and accompanying themselves with a guitar usually does. He approached the guitar as a painter, someone who saw music in visual ways, and thought of the guitar neck as a landscape, and each note or cluster of notes as objects – trees, streams, rocks – in that landscape. When Visconti watched him play, he noticed he knew lots of unusual chords, and would juxtapose them in surprising and delicate ways, possibly because he was thinking visually rather than musically, in terms of mood, shape, architecture, colour, texture. Visconti had been used to working with Bolan, who built his vast repertoire based on six or seven basic chords roughly borrowed from the blues. Bowie had built enough mystery chords borrowed from jazz, classical, Broadway, tradtional folk, avant-garde rock and baroque pop to last him a lifetime.

He'd pass on the playing of his chords, or his ideas for chords, to his guitar players, from the hard, visceral rock of Mick Ronson in the early 1970s to the intuitive, unconfined impressions of 2016's *Blackstar*'s Ben Monder, via himself – for the polarised, pulverised deadbeat energy of *Diamond Dogs*, he directed his own guitar playing, generating a dystopic punk blues – and then Carlos Alomar, Robert Fripp, Ricky Gardiner, Earl Slick, Adrian Belew, Stevie Ray Vaughan, Reeves Gabrels and David Torn.

It was like he wrote lines of dialogue, or scenarios, occasionally just abstract suggestions and sketched-out blueprints, for actors, who followed them to the letter or improvised around them, adding their own character, their own influences and style. This 50-year guitar trail and the blueprints all began with his 12-string acoustic, and the songs he started to write on them, which focused his mind and set up his meticulously detailed songs, rather than weighing them down with ornamental over-thinking.

Visconti encouraged this enhanced, evocative take on folk expression and jazz structure, and hints of the structural ambiguities of the Velvet Underground, so there could be a consistency throughout *David Bowie* (II). For this album, Bowie's 12-string would be the band, the identity, with added electric guitars and drums and bass, so that wherever Bowie went lyrically, it was kept inside a vague, identifiable, psychedelic folk world that would satisfy the business with their boxes and labels and their ultimate fear of the unknown. It was Bowie's fascination with the unknown that was keeping him unknown.

Creating consistency from a rapturous muddle of ideas and impressions was what Visconti had done with Tyrannosaurus Rex, but with Bowie, Visconti was dealing with a darker, more supernaturally observant and deviously autobiographical mind, dealing with Bowie's troubled tenderness, his experimental chords and melodies. Bolan was an ebullient fantasist and fun to be around; with Bowie, there was more going on, which sometimes wasn't necessarily fun, and a powerful compulsion to work out who and what he was.

Unlike Bolan in Tyrannosaurus Rex, Bowie wasn't frolicking in the woods, chasing alluring fauns and drumming up ancient dreams. At least, not in his songs. He was writing about not finding ways to fit in, translating his experiences of feeling left out, at the edge of things, unwanted and unloved, however hard he tried, however many friends he made, whatever scenes he created for himself. They were songs about finding refuge and the songs were themselves his refuge, where he could invent worlds and characters mirroring his own dilemmas and despair, creating them to work himself out, how and why he sometimes felt scared of his own mind.

These characters found themselves in a dystopia sometimes of their own making, living in a world dominated by technology and disconnect, alienation, loneliness and dysfunction. As much as he travelled and changed – forced change on himself and had change forced on him – over the next few years, as famous as he became, those obsessions and the feelings of loneliness, the need to explain the inexplicable, were at the centre of everything he did.

In America, the album was given the sombre title *A Man of Words/A Man of Music* because, as much as Visconti and Bowie had straightened out the zig-zagging quirks of the debut, the follow-up was still a warped if luminous variety show. It seemed, at least to a record company ushering a complete unknown into what in the end was the marketplace, that an audience needed to be told, literally, who Bowie was and what it was he did. As he took more control and gained more confidence, he would soon sort out these problems with the carefully chosen titles of his albums.

Whatever the second album was called, with Visconti helping to create the space for him to move and find his own space, Bowie had begun, musically, to live.

SHADOWS AND DUST

Fifty years later, beginning all over again, Bowie and Visconti were still taking walks, this time on the streets of New York, still talking about music, theirs and in general, and how to organise their thoughts. The title being used this time to tell an audience who Bowie was and what it was he did had become much more abstract and much more accurately muted; to some extent, it wasn't even a word, just a symbol.

The making of *Blackstar* began, as all David Bowie albums would begin, after the second album – which began with the 12-string guitar – with a live band, the latest band that Bowie would use to create the sonic style he was looking for to fit where his mind and mood was. A jazz fan from an early age, he thought like a jazz musician as much as a pop or rock musician, planning the instruments and groups of musicians he would use for a particular album.

For this album, knowing he was heading into his final years, if not necessarily his final months, he was going to make the kind of jazz album he had always had at the back of his mind, using as the core of his band the Donny McCaslin Quartet – McCaslin on saxophone, Tim Lefebvre on bass, Mark Guiliana on drums and Jason Lindner on keyboards. Ben Monder was the latest of Bowie's rotating and overlapping guitar players – his final guitarist a technical marvel, suitably floating free of any particular genre whilst aware of them all, existing in an ethereal, adventurous, mysterious rare groove.

Somehow, there were discreet echoes of all the pop, rock, soul, funk, avant-garde guitarists Bowie had used, an oblique tribute to their continuing importance in setting the mood and style of each album since his touchstone 12-string, letting them drift out on this record as far as possible.

Bowie had come across the quartet on one of his regular jaunts into New York nightlife in 2014, always on the hunt for potential collaborators or just music that might inspire something in him as a fan or songwriter. McCaslin had been releasing acoustic jazz albums since the late 1990s, incorporating electronics and new areas of rhythmic work after hearing probing, textural electronic music by drum'n'bass deformer Squarepusher and the cryptic, mesmerising electronic duo Boards of Canada.

Bowie responded to a progressive, speculative mix of tradition – in this case the jazz, the influence of Archie Shepp, Sonny Rollins and Weather Report – and the modern progressive – here, the abstract, mystical electronics – he'd always favoured in his own music. It was jazz plus, jazz at some kind of edge of becoming something else, and Bowie heard the sound he was looking for to take his words about where he was, in the moment, leading to the moments that were becoming more dramatic by the day.

Applying vocals to musical structures and songs played by musicians who usually improvised would be something new for someone always keen on trying something new, even this far into his musicmaking. There was no thought of sticking to a formula or repeating an old one; the only thing staying consistent from album to album would be a certain spirit of adventure and a certain shared ambition to make 'the one', the best Bowie album yet.

At first, making the best Bowie album was easy, after the madcap, mixed-up overly quirky debut, released with terrible timing the same day in 1967 as the album Bowie and Visconti held in 1969 and 1970 as their gold standard, the technological and cultural marvel, *Sgt. Pepper's Lonely Hearts Club Band*. (Bowie and Visconti together had different opinions about music and pop history as Bowie and Visconti separately. Bowie's loves were often more awkward, eccentric and challenging, Visconti's more straightforward and delightful. Together they found a middle space where they could work from, satisfying each other's perfectionism.)

The second Bowie album, *David Bowie*, or *A Man of Words/ A Man of Music*, later known as *Space Oddity*, where Visconti helped sort out various problems caused by Bowie's almost manic youthful eclecticism, was the best Bowie album up until then.

The follow up, 1970's *The Man Who Sold the World*, where Bowie began to put together his first great rock band with guitarist Mick Ronson, drummer Woody Woodmansey, hard but nuanced rockers from Hull, and Visconti on bass, replaced it as the best ever Bowie album. Bowie and Visconti were working together with increasing confidence, connecting Bowie's imaginings, musical eccentricities and fantasising, and Visconti's skills as coordinator, musical arranger and sound technician.

The arrival of the shy, slight Ronson was huge for Bowie – here was a genius on his instrument who was prepared to be guided and even controlled by Bowie, as though he was the paint that Bowie was using, but somehow paint that could change its own colour. Live, Ronson would concentrate on his playing, the most important thing to him, allowing Bowie to use him as a kind of prop, a living foil, in a dance he was choreographing, touching him, using his energy, eventually even mock fellating him, stoking Ronson's energy as part of a greater performance. The inventive, urgent guitarist and imaginative song arranger, the kind of musician who if he'd never met Bowie would have been content staying behind the scenes, committed himself to the provocative theatre Bowie was setting his songs inside. Which eventually meant playing his part as a made-up and costumed Spider from Mars, carried into the future and living someone else's dream.

THOUGHTS AND PRAYERS

Hunky Dory came next, not produced by Tony, now busy elsewhere, which became not only 'the one' at that time but a record which would stay permanently as 'the one' in many minds, as if Bowie as songwriter and cultural antennae had peaked in the studio as the Beatles had, and the rest was history, the rest was clarification, a variety of extensions and elaborations.

The idea of making 'the one' then went through various stages of difficulty, as if Bowie had uncovered some kind of secret. Between 1972 and 1980, Bowie made a few albums that could be said to be 'the one'. Some were produced by Visconti, including the three albums seen by Bowie as an artistic triptych during one of his very distinct periods of focus, *Low*, *Heroes* and *Lodger*, and known in the wider world as the Berlin Trilogy. It was his most potent period of breaking down form and tradition – he'd pick up the threads most notably on *Outside*, when he reconvened with one of the more elusive, unattached and quizzical members of any of Bowie's irregular bands, Brian Eno, in some ways the abstract band leader on the Berlin Trilogy and even in a way on the final two albums, *The Next Day* and *Blackstar*, when the past and the future were becoming one and the same thing, and the vagabond life of a wandering magician was drawing to a close, heading towards a day that would be the shortest of his life.

The elaborate, exquisite 1980 album *Scary Monsters (and Super Creeps)* concluded and to some extent summarised an extraordinary series of shapeshifting, sound-bending albums that dominated the seventies as the Beatles had dominated the sixties. It was like a manifesto after the fact, taking stock of ten years of conflagration, disintegration and reinvention.

After Visconti produced *Scary Monsters*, there was a long break following a perhaps inevitable falling out before he returned for *Heathen* in 2002. For the final four albums, the mantra had shifted slightly. *Scary Monsters* was Visconti's own favourite Bowie album, where he felt they had enough time to produce their Pepper-like masterpiece. It replaced *Sgt. Pepper* as the album they needed to outdo.

The joke between them was that as each Bowie album in the 1990s after the non-Visconti 1980s, whatever its quality, was greeted as the best since *Scary Monsters* – where prime, God-like 1970s Bowie was generally seen as having peaked – the next one needed to be at least as good. The disciplined but daring sense of adventure Visconti and Bowie established as soon as they started working together, leading from *David Bowie* and *The Man Who Sold the World*, and the collaboration of *Diamond Dogs* which Visconti helped Bowie finish off, via the Berlin triptych to *Scary Monsters*, was revitalised in the twenty-first century. The 22 years they didn't work together somehow didn't exist; they carried on from where they had left off in 1980.

To outdo Bowie's own history meant making a masterpiece; it's difficult to think of an album made at the end of a rock or pop or even jazz musician's life that could be considered their masterpiece, their finest work. Late life, end-of-life masterpieces belong mostly to classical composers, from Beethoven's late string quartets to Shostakovich's late symphonies. Energy, relevance, subject matter all tend to have dried up for the pop and rock musician, whose last years swing towards retreading and archiving old material and celebratory performances more than any extension or radical development of their earlier work.

For the classical musician, diminished energy can be transformed into beautiful, melancholy music; relevance does not fluctuate within their own lifetime as much as it does for a musician stuck with the changes and transformations attached to popular culture, and facing death is more of a subject matter for the classical composer – attached to centuries of history, with a constant connection between inspiration and spirituality, and between the moment and eternity.

By the time they came to *Blackstar*, the album after the Visconti-produced *The Next Day*, which was released in 2013, ten years after he produced *Reality* as Bowie's health faltered after a 2004 heart attack, Bowie was nearing his seventies. He'd completed 25 studio albums. He was an old man, relatively speaking, although it was never spoken in those terms. It was David Bowie, after all. If he's an old man, revisiting lost loves, creative highlights and once-upon-a-time moments, drifting into silence, then the world is in real trouble.

The Next Day had looked to the past with nostalgia, quiet wit and deep emotion, but still looked forward, still trying to be different, noticeably connected to where he'd been, as enigmatic entertainer and elusive avant-gardist who used music as a way of defeating the terrors and trauma of life. It appeared as the *David Bowie Is* exhibition began, as though to make clear, yes, there is this majestic presentation and reassessment of everything he had done, a way of signalling everywhere he has ever been, all the things he saw and did, many of the costumes he wore on the way, but there is more to come. He was leaving behind hundreds even thousands of clues and reminders, but there were still more to come.

The Next Day was about days before, a collection of disjointed memories, the kind which thrive in the dark, some of which seemed more real than ever, some which seemed to be constantly changing, some of them doing funny things to his mind. But it was also building a path into the future, indicating that the journey he was on had not come to an end. There was still tomorrow and what it might bring – the title said so. There may be an ending, but an ending that would always contain beginnings and shadows.

There was time for a final album, some summing up to be done, an exit to be made, a last adjusting of the sails.

SOMETHING AND NOTHING

After a few months in 2015 spent rehearsing and sketching out ideas, a couple of days before the recording started, Bowie told Visconti that he was seriously ill. He seemed optimistic that with treatment and therapy he could recover, but he needed to let Tony know that there would be days when he might need to leave the studio early if his energy ran out.

The extent to which Bowie was ill and suffering deeply was a shock to Visconti, who had thought he was recovering well after previous scares. Visconti seemed more shaken than his friend when he was told the news. Bowie had to console his producer. The next day, Bowie informed the band, who were also deeply upset but took on board when Bowie said it was serious but not terminal. He appeared to believe he would recover and there was no need to stop the sessions. When he started singing, he didn't seem weakened. He had the vocal power he had always had, if not more.

The words seemed alive with beguiling intensity, a unique mix of fantasy, memoir and guidebook. The songs were about journeys, and journeys within journeys, all of them spinning around the long-established rituals of Bowie's music, reporting how all of us find ourselves all the time whether we acknowledge it or not in an extreme, challenging situation in between life and death.

The work in the studio took over, as Bowie was always committed, even under these circumstances, to ensuring that the focus was on the music. That was what you always concentrated on. He wanted this record's combination of style and reflection to work, he wanted to find a new way to combine voice with jazz, and he was excited that he was working with the best possible musicians he could to achieve what he wanted. He always loved making records, which meant finishing off songs as a method of self-enlightenment, and this was no different. Except the self-enlightenment had an extra edge. He never liked to be idle and, as ill as he was, he wasn't going to stop working. Music for him had been a place where the brain and the universe met, and his illness, with all the life it brought to the very idea of death, made this particular studio time more intense.

He knew that feeling would make it into the music and felt that remaining inventive to the end – if this was the end, and if it wasn't, whenever that was – made sense of all the work he had put into his music, his art, over the previous 50 years. His attitude had always been: live every day as if it is your last, and be ready that it might not be. Through the years, even before his 2004 heart scare, he had this in him – that death was never far away in the future. Now, it seemed, it really wasn't. It was time to concentrate on producing a unique kind of artistic testament. He had explored the death of characters, had killed off characters, thought of death and sang about death, and now he was exploring his own death, coming to terms with it, bringing it out into a public space.

At the end of 2015, Bowie started to make calls to friends and colleagues, just to catch up, perhaps, but there was something else, not necessarily bleak, in between the words. He was still laughing, and reminiscing, still thinking of music to be made. You might have had some questions after the end of the call, the same way you'd have some questions at the end of November when a song called 'Blackstar' was released as a single, edited down to 9 minutes 57 seconds by Bowie and Visconti, as Spotify – where seven-inch singles and 33⅓ albums had washed up after 60 years of drama and dreams – wouldn't play a single track longer than ten minutes. How much better the world might be if they'd chosen a more random time, like 11 minutes 34, but Bowie lived to see the days when the original magic of the seven-inch single and the record album had reached a voluminous, sterile end point.

Despite the cultural and personal signs, Bowie was still experimenting with pop, with music, with the studio process that had led to 'Space Oddity', with the idea of being David Bowie and imagining what he would be thinking as the air got thinner and the world got darker and there was only so much time to process what was on his mind, weighing it down and lightening it.

You'd be asking yourself questions, though thinking you might be reading too much into it – you might have been one of those people who couldn't help reading too much into 'Life on Mars', into 'Station to Station', into 'Ashes to Ashes'. Is he saying that he is dying, is he being so deliriously unsilent and livid because he's got to get it out of his system, quick? Is he done and giving anyone who is interested time to digest the fact?

Or was this just how Bowie was going to grow old – keeping a list, wandering the forest, watching the news, staring at the sunset, delivering strange messages, singing like an angel, discussing the past, present and future from a weird distance, stretching sound into diabolical new shapes, because who the hell was going to stop him? Spotify?

Blackstar was a meticulous commercial release, produced, packaged and presented like an album, that fragile, temporary twentieth-century canvas that allowed him to do so much. Therefore, because it was him, it was also a fluid work of art fighting the confines of the world, imagining new realities, confronting the dying world before him and inside him.

Two days later, the killer punchline: he's visiting one more country, taking one more walk, beyond the sea, beyond the sky, into the invisible country far away. He's alone. He's not alone.

Give me your hands.

His death was given the headlining, analysing attention a majestic fairy-tale monarch might have received. When he started making records in 1964, with some of the moves and mannerisms of a giddy light entertainer, and flickering hints of a provocative deep-thinking outlier, imagining such a thing would have seemed preposterous, like something from a science fiction future.

The announcement of his death came two days after the appearance on his sixty-ninth birthday of what turned out to be his final album. He was alive on the Friday and then he was not on the Monday. Overwhelming sadness changed the very nature of the album and also made people think; when something like that happens, things will never be the same again. It felt more than just the end of a life.

As a final appearance, a final, intended work, it reshaped his entire musical story, reordering things, even to the extent of putting *Blackstar* at the centre of his art life even as it came at the very end. It emphasised his experimental and esoteric instincts, and lifted up and clarified everything he had sung and sung about. It surrounded everything he had done and was surrounded by everything he had done.

His death came without warning, other than two signs at the end of 2015 that he was thinking particularly deeply about death as a phenomenon and a certainty. It was known he had been ill. After decades of seeming ageless and looking youthful and eternally stylish, even as he was 50 and then 60, even as he had fought addictions and had heart scares and smoked as if it was saving his life not burning a hole in it, there were physical signs he couldn't hide. Not even the star man chameleon, the defiant changeling, the man who liked to look the part, whether it be exaggerated rock star, alien visitor or genial public intellectual. Whatever begins also ends. The meaning of life is that it stops. Accept it.

The day Bowie died, of all his famous songs that were played around the world in private and in public, as grief was processed, shared and a communal gratitude spread, one in particular seemed particularly prescient. It was one of his anxious songs that he wrote to sound an alert, which came with the kind of theatre he relished. 'Five Years' was the audacious pitch-black opening track setting up the *Ziggy Stardust and the Spiders from Mars* album that launched him as a real-world superstar sensation after years of trying.

'Five Years' said, before we get to the cities, speed, promises, frenzy, paranoia, sex and irresistible drama inside the album, don't take any of this future for granted. The song had the detail and intensity of a film or a novel, one that opened gateways to new possibilities and potentials of being. It announced that Earth was really dying; the planet had five years left – no reason given, no cause, no one to blame except perhaps everyone for not taking enough care. It was just the end of civilisation and, with a heavy heart, and a heavy drumbeat counting down the days, Bowie described the fear and panic, the resignation and desperation.

When Bowie died, the song seemed to activate a deeper meaning behind this dazzling fiction. We've got five years left. The world might not be coming to an end but everything we held dear was.

ETERNITY AND A DAY

The Rise and Fall of Ziggy Stardust perfected ideas Bowie had had about the potential of the record album to create an imaginative framework to work within, provisionally presented on the previous two albums, *The Man Who Sold the World* and *Hunky Dory*.

There were those who had got there before, the obvious British ones like the Beatles, the Who, the Stones, Pink Floyd and the Kinks, and the Americans Bob Dylan, Iggy and the Stooges and the Velvet Underground, but their 1960s looked decades out of date by the early 1970s, separated by the Moon landing of 1969 and the American winning of the Space Race that had run concurrently with the Cold War.

He hadn't yet completely become David Bowie before the Moon landing. Or, rather, he actually had become David Bowie, after a few false starts, but that wasn't quite enough yet to make him something more than a cult artist, a name to know amongst the cognoscenti. Perhaps a cult artist who'd had a surprise hit single with the immaculately constructed 'Space Oddity' that meant he might never be taken seriously, frozen for the rest of his life inside his deliriously opulent song about the mysteries of space and an altered perception of time.

Visconti wasn't sure when David presented the song to him for inclusion on the album they had been carefully preparing. For the producer, it didn't fit with the tone and perspective of the other songs, and in his memorable words, it seemed a bit of a cheap shot, a desperate, obvious attempt to grab some second-hand attention from all the hype surrounding the imminent Apollo 11 American moon mission.

He knew where the idea for the song had come from – along with a doctor friend, Visconti and Bowie, happily stoned, went to see Stanley Kubrick's transcendent film *2001: A Space Odyssey*, the cinematic experience of the moment, and Bowie reacted as though he had seen God, and God was playing a 12-string guitar. He also seemed to have seen into the dream he had of the kind of songs he wanted to write.

He viewed the film as being about the feeling of isolation that was becoming the central theme of his songs. The film gave him a clear way of crystallising this isolation, where an astronaut in a small capsule is floating in space with billions of people below him on Earth and billions of stars surrounding him, but he is completely on his own.

Visconti had the kind of countercultural energy more prevalent at the time. Having been determined to sort out Platz's Bowie problem, he felt this was repeating one of the problems of the first album, packing too many styles into one place in search of an elusive hit. He said to Bowie that he didn't think it should go on the album and unbalance it. None of the other songs were like it, and Visconti didn't think he'd ever write another song like it. Which he never did, not explicitly.

It stood alone. It was nothing like what they'd been rehearsing and it felt to Visconti like another one of those novelty sounding one-offs he'd been determined to avoid on the new album.

Bowie admitted to Visconti that unless 'Space Oddity' was on the record, his new American label, Mercury, was reluctant to give them the money to go into the studios to make it. In classic record label terms, it didn't have a radio-friendly hit single on it. The London-based man from Mercury's UK label, Philips, was convinced 'Space Oddity' was a hit and put some money into making a demo without the head of the American label knowing. When Mercury heard it, they agreed it felt like a single.

To their ears, 'Space Oddity' wasn't a song about loneliness and an innate, universal search for connection. It wasn't a song about a cold universe and not knowing what's out there, nor about how we miraculously find ourselves against all reason and logic in this tiny, fluky pocket in the cosmos where there's a sun, nor about how all we have is love and the need to guard ourselves against all that loneliness and isolation. The label didn't see it as a song about an astronaut who doesn't know why he's up there in space, who, at the end of the song, is just left there, where there's nothing; everything in the universe he knew is on Earth and he can't get back there.

To Mercury, it was set in space. It had astronauts. There was the moon. There was some kind of jeopardy. It was a space song with a catchy chorus in the year of space. It was what made signing Bowie a more attractive proposition for Mercury Records. Bowie hadn't fully explained this to his producer.

Visconti was stubborn and didn't want his plans for the record – and, as he saw it, his career – to be compromised by working on this trivial 'cheap shot'. If he had to go ahead and record it, his recommendation was another of the producer/engineers in Platz's production department, Gus Dudgeon, who loved Bowie and really wanted to work with him on something new.

Dudgeon was a friend; he'd contributed the potty pixie laughter to Bowie's daftest, most clownish, Danny Kaye-esque song, 'Laughing Gnome', from his debut album and he was based just down the hall from Visconti. Bowie took Visconti's advice and played the demo to Dudgeon in his office, who couldn't believe his luck. Are you sure, he asked Visconti? He's all yours, Visconti laughed.

Dudgeon heard a potential, dramatic space opera and immediately knew what he wanted to do. He took the opportunity, in the spirit of Visconti, to use the chance to try out a host of studio ideas he hadn't been able to place.

Early, relatively primitive and low-key demos of the song include one written for the temporary neo-Simon and Garfunkel duo Bowie had formed with John Hutchinson of Feathers. There is a solo version on a homemade tape of new material for Mercury, which shows Bowie moving the pieces around, focusing the story and finding a place for the pocket-sized Stylophone – a cheap, gimmicky toy synthesiser where you played a small keyboard with an attached metal rod. Depending on which story you prefer, one had been sent to Bowie's manager Ken Pitt by a marketing manager looking for musicians to use it, or it was sent to his friend Marc Bolan who threw it out because it was too fiddly and made a horrible noise; he'd stick with the toy xylophone. The inflexible robotic sound gave the demo a thin thread of fragile Space Age interference. Like Bowie's song, the futuristic-looking little machine was in the shops at just the right time to seem connected to a man walking on the Moon.

Even though the words lacked even a hint of the sometimes awkward transitions and over-involved imagery of Bowie's Deram songs, it still seemed to exist in a folky limbo between those songs and his later, more certain and often incandescent songs. Dudgeon thought of it as a short radio play, almost an audio film, which involved losing the strumming folk element and creating an elemental, one-off planet-spanning genre. To help him achieve the seemingly impossible atmosphere he was looking for, Dudgeon introduced Bowie to Paul Buckmaster, a young classically trained cellist who'd failed in his dream of becoming an international concert cellist. He was currently playing on tours with various bands including the Bee Gees and had limited arranging experience.

When Bowie met Buckmaster, he was excited by the untested originality of his ideas and the fact that he would be the first musician to use them in his songs. After desperately chasing fashion in his early few years, Bowie wanted to make sure that in the future, he would be the first to discover a new style, an unusual way of doing things. He would lead, like George Martin's Beatles, like the Velvet Underground.

'Space Oddity', reflecting new adventures and new states of mind, was, in an ideal world, the kind of song that needed something sonically new, so that it sounded like the future that at the time seemed to be actually happening around us. The number of early versions there were of the song suggested there might be no ideal world, especially when Visconti turned it down. In a way, that was an act of production because it was an artistic decision, a deliberate act of omission. It led to a kind of magic that was destined to happen over to the side of what Bowie was developing with Visconti. Time and space overlapped. Bowie could be in two – or more – places at once.

The freedom Dudgeon and Buckmaster were given to experiment with Bowie and not have to explain what they were doing to anyone outside the inner circle led to something uncanny that brought out the fantastic power of the song's words. Initially, the depth and clarity weren't so noticed in the middle of all the sixties happenings, where plenty of other folk songs were drifting into psychedelic areas. When 'Space Oddity' was more a folk-like song, the lyrics simply told a story, a far-fetched fable. As part of an enigmatic, innovative soundscape, they were the experience itself, set apart from current trends and fashions, that would only grow over time.

On hearing what the Stylophone was doing on the demo, Dudgeon knew that a mellotron was needed, the electro-mechanical sampler used by the Beatles for the flute introduction to 'Strawberry Fields Forever'. It was all over the steamy pop orchestration of the Moody Blues' 'Nights in White Satin', as if the band were on a royalty for all mellotrons sold. The mechanics of the mellotron were a mystery but if handled well, it led to mysterious music. The early problem was finding a player that could do more than merely use its pre-set sounds.

Tony Visconti was producing a single on Regal Zonophone by early John Peel heavy blues favourite Junior's Eyes, and booked a Royal College of Music piano-playing student, Rick Wakeman, to help out. Wakeman was happy to earn the £9 session fee for the Junior's Eyes session and, crucially, had found a way to make the mellotron work.

Wakeman was called in for one of his very first sessions and greeted with relief by everyone at Trident Studios along St Anne's Court, Soho, who were frustrated that they couldn't keep the damned thing in tune. The merry, determined Wakeman brought the mellotron to life and, in 20 minutes, created the unearthly string sound evoking disaster or deep, eternal peace – a hint of something infinite that reminds you that you are finite.

Because of this, and because he was funny, and without making much of a fuss about it, musically brilliant, Wakeman would become a member of solo Bowie's earliest wandering, make-shift bands. He also did his own shape shifting, from the spirited folk rock of the Strawbs to prog lords and masters Yes, and then his own conceptual historical extravaganzas.

Buckmaster also brought in bassist Herbie Flowers, another nomadic music specialist and a part-time member of Bowie's early ensembles, leading to the classic, contemplative bass part he gave the Bowie and Ronson-produced Lou Reed 'Walk on the Wild Side'. The drummer, Terry Cox, came from the folk fab five and dark power specialists Pentangle, who played a pure, courtly music that wasn't quite blues, jazz, folk, pop or rock. Guitarist Mick Wayne of Junior's Eyes, nicknamed 'One Take Mick' for his efficiency as a session player, had played on the classic James Taylor song 'Carolina in My Mind', released in 1968 on the Beatles' Apple label with Paul McCartney on bass – McCartney's first experience with eight-track recording equipment, which is why 'Hey Jude' was recorded at Trident while EMI Studios prepared their new eight track to what they called EMI Studios' standards.

For all of the players on 'Space Oddity', what initially seemed like just another quick, in-and-out session turned into something undeniably special, something they gave more to because they felt they had been called in for a reason, despite the usual casualness of the arrangement and booking.

It seemed initially like just another ordinary bit of basic playing, helping out friends or friends of friends, or just being paid to play on something formulaic; then you were swept up into a moment, sensing the emergence of something important, something beyond the usual routine.

The hairs stand up on the back of your neck as you listen back to the track. You don't talk too much about what you've just done because there's no way yet of really judging what you are doing, but in the future, you want to repeat the same feeling, the same emotional rush cracking through the money-chasing routine of freelance session playing.

Buckmaster knew grandness was needed to capture the spaced-out spirit of 'Space Oddity' and put together an orchestra consisting of eight violins, two violas, two cellos, two acoustic bass guitars and an organ, used in particular for the song's lift-off – organic sounds acting as a ghostly reflection of what once was, merging with the two extremes of the eery machine mellotron and the intermittent, tremulous Stylophone. Bowie kept the Stylophone, risking kitsch, even with the orchestra and the mellotron, three stages of music making that added inexplicable essence to the overall mood.

The song starts with Bowie's 12-string, as if, after all the clutter and offerings, things had now settled down to one man and his guitar telling a story that might be centuries old, that might not have even happened yet. It's what his publisher had asked for – one style to rule them all. Then, of course, all of space and time joins in, as organised by Bowie, Dudgeon and Buckmaster and their visiting musicians, as though this might be their one chance of glory, or at least a hit record, taken by surprise at what they were involved in.

It was rush released on 11 July, three weeks after it had been recorded just in time for the Apollo 11 launch on the sixteenth and the landing on the twentieth – the cynical ploy that made Visconti recoil. Someone at the BBC, finding a new release about astronauts that used some space terminology, not least a very helpful countdown, hoodwinked by Bowie's exquisite melody and graceful vocal, used it as background music in some of their coverage. The playing of it was soon stopped when it became apparent it was more a dark song of loss – of an astronaut's failure, despair and even insanity as he orbits the Earth – than a song of celebration.

Slowly, the song, written as an antidote to all the space fever, took off on its own initially slow journey. Bowie finally made an appearance on *Top of the Pops* in early October 1969, a gentle looking hippy with curly hair and sad alien eyes playing an acoustic guitar and Stylophone, which helped the song to reach number five in the charts and to gain the attention that none of his other hit-seeking sixties songs came close to receiving. Although the song became directly linked with the excitement surrounding the Apollo 11 Moon landing, and was Bowie's first commercial hit, it was as much a hallucinatory song about a fugue state, about losing your mind, as it was the jaunty, timely, novelty pop song celebrating America's space programme victory it became. For Bowie, escaping the Earth's atmosphere was a kind of nightmare, a hellish weightless loneliness, a terrifying retreat from reality.

Visconti had to admit that the Bowie, Dudgeon and Buckmaster 'Space Oddity' worked beautifully in isolation, but it really didn't fit on the album they now had the money to make. It opened the album and then the record went into another part of the universe.

'Space Oddity' was an event, it was a hybrid of oddball and masterpiece, not even really a single. It was in a world of its own, a kind of beautiful folly created by a group of youngsters enjoying a certain kind of freedom from responsibility. It was Bowie's determination to prove he knew what he was doing turned into a work of art, and the determination and rush of liberation continued on to the quietly epic B-side. Recorded the same day with Bowie on guitar and Buckmaster bowing an acoustic bass, 'Wild Eyed Boy From Freecloud', instead of the usual throwaway B-side, was an oblique companion piece to the A-side's take on the cold, cold space between planets and the awful loneliness of the outside world. A boy in the mountains who lives a beautiful life and sees the future is feared by the local villagers who decide to hang him. Anyone unclear about the darkness of the A-side as a cerebral song about exile needed to listen to the B-side. With its sense of nothing being permanent, it revealed a lot about Bowie the wanderer's sense of estrangement at the time. No one understood him.

Without the Moon landing, DJs wouldn't have played 'Space Oddity' on the radio. It was the kind of song that could only be made at that time, as culture and technology collided in the post-war decades. The combining of a singular mind, technicians with ideas how to create sound effects as if their real calling was as sound designers, and musicians who came to life when they found themselves in an exciting situation, challenged to stretch themselves.

After the initial hit single palaver, and a Special Award for Originality at the prestigious annual Ivor Novello songwriting awards, as if the music industry didn't quite know what to make of it, the song stayed where it was. It was very 1969, the year of the Moon landing, even though, ultimately, after two or three more years spent in the doldrums, it helped take David Bowie where he was going, as though the song itself was a kind of space rocket.

LUCK AND TRAGEDY

Bowie was beginning to experience different micro-communities that emerged when you worked on a song with others in a recording studio – and also when you were on a record label with other artists who were suddenly part of your world and who would provide ideas you might never have thought of.

One of the other artists signed to Mercury/Philips was madcap idiot-savant genius and self-styled Legendary Stardust Cowboy, the missing link between loveable oddball 60s vaudevillian Tiny Tim of 'Tiptoe Through The Tulips' and earthy, radical musical artist Captain Beefheart of *Trout Mask Replica*. The Cowboy fused an interest in space travel with an interest in the Wild West as if it was the most obvious thing to do. A debut single, the brightly cacophonous combination of gibberish and joy, crooked rhythms and slapdash voices 'Paralyzed', which got him his Mercury contract, somehow almost made the Billboard 100. He called his music 'not middle of the road, but middle of the galaxy'.

Mercury had no clue what to do with him and he lasted about 15 minutes and two failed follow up singles, 'Down in the Wrecking Yard' and 'I Took a Trip on a Gemini Spaceman'. In early 1971, a Mercury executive, knowing Bowie was a fan of uncategorisable outsider music, gave him the three singles. Bowie was in America for the first time, roaming the nation on a lonely radio promotional tour because he couldn't get a visa to perform live. He would take some of his early custom-built clothes with him, including the flowing Mr Fish 'man dress' he had worn on the British cover of *The Man Who Sold the World*, one of the few items from his life he lost and which, after it had become historic, never made it into the *David Bowie Is* exhibition.

He would wear the clothes when he was on the radio, especially the dress when he was travelling the vast, lost lands of middle America, which, to his surprise, could seem like part of the developing world, rather than the shiny futurescapes of New York and Chicago, although the future had only made it there in fits and starts. Enough future, though, or maybe enough select, local joie de vivre, that when he wore his man's dress in New York, hardly anyone turned a hair. They had characters cruising the streets he recognised when he worked on Lou Reed's 'Walk on the Wild Side'.

He would wear the dress for a radio interview in Akron, Ohio, to see what the reaction would be, to show he was a little more subversive than might seem from his shy, tentative Englishness, hiding how overawed he was by the endless differences and contrasts of an America beyond the films he'd seen and the songs he'd heard. He wanted even just a very few Americans to know that he wasn't another forgettable, fey folkie; he was a true, mindblowing performer. One day, he'd be back to show them.

Hearing the Legendary Stardust Cowboy, Bowie laughed out loud, but he loved him for his untrammelled innocence and sheer optimism. He loved this kind of American – someone making their own kind of sense out of this country that he was realising was always slipping from your grasp, most of it too far away to ever be seen or too hidden to ever understand fully. His first trip to America had fooled him, but it hadn't let him down, especially when he found characters like the Stardust Cowboy. There was something a little Syd Barrett about him – in the world but somehow untouched by it, bringing glamour to life even though, or because, they tilted towards the unpredictable and lost.

Bowie said Syd was the first male rock musician he ever saw wear make-up – eye shadow, mascara, black nail polish – and that there was something so unworldly about him, like he was hovering six inches above the Earth. Both Bowie and

Bolan adopted a lot of Barrett's style and presence, especially his elaborate emphasis on an arch British accent when singing.

Syd had problems working out reality, seeing the world in extremes of good and evil, needing to create and evolve so much he couldn't keep up with himself. He ended up keeping himself to himself after early pop stardom as a dreamy, dreaming pop star with Pink Floyd, uncomfortable with the pressures of even out-of-the-way, underground success, leaving to briefly make his own wonderfully wondering music as he attempted to steady, or unsteady, himself, before more-or-less vanishing into his own mystery.

In Barrett and the Cowboy, Bowie recognised similar spirits, not part of any particular generation but maybe a mad one, one Bowie himself felt connected to, perhaps getting guidance how to deal with it from watching his half-brother Terry, who would increasingly break away from reality. Someone who you would be chatting to quite normally, laughing, listening to music, and then suddenly, click, that stare, out towards nowhere, outside himself, losing all motivation, difficult to reach. Syd and Terry showed Bowie his own possible futures; he loved them and lost them, and sometimes thought he was heading their way, dragged by forces unknown he felt he'd let inside him. It was perhaps the price he had to pay . . . Bowie identified with another Mercury artist who had a (sort of) hit and thought he'd made it, but then nothing happened, and the world seemed to be pushing against him.

Bowie couldn't get the name of the Legendary Stardust Cowboy out of his head and would realise he'd found the surname of a character he was working on who was based on an ultimate rock and roll star. One performance artist playing with the idea of being a star paying tribute to another.

The Cowboy – Norman Carl Odam from Buddy Holly's Lubbock, Texas, truly in a world of his own – didn't find out that Bowie had nicked his name until 1984, when he read about Bowie and Ziggy Stardust in a magazine. Any thoughts of taking some kind of legal action were dashed when it was pointed out that Bowie hadn't taken the whole name. Clever. A born thief. Take just enough that it might be noticed and you'd get away with it.

Bowie, in turn, would find out years later that Norman was upset when he came across a rough, two-page Legendary Stardust Cowboy website where Norman said, in a handwritten note, that he was having money troubles. 'That English guy called David Bowie stole my name and I think he should do one of my songs – he owes me.' Bowie felt so guilty, he covered 'I Took a Trip on a Gemini Spaceship' on his 2002 *Heathen* album – his return to working with Tony Visconti after 22 years. This time, his producer looked after the space song – taking it as seriously as covers of songs on the album by Neil Young and the Pixies.

Bowie slips the song back in time to a place where Odam had begun, doing a gleeful, Residents-type deconstruction or hallucination of the 1939 song 'I Thought About You' about a train trip written by Jimmy Van Heusen and Johnny Mercer, sung and performed by the likes of Frank Sinatra, Miles Davis, Billie Holiday, Dinah Washington and Stan Getz.

Some royalties for Odam did start to come through, and when the pair finally met, after *Heathen*, Bowie reverted to a teenage fan and was more in awe of Odam, as a significant influence in his world, than Odam was of Bowie.

The Legendary Stardust Cowboy decided to return the favour by doing his version of 'Space Oddity' in 2013, as a Scottish Elvis on Benzedrine backed by the Fall, somehow without smashing the song's intrinsic beauty – and, more poignantly and appropriately, not shattering the 'Ledge's' own loneliness. It was hysterical; it was totally moving; it was stardust.

HOPE AND VISION

As he made 'Space Oddity' in the studio, a band of transients assembled around him and his song, Bowie was beginning to understand that one of his roles, apart from being the writer and singer, was to inject positivity, playfulness and purpose into proceedings, to make everyone believe in the project and concentrate on something they might not have been thinking about the night before, but which for the time they were in the studio became the most important thing in their world. Those early experiences with Visconti and his team created a template that Bowie would develop over the years – his recording sessions would become all-consuming for everyone involved.

He was extremely calculating when it came to fulfilling his desires for a particular project, even as he created comfortable settings in luxurious but isolated surroundings. When he was rehearsing the band for *Station to Station*, he decamped to Jamaica and put them in a deluxe location where they were hard to get hold of and could only really think about David Bowie and his current concerns, which involved the demons and drugs of Los Angeles, and a desperate need to flee both.

It was out of time, as though it had taken the world a few years to catch up, but 'Space Oddity' had become Bowie's first UK number one single when it was rereleased in 1975, while Bowie himself, in another kind of time distortion, was suffering the fall-out of an international, more permanent fame that 'Space Oddity' hadn't originally given him but that had, by now, warped his reality.

The songs the 'Space Oddity' studio experience quickly led to – 'Changes', 'Life on Mars', 'Starman', 'Moonage Daydream', 'John, I'm Only Dancing', 'The Jean Genie', 'Drive In Saturday', 'Rebel Rebel' – meant the 'Space Oddity' re-release eventually made number one in the UK charts, as though it was always meant to be that way, an out-of-this-world venture representing the now out-of-this-world famous David Bowie. There was a glitch in history, time played a trick, but it all worked out in the end, even if David Bowie himself was by then in a very different state of mind – stuck in an otherworldly place where there seemed no way back.

'Space Oddity' had shown him that seduction, confidence, ambition and a little danger should be in there somewhere when he made a single. Also a chorus that's pleasing and a little off-balance, and leaves the listener believing that there is something right in the world. Mostly, though, it should be made of David Bowie, always dealing with the mystery and chaos of himself. It was something he started to learn during the making of 'Space Oddity', a song that used the studio to take a picture of his imagination.

In the studio, Bowie would be the community leader; his was the ultimate vision, the key to the sound they were all looking for. Working for and with Bowie, you must believe in Bowie, in the higher purpose. He was the one in possession of all the facts. If Bowie needed to be out of the way, as far away from temptation as was possible, then everyone else did too. The studio could be a safe space in which to learn and grow through experimentation and creativity, and it could be a dangerous space, its isolation from the real world and the increasing number of options leading to indulgences and time-wasting. The key was finding the right balance between the opportunities and the playtime, between the time when something was happening and the time when you were just hanging around waiting for something to happen.

The studio was an environment unlike any other, a place filled with technology and hardware which could produce magical moments if the stars, and the people involved, were aligned. It could be a cold, unwelcoming, alienating place; it could get in the way of your ideas. But if you knew what you were doing, and were surrounded by others who knew what they were doing, it could become a holy place, where spirits and dreams could be transferred into sound and pieces of music materialising out of nowhere.

Bowie would sometimes watch Tony at work, both because it was such a unique experience to witness and to find out for himself how it worked, what the machines and buttons were for, how the microphones were placed, how the tape was edited and the sounds and effects manipulated. For the writing of his own songs, Bowie needed to know that – how a song written on one instrument, a piano or a guitar, sometimes just a rough collection of moments and ideas, could be transformed into a world of its own. You could take things to the limit and then sometimes, when things were working really well, cross that limit.

The studio in the rush of the sixties had become the best method imaginable at the time for doing that thing all artists and musicians hope to achieve – the altering of consciousness.

PEOPLE AND PLACES

In his small, end-of-sixties world, which for a time mostly included recording studios, Bowie came across the San Francisco-born Tucker Zimmerman, another obscure, outlying, loner musician who was recording an album for Regal Zonophone, produced by Tony Visconti. They were two Americans who found each other in London at a time when they could make a record together because of Visconti's connections with Denny Cordell and David Platz.

Bowie would sometimes be in the control room at Trident as Visconti and Zimmerman put together the songs for a largely neglected album called *Ten Songs by Tucker Zimmerman*, as though a title was the last thing on their minds or just too commercial a conceit for two dreamy hippies. It was intense, troubadour folk, fanning out from Bob Dylan's abstract expression of emotion, like Tim Hardin, Cat Stevens or Richie Havens were folk. It was straighter and more conventionally angrier and bluesier than Bowie's more trickster, fantasist folk, but Bowie never forgot being around the studio as the record was made, soaking up mood and technique that would come in useful somewhere along the way.

Bowie quietly watched the recording process, seeing how Visconti worked with Zimmerman. If Zimmerman saw Bowie in the control room and came in to say goodbye, by the time he had got there, Bowie had slipped away. He didn't want to interfere. Sometimes it seemed as though he was at his most silent when he discovered something new, an artist he hadn't heard of before, an idea he thought was interesting. He'd go quiet, wondering how he could use that idea in his own work, interpret it in a way unique to him. Bowie was in awe of those who he made into a private influence, like the Legendary Stardust Cowboy. But when he got over his reserve, he would sit with Zimmerman and they'd sing their songs to each other, telling each other what they thought.

The experience left a deep impression and maybe, as Zimmerman drifted further into the margins, making albums with little impact, Bowie recognised a remote, itinerant musical life he might have had if he'd never been able to follow the dangerous success of 'Space Oddity' and he lost contact with his manager, publisher and producer. It was cold out there. It was easy to lose contact.

In 2003, when Bowie was asked for a current snapshot of his 25 favourite albums by *Vanity Fair*, *Ten Songs* was one of the lesser known, amongst Robert Wyatt, Little Richard, Steve Reich, the Velvet Underground, John Lee Hooker, Linton Kwesi Johnson, Daevid Allen, the Incredible String Band, Glenn Branca, Syd Barrett, George Crumb, Toots and the Maytals, Charles Mingus, James Brown, Igor Stravinsky and the Fugs.

Bowie helped Zimmerman, in need of some money, get a couple of London gigs, including one at the Arts Lab he was helping run with Mary Finnigan in Beckenham. For a laugh, but maybe hoping for some interest, they billed it as a guest appearance by Tuck Zimmerman, a cousin to Bob Dylan, as in Robert Zimmerman. The enthusiastic Bowie took care of the light art and projected a primitive liquid light show in the direction of Zimmerman as he was singing, hitting his face. Zimmerman shouted, turn it off, turn it off. Bowie thought they were the lyrics to the song and kept the lights on Zimmerman's face.

One day, as they sat in Visconti's office playing each other their latest songs, Bowie sang 'Space Oddity'. Zimmerman said, after Bowie had finished drifting into space, that's a pretty good song, but you should lose the bit about Major Tom. That's no good. David nodded, politely.

TOUCH AND GO

In one way, Visconti had been right about the song: it created an alternative world where Bowie seemed to be a success – at last – but it wasn't where he really was as a writer and performer. To the discriminating, even snobby fans of underground and rock music at the time, a misplaced if welcome hit could threaten the audience you did have.

The lovely but more grounded follow-up single, 'Prettiest Star', sent Bowie back to where he had been before his hit, as marginal cult figure loved by a few in the know, with the extra burden of now appearing to be a one-hit wonder. Some say 'Prettiest Star' is Bowie falling in love with his free-spirited new girlfriend, Angie. A couple of years younger, a Cypriot who'd spent some years in America, she would become so impatiently committed to helping him succeed it was as though to support and collaborate with Bowie practically, emotionally and conceptually she was prepared to sacrifice the parts of her own life that had made her the kind of free-thinking person who loved music and musicians, art and artists, that he was first attracted to. She would become the perfect foil, the perfect cheerleader – and the muse always challenging the traditional binary of artist and muse – and in March 1970, his wife. She created for herself her own voracious characters – Rock Star Wife was one, Driving Force behind the throne, scorned Ex – as she stuck by Bowie as he repeatedly transformed – and immersed – himself in the 1970s.

'Prettiest Star' featured poetically deviant soul-searching guitar by Marc Bolan, who was also on the outside looking in, envious of Bowie's sudden top-ten breakthrough, with the help of his own bloody Stylophone. Who on earth would have thought that would have worked, but they were still friends.

They loved each other, identifying with the insecurity and underachievement of the other, but not prepared for the agony if one of them made it and the other didn't.

The song was a plaintive duet between two close friends being exiled from their hopes and dreams, mildly puzzled, sometimes deeply frustrated by the delay in their divine calling. It was a hybrid of two different types of imaginative showmen who liked company but loved time spent on their own, learning to live with the characters and creatures they created.

They were urging each other on. They had different views on the meaning of the word 'boogie' – for Bolan, it was sex and sensation, for Bowie it was at root the same but a little more holy and sacred and also profane; they needed an audience to complete them and shared a producer working hard to crack the code and find the secret of what made them click. They weren't loved by many fans, but those who did love them, really loved them, on account of a difference only they could see. Angie, and Marc's equally devoted and convinced wife, June Child, pushing him hard when all seemed lost, understood that. There had to be a future there somewhere, a way of breaking free of the gravity that was somehow holding them back.

Bowie wasn't ready to keep up with the chart success of 'Space Oddity', but returning to the plan he'd made with Visconti, he was ready to catch up.

He was now definitely David Bowie, performing songs as himself but once removed, by name if nothing else, and this slight distance from himself gave him hints at how to give characters life and a future, and perhaps give himself life and a future, by becoming someone else. By adopting a new identity constructed across intersecting and antagonistic thoughts and positions. His identity crises, represented using a multitude of ways and means over the next few charged years, made sense to those having their own identity crises.

ONE AND THE SAME

David Bowie was himself, at a distance, dramatically revealed on the album before *Hunky Dory*, the ornate, desolate, neo-heavy metal of *The Man Who Sold the World*, a kind of uncanny fantasy blues tangling and rethreading an obsessive network of themes, epiphanies, symbols and images to do with historical, social, individual madness, imaginary doubles, personality disorders, existential crises, religious belief and spiritual uncertainty, heaven and hell, and various illusions and delusions.

He presented himself on the cover with a tongue-in-cheek, daydreaming Pre-Raphaelite look, an extremely beautiful figure with supernatural energies. Someone taking pleasure in exquisite sensations, enhancing the aura that here was a record revelling in the idea of 'art for art's sake'. The Pre-Raphaelite Brotherhood was formed in the mid-nineteenth century by a collective of youthful revolutionary thinkers cultivating their own images, who Bowie would fantasise being part of. He was now writing his best ever songs – full of stories and full of wonders – not so much inspired by medieval ballads about star-crossed lovers and the simple beauty of a flower but the blurring of the sacred and the profane, and madness as a kind of elevated self.

The record is steeped with out-of-body experiences, as though he's floating above himself, seeing himself from outside, having dangerous experiences and getting a better view on the meaning of things. Bowie jumbles up a recent fascination with the writings of hypersensitive, megalomaniac moral philosopher Friedrich Nietzsche – a belief in God is unreasonable in the modern age but people will still believe – and dark-side royalty Aleister Crowley with fading childhood memories from Sunday School lessons and his family's Protestantism. Nietzsche approved of Buddhism as being a hundred times more realistic than Christianity, with its ability to face problems objectively and coolly. 'Buddhism promises nothing but actually fulfils; Christianity promises everything, but fulfils nothing.'

Nietzsche's 'mad man' in *The Gay Science*, plunging from total confusion to devastating clarity, urging people to understand the nihilism and crisis of values that will follow once God is killed, parallels the schizophrenia of his half-brother, Terry, and Bowie's own search for new opportunities.

Bowie read Nietzsche with his theories of the Superman and how life could be like a work of art, how you too could be a worldbuilder, directing the action of your life according to your personal vision. The individual could use creativity to develop their own style of living. Post-God, post-Christianity and now very much post-war, Bowie learnt how the nihilism of Nietzsche could be life affirming, a way of accepting both the pleasure and the suffering of existence.

It was the passing phase of a restless thinker committed to finding out all he could about feeling alive fascinated by the emotions associated with reading, listening and looking, and identifying with Nietzsche's 'Buddhism is a religion for late human beings, for races grown kindly, gentle, over-intellectual who feel pain too easily.' But the shadow, the thinking and Bowie's thinking about the thinking would remain, sometimes less explicitly, all the way to *Blackstar*.

One of the next stops on Bowie's journey through knowledge, which, unlike most of his peers, he kept pursuing to the very end, was Freud, who interpreted Nietzsche's 'will' as 'libido', the energetic subconscious, and from this seething energy, Freud articulated the fundamental competing drives Eros (the life instinct/being/attraction) and Thanatos (the death instinct/non-being/repulsion). Another stop was

William Burroughs, with his hollowed-out paraphrasing of Nietzsche, and, in a way, Aleister Crowley: 'nothing is true, everything is permitted.'

When Bowie came to this quote, it was Burroughs imagining a basic disruption of reality by art, the literal realisation of art moving off the canvas and penetrating the world. He burrowed into the world far more than most experimental literary writers, and took his place next to Marilyn Monroe as part of the collected influences on the cover of the Beatles' *Sgt. Pepper's Lonely Hearts Club Band*, one of the records that reflected a social revolution of peace and love and a world of change. (Crowley also appeared on the cover, next to Mae West. He was nominated for the club by John Lennon, who also suggested Nietzsche and Hitler – who were both blackballed in the final count and do not make an appearance.)

By the time Bowie died, 50 years after being intimately caught up in the 1960s and '70s shock of the new, with truth and reality now being fought over in a hypermediated and conflicted world, we were on the verge of seeing a collapse of empathy and compassion. Progress and freedom were being reversed, encouraged by stunning election results and the contorted and contorting impact of social media. The consequences of the quote where nothing is true and everything is permitted were enabling power-hungry media-savvy opportunists, alt-right conspiracists, tech dictators and amoral, corrupt forces savaging liberal humanism to take it literally. Harbingers of a new Dark Enlightenment, they exploited the precariousness of reality for different, meaner, diabolical purposes than Burroughs, and his pupils, like Bowie, hoped for.

Nietzsche and libido flowed through *The Man Who Sold the World* – produced by Visconti who as the bass player in the band, with his non-rock jazz roots, was told by Mick Ronson to listen to Jack Bruce of Cream, with his more dynamic electronic bass take on jazz bass playing. Visconti did so, and mixed his own rampant, energised, sometimes berserk bass playing at the front of the sound – one way of paying tribute to the mind of Nietzsche and the madness of Crowley. Nietzsche and Crowley were still lurking in the shadows of the next album, *Hunky Dory*.

It was produced by Bowie and Tony Visconti's engineer Ken Scott, with a lighter, sparkier touch, now that Visconti was occupied with continuing the success of Marc Bolan's T. Rex, the made-up, sexed-up, electric guitar version of Tyrannosaurus Rex.

T. Rex was getting to pop stardom and glam rock months before Bolan's friend, possibly because Marc's journey though knowledge was taking in no discernible Nietzsche and Burroughs. T. Rex, though, and Bolan's innocent, aesthetically populist flirtations and obsessions were preparing the way for David Bowie and his more fragmentary, knowing stylistic innovations, his deeper, darker sense of strangeness, his commitment to finding the telling image.

MYSTERY AND ACTION

Bowie was himself, at a distance, not yet a character; the first was perhaps to be beautifully revealed on *Hunky Dory*, the follow-up album to *The Man Who Sold the World*. It was another way of leaning on the work that was still in the future, and a different way of writing and sounding whilst still being himself. *Hunky Dory* was a fantasy autobiography of a darling, loosey goosey, turned-on and tuned-in bohemian drifter with a sartorial edge and a florid artistic imagination, already up to speed with the disappointed retreat from and/or still hopeful reshaping of the sixties counterculture that had helped shape him.

He collected in one mythical place loves, kinks, infatuations, curios, idols, charismatic figures, dreams, nightmares, fragments and beliefs. It was a world of wonders, flights of fancy and influences twisted by his singular, outré Englishness, his inquiring mind and a unique way of aligning his more disquieting, experimental instincts with heartwarming and heartbreaking melodies. He was beginning to see the creation of a memorable melody as a surrealist act, one that balances a rational vision of life with one that asserts the power of the unconscious, something that could be enhanced by the correct use of rhythm and lyrics revelling in the full wildness of dreams. There was also, he conceded, thinking of his love for noise, dissonance and the freedom of cacophony, something quite nineteenth century about his devotion to melody. It's a form of handicraft as much as an art. He wasn't perturbed that his melodies might stray into the corny or needy. Sometimes that was the point, and somehow with his particular form of self-awareness he could do it without his songs sounding instantly dated.

He simply liked melody and he wallowed in it on *Hunky Dory*. At all stages of his writing life, nothing would give him greater pleasure than finding ways to bind together churning chaos with a melody that turned his fastidious late-twentieth-century method of cutting up words and sentences to create lyrics into glorious, transcendent choruses, into compressed delight.

He didn't immediately know how to present these songs, so the Hollywood movie goddess cover image never made it outside the record sleeve and onto the stage, as Ziggy would, from his next set of creations.

Hunky Dory's songs seem as though they are from a different jigsaw puzzle but one restless mind, all jumbled together in Bowie's own world. He wanted to make as many people as possible believe in what he believed in. Containing at least two of what would become Bowie standards – 'Life on Mars' and 'Changes' – it was both the perfect introduction to David Bowie and also, for now, a farewell, before Bowie fully became A Character, in costume, making himself up out of concepts, with something specific to prove. A farewell with its very own farewell song.

The busy, hustling David Platz and his team had a strategic knack for creating collaborations amongst his collective talents, including ones that led to the writing of the anomalous epics 'She' that Charles Aznavour would sing, and Procol Harum's 'A Whiter Shade of Pale', perfectly timed for the 1967 Summer of Love.

Platz had arranged for the journalist Herbert Kretzmer to write the lyrics for 'She' with Aznavour. Kretzmer had written the sparky Sophia Loren and Peter Sellers comedy duet 'Goodness Gracious Me', and 'In the Summer of His Years', the powerful show-stopping Millicent Martin tribute to John F Kennedy on the weekly BBC satire show *That Was the Week That Was*.

The elaborate, stylised words for 'A Whiter Shade of Pale' were written by the 20-year-old poet Keith Reid, who would sit on Platz's office windowsill, full of ideas about words, and the images words could create. Platz had signed a poet, thinking that maybe he could write lyrics, in the way Kretzmer the journalist turned into a distinctive lyricist. Platz would find musicians he was publishing to put these words to music. It seemed a long shot – Reid's words seemed too impressionistic to become songs, written as though remembered from a dream.

Mod star, influential soul and R&B disc jockey, and conceptual whizzkid Guy Stevens at Island Records introduced Reid to Gary Brooker, who was then playing in Eurovision winner Sandie Shaw's backing band. Together with the organist Matthew Fisher, they put together Procol Harum, who took the words of 'A Whiter Shade of Pale' and found the only music that could possibly go with them, adding Bach to a beat and burying the song in spiralling grandeur to come up with a delicate fantasy of a pop song. It became the single of the summer in the way *Sgt. Pepper* was the album of the summer, made the group's name and brought them a success they could never equal and never fully escape.

Eventually, Platz funded the recording of one of the first heavy metal albums, the debut by Midland maniacs Black Sabbath, when its murky, ominous power and the bands' love for fighting amongst themselves and shooting neighbours' cats was beyond the understanding of even the hippest label. Platz could see showbusiness in the oddest places – if there was a song and a personality, and preferably some potential publicity, it had a future.

Platz was good at thinking ahead to where pop might be moving and, with his company of different talents, at hearing something that to others might be nothing. In 1968, he was sharing an office with another publisher who had the UK rights to a French song, 'Comme d'habitude' – 'As Usual' – composed by Jacques Revaux with lyrics by Claude François and Gilles

Thibaut, a minor French hit about a failed marriage. It had a particular French pungency, suggesting bad breath might be one cause of the marriage breaking up. Platz was asked if he knew of anyone who could come up with some English words. Hearing it, he thought that an English version could be a hit. Bowie's manager Ken Pitt was also keen, believing in Bowie as more of a behind-the-scenes lyricist – as with Kretzmer and Reid – than the creator of instant hit melodies.

The constantly insecure Bowie would complain sometimes – protesting too much – that he didn't like his voice, that he wished he could write for other singers. Being simply a writer would mean he wouldn't have to bother with the performing, the revealing himself, something he often felt was beyond him. Reid was an interesting example of what he could become – like Bernie Taupin later with Elton John. A songwriter, even a member of a group, who never had to record and didn't perform.

Bowie had already tried a few translations for some of the songs Platz published, looking for international releases, and he was called in to work on the English version of 'Comme d'habitude'. Writing one of his precious, detailed lyrics to a classic melody might crack the code of how to make him succeed.

His English version, from a mind still struck by the intense, intimate lyrical style of Anthony Newley, was called 'Even a Fool Falls in Love'. It was rejected by the French publishers, not least because they hadn't heard of Bowie and were looking for some star power.

The singer and composer Paul Anka got the rights to the original on a visit to Paris; he didn't think much of it but his friend Frank Sinatra kept badgering him to write him a song. Frank felt he was getting old and hated it, baffled by the Beatles and the new world. The Kennedy years were over, with their addictive blend of politics and glamour; the Rat Pack, no-nonsense men's men always on the prowl, were out of touch, and the FBI were hassling him. He felt his time was up and he repeatedly threatened to quit.

Anka turned to the song he'd bought the rights for, which seemed to have the kind of melody Frank would relish, and put all Frank's angst into some tender-but-tough-guy words he imagined would be the kind Sinatra himself would say in casual conversation, about ageing, about the end of the road.

Frank loved it, turned it into a song he owned – Elvis and Sid Vicious would try to make it theirs – his grand adios. In the end, it helped give him a new lease of life, and another 25 years of saying goodbye, its success forcing him to repeat a song whose novelty soon wore off and keeping him permanently on the wrong side of hip, whatever hip was and wherever it went.

After the rejection, Bowie sulked for a year, convinced he could write something as ambitious and perfectly presented as Anka's 'My Way' but something that summed up a different life, a different chain of events, a different twentieth century. A different history. Being so close to the emergence of such a song, which grew in power once Sinatra had taken it over, he turned his longstanding feelings of rejection by the wider pop industry into a personal anthem, its own kind of revenge on those trying to dismiss him.

With his jazz experience at vamping on a theme, Bowie was inspired to write 'Life on Mars', which shared some of the original's chords and in the final version used Rick Wakeman's piano majesty to echo and exaggerate the conspicuous classical and film soundtrack allusions.

The words came from various sources: impressions, dreams, in-jokes and memories – the caveman reference came from a 1960 novelty hit 'Alley Oop' – mostly to decorate the meticulously organised vocal line, which was Bowie's main concern, now he was absolutely sure that he was a singer, an entertainer, and only he could inhabit such a song. Any meaning is left to interpretation because this is a song meant to mean different things to different people at different times.

He's writing about a world becoming increasingly obsessed with movies, music and television. He's capturing the essence of a teenager's life. He's coming to grips with the ineffable. He's knowing better than anyone that pop stars are meant to be weird. He's saying that sometimes words are too much and sometimes they are not enough. He's becoming a master at understanding the yin and yang of major and minor chords, how words symbolise language and music symbolises words. He's writing a song about plagiarism. He's writing a song like no other because it occurs to him he can. He's showing he believes in magic by making something magical. He's working out how to create all the art he dreams of.

'Life on Mars' was driven by the pain of rejection, the embarrassment he felt at the flatness of his first attempt, and he piled up the possible meanings and reflections of the madness of his own life, the vivid quality of his daydreams, as a reaction to how he felt his songs were being misunderstood. He had so much to say, and so much he wanted to say, and he let out his frustration at being turned down by writing an assured, uncompromising song overflowing with information and sensation.

There was so much left to interpretation that the song seems to reach deep into the mind of the listener, telepathically connecting with their own life, their own reality, their own 'Mars'. What started as an embittered, sarcastic parody of 'My Way's' self-indulgent Rat Pack bombast bloomed into a wonderland all of its own. The rejection Bowie felt was transformed into an abstract, humane anthem of abandonment, loneliness and longing.

There was no stopping him now.

IDENTITY AND OPPOSITION

If, in particular, you were 16 or 17 and having an identity crisis, watching him on television in 1972 singing 'Starman', the first single from *The Rise and Fall of Ziggy Stardust*, set you up for a lifetime of believing in Bowie and the things he believed in. For many, it was the first time they had come across him, the first time they had seen him in action, and it was truly as though he had landed from another planet. Look into those eyes . . .

Careful . . .

The look in his eyes as he looked at you through the screen and into your very being might even set you up for a lifetime of thinking about Bowie and his songs, and even a lifetime of writing about their meaning and magic. He was high on the idea of putting ideas in people's heads.

He looked like he thought he could do no wrong. He looked like he thrived on volatility. He looked like he knew he had arrived, as he always knew he would, flinging his arms around guitarist Mick Ronson with loving care and a bit of cheek, clapping along to his own audacity as the song fades away, roaming the stage he now owned to see if he could see himself make his breakthrough.

The funny thing was, you knew as soon as you saw him point straight down the camera into your own life, your own world, that you had been hooked. You had been won over, brought into the fold, given the code. Taken, seen and changed. He had got under your skin and would remain there come what may.

And he needed us, the watchers, the devoted fans, to affirm his identity, to complete various circuits, as much as we needed him. He needed followers in order to pass into history, to find a platform where he could play with his new role as a creature of the mass media, and exploit the cunning world of television, which gave him powers to construct a world and unsettle his fans' historical, cultural and psychological assumptions.

Those having an identity crisis at another time, finding Bowie later in the 1970s, in the 1980s, '90s, '00s, after he died, would still find a sympathetic spirit, a soulmate at one with their dilemmas and angst. Someone on the inside track when it came to seeking and finding their own elusive, tricky, sometimes increasingly hunted and aggressively hated self.

FANTASY AND ECSTASY

Changing his name from Jones to Bowie wasn't enough of a disguise to conquer his folksy shyness, a peculiar kind of English reticence considering how extrovert and assured he seemed, how much he liked to meddle with other people's minds. What he needed to do was to not be himself, to build on these themes and fragments, to take them beyond sounding like flamboyant pastiche or skilled rearrangements. Not being himself could mean losing himself, but at the time it was a risk he was willing to take.

Things were moving fast. He set himself, now not himself, in the future, where everything, for better or worse, would be different. Along the way, still young and brazen enough to have crazy dreams and wild hopes, he might even get to design the future, send his songs back from fantasy into reality with enough force to shake its foundations.

He approached from different angles the rock music and miscellaneous avant-garde experiments he loved to death as a fan and enthusiast, with different intentions to his heroes and influences. There was a whole new world of social and sexual philosophy to play with; a new vocabulary was needed to deal with the present, let alone the future. And now he wasn't himself but a someone else, he was liberated as a writer and performer. He could go to all sorts of extremes, send Ziggy to the edge, over the top, round the bend, through the wringer. He could sing Ziggy songs as if he was interpreting them, playing Ziggy in a musical setting, always aware of himself as a strong interpreter of songs more than a great singer.

Hear him say in interview after interview that he had dreams he could play Elvis, as if there must be a reason they were born on the same day, but he knew in the real world he didn't have the talent for it. He started developing characters so he could hide behind them and let them pretend. They could do it, become it, even if he couldn't

Ziggy was his messiah who twanged a guitar. He was a simplistic character. He took on a lot of facets in other people's eyes, created so many different ideas in the people who reacted to him, and that was part of the fulfilment for Bowie, which he then wanted to replicate in other characters. People saw so much in his characters that he never planned or saw himself. It created so much momentum, much more than he anticipated.

He could issue a series of momentous show stopping performances, avant-garde cabaret as much as dynamic rock and roll, climaxing *The Rise and Fall of Ziggy Stardust* album with another eventual Bowie standard, 'Rock 'n' roll Suicide', an intimate self-examination at the other side of life and death to the communal 'Five Years'. Everyone's alone at the beginning and at the end, you're not alone.

On behalf of nihilistic, mixed-up kids everywhere facing an uncertain future, including himself, some hoping they died before they got old, he could send Ziggy to the limit and, apparently, walk away unharmed. As Ziggy, he was giving everything to his cause, giving his audience a helping hand, in return for their help. With Ziggy to play with and write for, he could imagine Baudelaire writing for Edith Piaf, the Who writing for Jacques Brel. In a way, Ziggy was writing for Bowie as much as he was writing for Ziggy. He could send him to his death, sacrifice him for the sake of a sublime ending.

Bowie understood as he was writing Ziggy that the character mustn't endure, that he would need to be disposed of before he became too clingy and suffocating. But as quick as he was to mark his death, the character would linger. Ziggy ended up dying a few times, as Bowie moved on to other faces and fables, but he was so potent a creation, amplified by the adventures and iconography of *Aladdin Sane* – that he wouldn't truly fade away.

Aladdin Sane was effectively Ziggy in America, but it was also Bowie's first time in America as performer and the two started to get tangled up. Playing and writing for a character was working, but it was also taking over his life as though the role an actor was playing followed him into reality.

Sometimes, it was as though Ziggy was chasing him – give me one more chance, one more life – and by the early eighties, Bowie didn't even want to think about him, even if for some it was the most fascinating thing he'd done. Thinking about him might start to bring him back.

When Bowie retired Ziggy live at the Hammersmith Odeon, confusing some who thought it was Bowie retiring, he had the spellbinding farewell song, the rock and roll suicide, ready and waiting. Ziggy fell but he kept on rising.

The Rise and Fall of Ziggy Stardust and the Spiders from Mars contained a surreal clash of influences and inspiration, selves and visions, sensuality and seriousness, as well as dust and shadow, lust and longing, agony and ecstasy, and signs of a future that kept unspooling, spinning between technological alienation and searing musical thrills.

MAD AND BEAUTIFUL

Bowie put together a one-off version of an extreme fantasy variety show for American television in October 1973, a one-hour special for NBC's *The Midnight Special*, at a time when Bowie in America was still at best a cult artist. He agreed to do it as long as he was given the blessed 'complete artistic control', and the show was filmed over three days at the famed Marquee rock club in Soho, central London.

Bowie had first gone to the Marquee in 1964 when he was 17, not long after it opened new premises on Wardour Street, changing from promoting jazz to catching up with where the in-crowds were now heading. Groups like the Rolling Stones, the Who and the Yardbirds built their early audiences down Wardour Street, and would spend a lot of time there. It was a dirty, unpromising hole with a carpet that felt like squelchy mud under your feet, but at the time it seemed to be the most special place in the world. For regulars, the place smelt like rock and roll.

Bowie first played at the venue later in 1964 with one of his early groups, the Manish Boys, supporting the Moody Blues a couple of times wearing long blond hair and knee-length boots, playing many more times in the mid-sixties in his other struggling early bands, especially with the Lower Third, who viewed it as something of a home venue, and the Buzz, who played regularly on Sunday afternoons.

Thinking ahead, he called his episode of *The Midnight Special* 'The 1980 Floor Show', and even before he had appeared on the new kind of American TV show picking up on counter-culture influences, he was contributing ideas to a new kind of spontaneous, visceral rock and roll television.

One aspect of the show was that it would be the last time Bowie would perform in costume as Ziggy Stardust. He reprised the role for an American audience three months after he more formally announced his retirement as Ziggy at the Hammersmith Odeon, at the end of 17 months of ascendant Ziggy activity, which took him from the edge of fame playing small venues as some kind of curious underdog deep into the flaming centre, emerging victorious as a virtual hero.

Along the way, he evolved into Aladdin Sane, the alter ego and philosophical soulmate of Ziggy Stardust: Horatio to Hamlet, a shadow, a distorted reflection. He was bursting at the seams with ideas and intentions, desperate to try new characters and settings, and made the decision to split up Ziggy Stardust and the Spiders from Mars because that was in the 'script' he'd written. It was part of the fantasy and now it was part of Bowie's reality, of his performance art, leaving an audience anxious and excited to find out what was going to happen next.

The dramatic onstage announcement he was quitting as Ziggy and breaking up the band was a classic strategic manoeuvre which quickly became part of rock legend. It surprised the rhythm section of the actual group now known as the Spiders from Mars, if not guitarist Mick Ronson, who had been alerted to Bowie's intentions.

While he planned the next stage, Bowie released *Pin Ups*, quickly conceived after the grand retirement of Ziggy, an album of some favourite songs from the 1960s, when the Marquee was at the centre of London's mod scene and he was a manic, besotted fan becoming tenacious participant. He shared the record cover with Twiggy, the quirky, sublimely gawky model who became one of the main faces and forms of the decade, symbolising the moment that was rapidly relaxing the stiff 1950s, taking it into the fluid 1960s, alongside the clothes designer Mary Quant and the miniskirt, and the graphic, more androgynous hair styling of Vidal Sassoon.

Somehow, for those questioning the significance and aesthetic merits of fashion and popular culture, it was part of a wider reaction against sociopolitical inequalities and systems of oppression, championing the freedom of sexual expression.

Twiggy became, briefly, another alter ego, a double of Ziggy, a further echo of Aladdin Sane, temporarily bringing themselves to life in the same make-believe world. Bowie's knack was to turn an album sleeve into a profound piece of contemporary theatre that helped turn the songs inside into a complete magical world.

'The 1980 Floor Show' was as much promotion for this as it was the final bow of Ziggy; *Pin Ups* and the Floor Show saw him shedding the costume and the story, reframing his mostly unspectacular 1960s as though he was at the centre of it, imagining certain songs as though they were part of his repertoire, part of his history. It was nostalgic, Bowie saying directly from his experience how great it was to be a teenager in the 1960s, with all this new music directed their way. It was an expert's insider insight into the kind of influences that had formed the glam rock he used as Ziggy's music, but also part of some research for where to go next. He was looking back to look forward. Acknowledging the 1935 words of Surrealist original André Breton, himself acknowledging the words of Karl Marx, Bowie believed that the activity of interpreting the world must be linked with the activity of changing the world.

He's looking back to the sixties – even by 1973 seen as the distant wonder years when British rock created itself out of disparate, mostly American sources – and forward to 1980, which in 1973 seemed a long way off, in a distant future, which would surely seem more obviously a future. The Marquee was the natural venue – where it had all begun, where he came across many of his influences, where he played some of his early important shows. And where he never quite found an audience. Now, he could use it as a bona fide star as the stage to say a televised goodbye to Ziggy, who had helped him rise, and dramatically pretend to fall, and set his sights on America, which you needed to conquer if you really wanted to feel you'd made it, even if as part of a fantasy.

A few songs from *Pin Ups* made it into the Floor Show – an almost confessional, post-Ziggy, exhausted 'I Can't Explain' by the Who, the elaborately retooled Merseybeat of the Mojos' 'Everything's Alright' and an elegantly baroque version of an American melancholy folk-rock song 'Sorrow' that he'd heard sung by the Merseys, which obliquely seeped into one of the most adventurous Beatles songs, George Harrison's 'It's All Too Much'.

There was also a version of the Sonny and Cher song 'I Got You Babe', which probably didn't fit into the British aura of *Pin Ups*, but Bowie as Ziggy paid homage to the proto-glam surrealism of the duo's appearance in 1967 using Marianne Faithfull as his appropriately unearthly divine other half. They were born ten days apart; it was a meeting of minds and bodies, both drawn to black humour and playacting, both with a self-destructive tendency that was part of their creative energy.

They'd been friends for years. When he was Davy Jones in the mid-sixties, he had been at the bottom of the bill on one of her solo tours. He really wanted her to sing one of his shadier, more disorientating songs, 'The Man Who Sold the World', but she found his intensity, that look in his eyes, a little frightening and she said no.

Recently separated from Mick Jagger after some torrid times, Faithfull was a delicate doll-faced flower chucked to the floor after he'd bound her in scandal and used her up. She was beginning her own long, dark drift into the margins after sixties notoriety, condemned to wander, living through a version of the post-fame hell Bowie was heading into, a world of freedom and addiction. As attracted as she was to dangerous, hedonistic flames, something in the black stars told her they needed to keep apart, as artists and doomed romantics.

Moving from the depravity and stampeding wild horses of the Rolling Stones to the insatiable appetites and outrageous hedonism of the jean genie of Bowie was a recipe for tragedy.

She'd given Jagger a copy of Mikhail Bulgakov's Soviet era satire *The Master and Margarita* in 1967, three years before he appeared in Nic Roeg and Donald Cammell's spiritually intense avant-garde thriller *Performance*, about a reclusive, burnt-out rock star in decline, holed up with a cold-hearted gangster looking for refuge. With the Stones, Jagger had had Number One singles with 'Satisfaction', 'Get Off My Cloud', 'Paint It Black' and 'Jumpin' Jack Flash', which made him the epitome of the idealised decadent rock star freely adopting personas before such a thing had entered the mainstream. The film cut up and turned inside out the troubled, freedom-seeking mood of the times, itself cut up in the first place, and Jagger, playing some devious, debauched double of himself, acts as if this extreme pastiche of his world and character is as real as his life outside the film.

He'd been reading the nineteenth-century French poet, philosopher and harbinger of modernity Charles Baudelaire, because this was when rock musicians, often vociferous readers, were taking their influences and imagery from where they could. Baudelaire was fascinated by the devil and wickedness, and dualities and doublings, the divided personality of a character, the notion that Satan and God were the same and good and evil could exist within the same person.

For Jagger, it all led to a casual, or more deranged, fascination with the occult, and a song originally called 'The Devil Is My Name', which became 'Sympathy for the Devil', an account of the devil as a diabolical, salivating, vice-ridden, Casanova-like socialite taking the credit for the historical sins and corruption of humanity, from the crucifixion of Christ to the Cold War, the Vietnam War and the recent assassinations of the Kennedys. Jagger, the shrewd cultural opportunist, naturally plays the devil himself, demonstrating how rock stars, crazy with power, were changing their image, character and face as they developed their songwriting, trying to outwit each other in some new kind of multifaceted cultural competition. Rock musicians at the time were driven to go further out than Dylan, than the Beatles, in documenting how in the sixties reality and appearance were being confused.

Faithfull is one of the backing singers contributing the gloriously seedy and repetitive 'woo woo' incantation that laces the song with menace and unholy joy. For Bowie, this meant she'd left abstract traces of her own soul on one of the most powerfully disorientating of rock songs, one which helped kill off the shallow love and peace dream of the sixties. One which helped open up how far you could go with the form and content of rock songs, and with the presentation of yourself as a character, a trickster, as light or as dark as you wanted.

You could play Lucifer if you liked – Bowie's version would be the repellent Thin White Duke, and he wasn't as able as Jagger, who was much more aware of his social status, his grace aristocratically devious not alien transfixing, to separate himself from the character.

When Faithfull turned down the chance to sing the enigmatic 'The Man Who Sold the World', a kind of inscrutable, feverish sequel to 'Sympathy for the Devil', where one self is eclipsed behind another, written three years later, Bowie turned to a less complicated and much less artistically restless pop singer, Lulu. This was like going from Marlene Dietrich or Nico to Doris Day. Something rare and wonderful failed to materialise.

Marianne said yes to his libertine variety show, still a little wary of his motives, a little nervous she was missing the point of what he was up to, but we get a hint of how dangerous and mystical she would have sounded being produced by Bowie. At the time, getting high and energised on his new star power, having visions of his own version of pop history, he was on the hunt for souls to save and minds to raid, and degenerate vagabonds and anti-heroes to elevate. He could have added Marianne Faithfull to a list of poetic pop partnerships and alter egos that he made part of a special collection that included Lou Reed, Iggy Pop and Ian Hunter of Mott the Hoople, with their own well-guarded sense of exceptionality. Working with these 'doubles' produced enduring songs, works of art, such as 'Walk on the Wild Side', 'Nightclubbing' and 'All The Young Dudes', all of which are helped as vivid impressions of experience by the sheer velocity of Bowie's thought at the time.

At least something rare and wonderful materialised with Bowie and Faithfull's masquerading rendition of 'I Got You Babe', a glimpse of an undiscovered galaxy, of a love that could have been truly something but might have ended with a gunshot.

This was their ecstatic, nefarious comment on the shock to the system seeing Sonny and Cher had been in the sixties, emerging from an alternative America into everyday, worn-down England. They'd turned up in hippy bohemian exaggerations of native American wear, which made them look more like they came from Mars than Oklahoma. Cher in particular was clearly fluent – as Bowie was – in the instant transformative language of fashion, both quite capable of making up their own words and phrases.

For their rushed, conceptual appreciation of Sonny and Cher and their playing lovers in real life, Marianne wore a full-length, backless, bum-bearing nun's habit and headgear passed on to her from Cleopatra. Bowie was tripping as more Ziggy as Ziggy ever got, letting him go – he thought – with one final, trashy flourish, wrapped in a black lather of feathers, with visions of the lunatic menace, the postmodern shaman to come leaking around the edge, his eyebrows shaved, the heels on his boots high.

David could be playing Cher, Marianne might be Sonny, they might both be both at the same time, making it clear in their own way that it's natural for humans to want to act in an absurd way.

Their collaboration was a one-off, a spectacular one-night stand. A few weeks later, Bowie went to see Faithfull in the John Osborne play *A Patriot for Me*, a response to sixties debates about countercultural protagonists at the Palace Theatre in Watford. Back to earth with a bump. She was playing the unconventional and seductive Austro-Hungarian Countess Sophia Delyanoff, appalled by the tragedy of closeted homosexuals and the establishment hounding of outsiders – not unlike the role she played for Bowie.

In 'The 1980 Floor Show', Bowie looks delighted with the extent of their mischief, the way the pair of them are jangling the keys to other worlds, confident that an audience will get the message in years to come, that no one will outdo this disruptive, cut-up cabaret show even 50 years later. This is the twentieth-century madness of youth, echoing around the internet five decades on, an attempt to escape the limits of reality. David is ready for the dead and aliveness of America, which will still take him by surprise.

FREAK AND SHOW

In 1975, his life is a blur within a blur. He's three years into a disorientating fame that is warping his mind, cutting up his emotions and taking over his life. The fame has moved him into an America he was once in boyish awe of – Jack Kerouac's shiny car in the night, Coca-Cola neon, the sensitive and vulnerable James Dean, Elvis Presley, Andy Warhol and all that jazz – as though it was all dream and no nightmare. He's found out it was an inferno which he was being swallowed up by.

Bowie didn't find the America he had read about in Kerouac. He didn't find the America that he had read about anywhere. He found a different one that he was nevertheless intoxicated by. There were parts of New York that had ghostly echoes of Kerouac's America, the aroma of his books. A few streets, a café or two. It was different because it was a couple of decades since Kerouac: he had started writing in 1948 and things had changed a lot. But it was still an adventure – there was always the next crazy venture. Adventures first, explanations later.

Bowie had a front-row seat in what he now realised was a freak show. Seemingly civilised, but there was so much wildness and so much wilderness. He'd moved out of expensive New York and was living in Los Angeles, his body shrinking into pure bony energy. He could see a long night settling in around him.

The album he was promoting was *Young Americans*, a record about and because of America, about the American soul and the soul music of America. He'd made it full of wild enthusiasm for Black American music, looking like the palest, coldest looking man alive, topped off with carnivalesque orange hair just in case you thought his eerie skin, the sallow complexion of the nocturnal and alcoholic, didn't make him look out of place enough.

An example of this emaciated, fragile Bowie can be seen in 1974 when, still only 27 years old, he appeared on *The Dick Cavett Show*, which ran from 1969 to 1975, as the stiffened glamour of old Hollywood segued into the wilder, more immediate glamour of the counterculture. Bowie is the shredded remains of when he was playing Ziggy Stardust with considerable zest, and then the so-called American Ziggy, Aladdin Sane, and then the desperado of cities, the short-lived *Diamond Dogs*-era Halloween Jack, used for the 'Rebel Rebel' video. Bowie saw him as an early version of the blank generation, a one-eyed member of William Burroughs' wild boys, a gang of drug-fuelled hedonists taking over the world. Jack was quickly devoured by America.

The suave 39-year-old Cavett – when 39 seemed a lot older than it does in the mid-2020s – was the most cerebral and conversational of the American late-night hosts, but still firmly embedded in showbusiness, slyly championing its more chaotic elements, playing up a shorthaired squareness that was part of his disguise. His carefully worn blandness was the blank canvas which his actor, comedian, literary, political, athlete and music guests could use to their own ends. He would calmly relish the idea of hosting the great stars of the day, from Mohammed Ali to Norman Mailer, Orson Welles to Marlon Brando, on the quiet as wised up as they were, and could comfortably deal with the unpredictable, conflicted ways of the flamboyant rock stars with alien manners like Jimi Hendrix and Janis Joplin. They seemed to be promising there was a world out there of ultimate freedom, where there were no limits on who and what you were, but both were on the way to having their already madly rearranged bohemian lives cut short at 27 by the excesses and dangers of the rock star life.

Bowie, right there at that dangerous age of 27, seemed to be someone in their camp, surely only famous enough to appear on a show where the famous and notorious were interviewed because his fame had begun to control him, doing its best to devour his sweetness and vulnerability, his English composure.

Cavett was having a genial but occasionally faintly sinister conversation with someone else in a celebrity predicament so extreme it had left deep cracks in their reality. Which made for great TV – the collected, sympathetic, relatively relaxed interviewer, looking like an off-duty undertaker, and the messed-up but undeniably fascinating and funny interviewee, a skeleton dressed to kill, slowly disappearing into his iconoclasm. Bowie was reaching Judy Garland levels of sucked-dry public breakdown, but still hanging onto his sense of humour; when a scattered, forgetful Garland was interviewed on the first series of the Cavett show, not long before her death in 1968, someone said to her it looked as though Cavett didn't know whether she was about to slit her wrists or break into '(Somewhere) Over the Rainbow'. Both, she said.

Cavett mentions to Bowie that for all his reputation, with some of his friends saying they'd be scared to meet him, he might bite their neck, he might bleed from the eyes, he seems to him just like a working actor. This nervy, niggly act is just a part he's playing, right? He's adopting the character of an elegant fuck-up, building up his own mythos, yes? Backstage, he didn't seem so antsy. Some see him as dabbling in black magic, while for others, he's just a very skilful performer. All of that, agrees Bowie with a batty smirk. 'I'm a person of diverse interests. I'm not really very academic but I glit from one thing to another. A lot.' Glit's like flit, he fumbles, but the seventies version.

There's too much going on in his mind, as though his skull has a thousand mirrors inside it. Nothing escapes him, not even the tiniest pin dropping to the floor.

The Bowie seen in the Cavett interview – perhaps one shifting between life and death, between clown and demon, between lean, hungry and neurosthenic coke fiend and bewildered charmer, between sleazy cabaret performer and deviant rock casualty radiating bad nerves, between his own creations Aladdin Sane and the Thin White Duke – would later be used as inspiration for Frank Miller's Joker talk show scene in his 1986 Dark Knight reboot of Batman. It's part of how Bowie ended up cutting up time, getting under people's skin, and through influencing others, appearing in different places at different times as various versions of himself.

Cavett had been a magician and in his own way, Bowie still was. It's as though, as shaky and lost as he might be in real life, he finds himself landing in what might in his mind seem like imaginary circumstances – a couple of years before, he was still playing to relatively small crowds in Britain and was yet to become the star of 'Starman' and beyond.

For Bowie, as jittery and disconnected as he was sitting with Cavett, this was him being himself, or at least trying to be himself, not dressed to the alien nines like Ziggy, or Aladdin Sane, on the edge of becoming the paranoid Thin White Duke, who consumed him from within, just a hardworking singer-songwriter singing his songs with a great band behind him. That had been his dream all along, really, and always would be. The best way of proving himself when he felt all at sea was to sing one of his new songs, one delivering an urgent message to whom it may concern, with a great, scintillating band behind him, as if all was right with the world.

Some theatrical instinct kicks in and he comes to taut, vibrant life. With a radiant kind of precision, considering he appears so detached, possibly in the middle of some form of delirium, he folds into *The Dick Cavett Show* a performance of 'Young Americans', months before it's released, of such fierce, fearless power and awkward grace it's as great as anything he did as an artist and entertainer. He's in his element; he's achieved his dream blend of saxophone and soul.

Incongruously, he strums the trusty 12-string guitar that took him from the space-folk of 'Space Oddity' to the rushing musical stardom of 'Starman', as if to make it clear he knows he doesn't belong with the effortlessly cool band he's fronting; he's a goddamn folk singer, but you can't blame a boy for trying.

LIGHT AND DARK

'Young Americans' on Dick Cavett's show is absolutely meant to be experienced 50, 100 years later as a kind of electrically delivered, spontaneous, unconquerable soul music that makes more sense as time goes by. History over time can be flattened of its original tension and turbulence, but through this version of 'Young Americans', under these circumstances, you get a sense of how much Bowie was on the edge, America was on the edge – and how little can explain that as sensationally as a fantastic, joyous song played as though it's the only thing keeping everything together.

(Bowie's antennae were twitching so much during his early 1970s American life, and then during his time in the deep end of Los Angeles, a city that had built itself up out of images, and images of itself, that he feared America was so much on the edge, it would one day go over the edge. He liked being on the edge because he could see things he couldn't from the centre of things – but there was the edge and there was The Edge, the edge of the world, the kind people only have an idea about when they've gone over it. One look over this edge will freak you out. Bowie at the time had clearly looked over The Edge more than once.)

It might have not made much sense as such when Bowie was in nervy, sniggering, incoherent conversation, trying hard to impress, but once he was singing and directing the band with crazed rigour, the world lit up.

He was leading a supreme, mostly American, mostly Black band – some of them forming the core of his band over the next decade or so – responding to him as a disciplined, inspiring, shape-shifting leader, charging through the mysteries of the song as if they're in some uncharted dimension between the razzle-dazzle gyrations of James Brown and the nightmare visions of Henry Miller.

Singing was saving Bowie, just as art did. It was his safety net. Art and music made him realise he was not alone. Art and music made him realise who and what he could be.

Cavett would say Bowie was the most unsettling, unpredictable rock star he ever interviewed, understating when he explained he didn't feel they were on the same wavelength. He described him as being a bit sniffly and, again with easy-going understatement, 'very weird.' There didn't seem to be much order or structure.

But at that point in his life, Bowie was storing up enough of the globetrotting rock-star bizarreness that audiences were then expecting to last for the rest of his life, however much he settled down in public. In the future, once he'd made it out alive, he managed to get some distance from the wrecked, burnt-out rock star, looking like someone who'd learnt a little from the clean-cut, unthreatening Dick Cavett how to position himself hiding behind a carefully cultivated politeness. If you needed to know anything else, about any kind of mental and spiritual liberation, it was there in his songs.

Over 50 years later, when his free-flowing interviews reached YouTube, *The Dick Cavett Show* proved they had a historical permanence that couldn't exist in the 1970s when the world wasn't recording itself and continually playing it back as it moved forward.

FUNK AND FOREMOST

The *Young Americans* album was artificial and inauthentic, even endearingly awkward, a sound he defensively described as plastic soul because he was a self-conscious English white guy pretending he knew the secrets of Ray Charles, Al Green, Ann Peebles, Wilson Pickett, Gladys Knight, Curtis Mayfield, Mavis Staples and Jackie Wilson. He didn't want to claim any authenticity for it, other than the authenticity given by using a Black rhythm section and Black backing singers. His contribution was the outsider looking in, making it as an experiment in mixing styles, not as a superficial appropriation of Blackness.

At the same time, as a knowledgeable, privileged and perfectionist fan's emotional celebration of soul music, it was true to the spirit and groove of soul and funk because Bowie worked with the best Black musicians, session players and singers in the Sigma Studios in Philadelphia – 'the city of brotherly love' – where some of his favourite soul music was made.

It sounded smooth, expansive and unruffled. The songs were mostly about romance and first love, but it could be as mysterious and melancholy as a seventeenth-century song by the English Renaissance composer John Dowland, which Bowie, in the mood he was in, with a lot of angst to unload, couldn't resist. It seemed to operate on a number of levels. In downbeat times, it was made with hope and courage in order to combat forces that divide and degrade us. It was still the blues – weary and defiant – but it was something modern and, behind the sheen and sophistication, something uncanny.

Desperate for a new sound for his American album, about a land of wonders and a culture in jeopardy, Bowie ambitiously wanted the ace house band of Kenny Gamble and Leon

Huff's Philadelphia International Records, MFSB, Mother Father Sister Brother, as the ready-made backing band for his next album. The musicians had played on the Gamble and Huff-written 'TOSP (the Sound of Philadelphia)' theme tune for the music television show *Soul Train*, specialising in soul and funk music. The first TV theme tune to get to number one in the Billboard 100 featured dreamy vocals and just two lines, inviting the world to party, voiced by the Three Degrees, beginning their association with Philadelphia International Records.

The MFSB Philly sound was wistful, more transitional than Motown, its label inspiration, and its elegant orchestral arrangements had an incongruous, lush, European quality. The use of almost supernatural widescreen orchestral strings on their three-minute records was one source of Motown records' uplifting and elusive power, especially on the Temptations 'My Girl' and 'Papa Was a Rolling Stone', and those parts were played by string players from the Detroit Symphony Orchestra. There was always an anonymous quality to exactly who from the orchestra was playing these strings, and this was the same with the strings beautifully played and arranged on the Philly soul records.

Philadelphia happened to have one of America's finest orchestras, for some the very best, and one of the world's best, the Philadelphia Orchestra, formed in 1900. The orchestra's third musical director, the rigorous, internationally renowned Leopold Stokowski, developed an intense, free-flowing and sublime orchestral sound that became known as the Philadelphia Sound. First in America to premiere works by Mahler, Schoenberg and Stravinsky, it was also the first American symphonic orchestra to make records and was the featured orchestra on the Walt Disney animated film *Fantasia* that Stokowski had encouraged Disney to make.

Stokowski was replaced by Hungarian-born Eugene Ormandy, who was musical director between 1938 and 1980, enhancing and extending the handsome, elegant Philadelphia Sound, bringing it into the contemporary movement of the city.

(Bowie would get to work with the Philadelphia Orchestra conducted by Ormandy when he narrated Sergei Prokofiev's imaginative 1936 musical symphony for children 'Peter and the Wolf' and Benjamin Britten's 'Young Person's Guide to the Orchestra', an artfully educational 1946 composition made to introduce children to classical music, both timeless pieces introducing the different sounds that make up an orchestra.

Bowie's son was seven at the time, and it seemed the perfect Christmas gift from the father who had just been tangling with Crowley, using his voice to charm and beguile in a different way and demonstrate that all was well with the world.

The shape shifting Bowie could become a duck, a bird, a bloodthirsty wolf and a mischievous cat, each animal an instrument. Bowie won over an initially suspicious and cranky Ormandy, who by then treated the orchestra as his own private instrument, seducing him with his timing and bewitching, weirdly dignified English accent and general benevolence. The album was released in 1978, another level of strangeness amidst Bowie's ongoing Berlin research and development, once more showing how he could be in different places at the same time.)

As well as this musical prominence, Philadelphia had inherited southern musical traditions between the early part of the twentieth century and the 1970s, as hundreds of thousands of African American migrants left the South as part of the Great Migration. Close to six million Black people moved their lives from the rural American South to industrial cities in northern, western and midwestern states, escaping racial violence and looking for new opportunities in these manufacturing centres.

This parallel existence of displaced African roots and European traditions adding a certain orthodox class produced a particularly unique musical character, and the coexistence of beautifully performed soul music and impeccably played orchestral strings on the post-civil rights pop music of PIR was the uniquely eclectic, late twentieth-century culmination, adding to a thriving jazz scene and the migration of the blues into white rock musicians' consciousness. While string players from the Philadelphia Orchestra were never directly credited as playing on the classic modern Philly soul records, the spirit of the orchestra was definitely present.

It's hard to believe some of its world-class players didn't moonlight on the sessions for songs like the O'Jays' 'Back Stabbers' and Harold Melvin and the Blue Notes' 'Wake Up Everybody', just as the Detroit Symphony Orchestra players did on certain Motown records – and players from the New York Philharmonic did on John Lennon's *Imagine* album, credited as the Flux Fiddlers after the 1960s Fluxus art collective Yoko Ono was associated with.

The label's house producer and arranger Thom Bell, fascinated by the eloquent entertainments of Henry Mancini and Burt Bacharach as much as the inspirational gospel of Ray Charles and Aretha Franklin, helped defined the sound on records by the O'Jays, the Delfonics and Billy Paul that caught Bowie's attention.

It was this fertile crossbreeding and hybridisation, and glorious, graceful grandeur amidst trying times, that Bowie was responding to, and because he never wanted to repeat himself, or sound like anyone or anything else, he'd got an instinct about taking this co-mingling of styles and attitudes even further.

In the end, Bowie couldn't get the MFSB or the label's ad hoc orchestra – it didn't make much sense when the wacky English guy with the orange hair and palest skin who'd sold himself as Martian came knocking – the man Miles Davis called 'Oh, that English guy in a dress' – as though he might be taking the mickey. (Five years later, which, considering what he went through in the meantime, were someone else's ten or twenty, he asked that the touching up of the cover illustration for his *Scary Monsters (and Super Creeps)* album involve giving him the red hair he didn't then have, because in America, they knew him as the red-haired bisexual.)

Bowie had to put his own Philly sound version together, his own consciousness-raising community in motion, which in the long run allowed him to maintain his experimental perfectionist quality that might have curdled with the moody perfectionism of the Philly ensemble and their symphonic soul – what the James Brown trombonist Fred Wesley called 'putting the bow tie on funk'. It was still coming out of the post-civil rights turbulence of the times, alert to injustice and political scandal; it wasn't as straight-out escapist as disco, where the strings and rhythm of the Philly sound, straightened out and boiled down, was heading, and beyond that, with added eclecticism, into house, and beyond that, spreading all over the twenty-first century.

The ragged, precarious America making mistake after mistake that Bowie was seeing and writing about – at a time of the Watergate scandal, the resignation of President Nixon, the end of the Vietnam War, the spread of urban decay – made him feel adrift, uneasy and flustered, but the American music and musicians he was honouring made the sound – which in the end was what mattered most – irrepressibly intoxicating. American music was always on the move.

Young Americans was his own intensely evocative enactment of the Philly sound, with extra loud guitars, the one thing linking all his records, whatever style or genre he was rewiring and sending into another dimension.

HEAT AND WONDER

Bowie's most direct, diagnostic song about the furies, and future, of fame, written with a contribution from the famous John Lennon, which could be called nothing but 'Fame', rolled out of a song full of funk he had performed on *The Dick Cavett Show*. It was a roughed-up reading of a 1961 song, 'Foot Stomping' by the Flares, with a voodoo rasp in Bowie's stressed, smoked voice that would never be heard again, and a clipped, clean, slightly giddy guitar riff tossed into the song playing tag with the perfectly present loud-ass drum that would be heard again and again and again. As much as anything, this was the statement of how far Bowie was going to escape what was beginning to trap him: the idea he was effete glam rock king and he was never going to change.

In America, glam was the whitest of music, a gimmicky English quirk, too small and narrow even as it borrowed some of the flamboyant clothes, beaten-up blues and boogie riffs from Black music. For Bowie, the quickest way out of the cul de sac was to dig into soul and blues, and how an American city, a location, a studio within that city, could add its own distinctive stamp.

It's why the theatrical British glam rock that was there at the beginning of the larger than life-sized, apocalyptically minded *Diamond Dogs* tour, after a break for some recording at the Sigma Studios, returned as the Philly Dogs tour, a lively musical revue fronted by some kind of fretful street hustler. Bowie needed to wise up to America and prove to himself if no one else that he'd got the funk, he'd seen the light, he'd conquered America. You could tell by the size of his set, which rose high into the night.

Key to this shift from alien spectacle to funk extravaganza was new 23-year-old guitarist Carlos Alomar, who'd added the high, nimble riff to 'Footstompin'', a Puerto Rico born, Bronx raised New York resident who'd played behind Chuck Berry, Ben E King, Wilson Pickett and James Brown. He'd also done time in an unlikely but esteemed musical academy, the highly sophisticated *Sesame Street* house band, which featured members of his own band, Listen My Brother.

Sesame Street was obviously set amongst the kind of inner-city neighbourhood where people of different ethnicities cheerfully and kindly co-existed. A TV show conceived to teach pre-school kids about numbers, letters and the language of life developed its own musical integrity, guided by its inspired first musical director, Joe Raposo, who helped make the music of *Sesame Street* one of its more consistently unusual, often surreal features, so it not only reached adults as well as its target audience, but was knowing enough to keep them engrossed.

Alomar had been called in to a New York studio to play some hired guitar on the Lulu version of Bowie's 'The Man Who Sold the World' – she'd acted in the 1967 Sidney Poitier film *To Sir, With Love*, and sung the theme song, and Alomar figured meeting her would bring him one step closer to Poitier, one of his heroes, the first African American actor to win an Oscar. Lulu wasn't Doris Day to Alomar; she was a great blue-eyed soul singer and had just sung the theme tune to the latest James Bond film, *The Man With the Golden Gun*.

She wasn't in the studio, they were still building up the track, but her producer was. David Bowie, ghostly white, all skin and bone, tangerine hair, with a lovely olde worlde accent that didn't seem to belong with the freak look. Alomar looked into Bowie's eyes and held his nerve. He had an instant flashback, remembering seeing him on *The Midnight Special* in orange tights and feather boa, some kind of faraway oddity he'd quickly forgotten, not something he thought would ever be part of his world. He looked like he could use a good homemade meal, to put some meat on the bones, which the gregarious Carlos and his singer wife, Robin Clark, were soon giving him.

Bowie turned up at their no-frills place in a limousine because, apart from whatever else was going on in Bowie's life at the time, this was the limo era, the beginning of the time when Bowie was being treated as a star by his latest manager, Tony Defries, whose job, he'd decided, was giving Bowie star treatment above his then current status so people would treat him like a star. Americans, anyway. The limo could also take a bodyguard who, along with the chauffeur, would keep an eye on Bowie, protecting him not so much from fans, who were thin on the ground in America at the time, but from himself and his wandering eye and mind.

Bowie went along with it, thinking it was what happened in America, or what happened when you were famous, not for a moment thinking about the economics of it all. He was paying but he didn't consider that. He was paying for a lot of things he didn't think about.

Alomar and Bowie quickly clicked, bonding over shared love for Black musicians from Thelonious Monk to Esther Phillips. Alomar was impressed by Bowie's musical intelligence and general openness. They educated each other – both liked learning things and seeing things in a new way, with new information. Alomar couldn't believe he was meeting this peculiar, gawky-looking Brit with see-though skin, who closely read the jazz magazine *DownBeat* and the sleeve notes for jazz albums on the Blue Note and Impulse labels. He'd started out in bands doing covers of Bo Diddley, Bowie explained. He quit one of his early bands because they wouldn't do a cover of Marvin Gaye's 'Can I Get a Witness'. Alomar couldn't imagine a British world – the fog, the pubs, Dickens and the Queen and all that – where there was such love for Black music.

Their flowing chat about music and musicians, the detours they took testing each other's knowledge and enthusiasm, became the foundation for how they worked together, each riffing off each other's ideas, their musical minds merging fantastically, heading off into new directions.

Alomar would give Bowie a tour of the bars, restaurants and venues of a Black New York Bowie had never encountered, giving him ideas, opening his mind to another level of experience and excellence. It was the kind of Black that made the Spiders from Mars seem very white, and very straight, and not so much from Mars after all. Or maybe an English Mars.

Alomar would soon become part of the fast-thinking session players Bowie was assembling for his *Young Americans* band and the *Diamond Dogs* live tour that was then taking a rest, and changing its identity – not least because of the Black bars and clubs he visited.

The riff Alomar coolly injected into the 'Footstompin'' arrangement, something he'd had on his mind for years, waiting for the right time, the right singer, because it had an elusive sparkle that didn't fit James Brown, became the backbone of 'Fame'. It was a riff he'd distilled from years of experience working in the house band at the Apollo Theatre on West 125th Street in Harlem, the great twentieth-century haven for Black American musical artists, the one that had caused such a fuss in Bowie's Bromley mind in 1964 when he'd heard James Brown's *Live at the Apollo* and imagined America as a place of promise where you could achieve wonders. It was a riff that came from seeing the great Motown vocal quartet the Temptations perform their exquisite dance routines, from watching Nancy Wilson elegantly prowl the stage sizing up the audience, from learning the art of timing while playing behind the righteous and raving due process of James Brown.

Alomar was one of three stage guitarists Brown challenged to keep him interested, each needing to get noticed, sussing out where the groove was that you mustn't get in the way of, so you moved around the space between the notes. Don't disturb the groove – that was the law. Lawless funk material-

Instrument; David Bowie with 12-string guitar, 1966.

Innocence; with Angie after their wedding in Bromley on 19 March 1970.

Self-reflection; backstage at Lewisham Odeon, 24 May 1973, during the *Aladdin Sane* part of the *Ziggy Stardust* tour.

Cigarette; arriving at the Hammersmith Odeon before the evening concert, 3 July 1973.

Storytelling; with arm outstretched for the final concert as Ziggy Stardust at the Hammersmith Odeon, 3 July 1973.

Uncanny; with Marianne Faithfull filming 'The 1980 Floor Show' for NBC's *The Midnight Special* at the Marquee Club in Soho, London, in front of an audience of fan club members, 20 October 1973.

Adventure; the *Young Americans* medley with Cher for her TV show, 23 November 1975.

Introspection; with Buster Keaton biography, 1976.

Entrance; bringing a message for the world at Victoria Station London, 7 May 1976.

Falling man; hand-painted billboard promoting the *Lodger* album, Los Angeles, 1979.

Fame; arranging himself for photographers in London, 1983.

Slings and arrows; holding a symbol of mortality on the *Serious Moonlight* tour, 1983.

Armour; wearing a well-fitted suit in London, 1993, photographed by Anton Corbijn for *Max* magazine.

Belief; on the set for the 'Jump They Say' music video in March, 1993.

Traveller; campaigning for Louis Vuitton in October, 2013.

ised from this law. (Bowie would inherit this jazz-based law from James Brown, so that Alomar would consistently play the steady, vital rhythm guitar, leaving the rotating 'star' lead guitarists like Earl Slick and Robert Fripp to bring the show off, the more obvious wow.)

The 'Fame' riff was the riff of someone who when he was working at the Apollo Theatre had an understudy called Nile Rodgers, who had just formed a group called Chic, influenced as much by the artful European style and refinement of Roxy Music as anything more obviously Motown or Stax. Rodgers would replace Alomar in the *Sesame Street* band and was there when *Sesame Street* hired a new bassist, Bernard Edwards, his future Chic partner. The Chic groove that launched a million grooves had its roots in *Sesame Street*.

Carlos Alomar brought some of his old *Sesame Street* friends into the studio when Bowie and his musicians were working on the 'Young Americans' song – his wife, Robin, and a friend she had introduced him to, another singer, the then unknown, undervalued Luther Vandross, who he'd known since he was 15. The road out of *Sesame Street* also led to Bowie's America, just as the roads out of Kerouac, Little Richard and Lou Reed had.

A chain-smoking Bowie overheard the two singers at the back of the studio instinctively responding to his call in the song of 'All Right', giggling at what they had done. Bowie, always alert to a fortunate chance moment, asked them if they could do that again. Sure, and they did it again. Bowie liked their idea. Can you do it into the mic? Sure!

Once future superstar Luther was in, part of Bowie's America set-up, he was full of ideas, coming up with the 'Young American, young American, she wants the Young American' part, throwing some deep, real swing into a song that needed some deep, real swing.

After Bowie asked him to appear throughout the album, Vandross in turn called in the backing singers he used and would use when he eventually recorded his bestselling debut album in 1981. Bowie got for his album an exclusive advance showing of the inspirational Luther Vandross vocal ensemble that was part of some of the biggest selling soul records of the 1980s. Bowie uses them as an instrument throughout the album, a Greek chorus commenting on the action, highlighting the messages and themes, imagining where the song's story might go, keeping Bowie in check, letting him fly.

Luther made all that space for himself and his ideas, encouraged by Bowie to build his part and that of the singers, and Carlos was making himself increasingly invaluable. As he would say, that's how the three of them got a lot of their paying gigs, turning up together at venues and studios, and worming their way into the process, into new musical settings, lightly showing off what they could do, which coming out of nowhere in a sometime clinical, tedious studio or rehearsal setting, was often amazing.

It was a hand-to-mouth living at the time and it took a few goes for Bowie, and Bowie's people, to get Carlos to come into the fold as more than a session musician paid by the hour because the money on the table was nowhere near good enough. They offered him a sad, mean couple of hundred dollars a week and he said no way – he was earning $800 playing with his regular group at the time, the long-running R&B group Main Ingredient, who were having hits and playing shows with the O'Jays, Edwin Starr, Harold Melvin and the Blue Notes, Ohio Players, Sly and the Family Stone. He'd joined at 19 and it was a hell of an education. It was one of the singers in Main Ingredient, Tony Sylvester, who had recommended Carlos for the Bowie-produced RCA Lulu sessions.

In the end, Bowie as a business had to pay up to land Alomar, but they got more than just a guitarist, as versatile and insatiable as he was, and as long lasting as he turned out. They got more than a band leader, coordinating the overall sound, helping assemble the rhythm section that would replace the Spiders from Mars rhythm section – the tough, hard-rock drums and bass replaced with a more oblique, more abstractly branded and entrancing jazz and progressive soul rhythm section.

Bowie was great at finding his people. He was a great collector of talent, quick to notice when something and someone was working for him, especially if it took him by surprise, in a good way, and he was fast to make use of it. He'd then place the name into his mental Rolodex, ready to retrieve the information when he needed that specific energy again. For a while, he only knew this new guitarist he'd found as Carlos. He didn't remember his surname. He just knew it was right; the other details would come.

Alomar had played with a smart, smiling and irrepressible jazz drummer, Dennis Davis, since the late sixties, including time with James Brown and jazz-funk pioneer Roy Ayers. Davis had studied with Coltrane's drummer Elvin Jones and the inimitable Max Roach, and toured with the Clark Terry Big Band. Alomar brought him in towards the end of the *Young Americans* session, just in time to play on 'Fame', and Dennis knew a bassist he loved working with, the impeccable and forceful George Murray. He completed the trio in time for *Station to Station*.

The Spiders from Mars band – one of rock's greatest looking and greatest sounding bands, especially if you were in your teens when you came across them for the first time – became, via the *Young Americans* sessions, the DAM Trio, with an almost ghostly, ingeniously sketchy presence on a series of culture-shifting, post-glam albums that Bowie made, moving on from playing characters to creating conceptual apparitions.

A different set of spiders from another kind of Mars, one first discovered by Sly and the Family Stone, nameless and ruthlessly efficient. A three-piece unit with one mind, reshuffling instrument roles, leaving the space for Bowie's speculations because they knew just how to make their presence felt without getting in the way of the star, the art, the experiments and other ways of describing the alienated groove of Bowie.

The DAM Trio of Davis, Alomar and Murray became Bowie's dream, no-nonsense, adventurous rhythmic centre for the radically transitional *Station to Station* and the following five albums, including the 'Berlin' three, the live *Stage* recording of the long, demanding Isolar II/Thin White Duke tour taking in a lot of 1978, covering the Ziggy album and *Low* and *Heroes* in chronological order, and Bowie's vivaciously heady end of seventies recap, *Scary Monsters (and Super Creeps)*.

HIRE AND HIGHER

By hiring Alomar, Bowie got someone reliable and consistent. He didn't clash with Bowie's lifestyle tendency to lose himself in time, especially on those tours that went on for months. Bowie got someone who was experienced in slipping into the rhythms of the hard touring he would do every couple of years, the easiest, quickest way of making some money.

Touring meant dealing with the amount of adrenaline flowing through the musician's system after a performance, making going to sleep straight away impossible, which meant partying and hanging out after a show finished. It takes a while to come down. It's not like you could curl up with a good book.

With Bowie, this meant possibly losing him in a city as he went out and chased experience and various extremes. His old friend from Bromley, Geoff MacCormack, nicknamed him 'too far' – he always went too far when he drank, when he needed to loosen up, when he did anything at all really, and around 1975 was the peak period of this never-mentioned character, the untamed extremist Too Far, better known as the Thin White Duke.

The Bowie team worked out a system whereby hotel rooms became part of the nightlife. Different parties in different rooms, different places to visit and meet different sets of people, tiring and drinking and inhaling yourself to sleep.

One of the problems after a tour finished was that moment about seven o'clock when you'd be at home, getting ready to eat, needing those quiet nights in, and then, out of nowhere, your body would be getting ready for the show you weren't going to do. You're wired to perform, and Bowie would need ways to perform even if he wasn't about to perform.

Having Carlos at his side, who could handle the parties and hit the night with the right kind of energy, but who also had a certain level of consistency in his life, helped Bowie make those coherent, if emotionally shattered records he was making in the middle of chasing and sometimes losing sight of his own soul. Alomar had the calm, level head that was required as Bowie's body imploded and his mind exploded.

JOHN AND DAVID

Bowie being Bowie brought actual fame into the studio when they were working on the song that became 'Fame', which existed because *The Dick Cavett Show* 'Footstompin'' didn't work in the studio the way it did when played live, as a temporary blast, a sort of theme tune for the street-smart, unEnglish character he was working on. It sounded flat and obvious, too much Bowie trying to copy Black music and losing his innate, untethered flair.

The one element that did work was Alomar's minimal, flickering riff, one of those moments Bowie relished, when the unexpected happens and then you get the chance to design the way that things evolve. They started from there on a new song.

One night, Bowie, accompanied by a new friend, walks into the Electric Ladyland studios where they were finishing the album they'd begun in Philadelphia. Alomar was there with the producer of the session, Harry Maslin, and various tape ops and assistants. Without any warning, Bowie turns up with John Lennon, of all people. They are giggling with each other, and the studio freezes.

Fame had arrived, changing the game. Bowie had brought in Lennon to contribute to, or just artistically approve, a version of a Bowie Beatles favourite, 'Across the Universe', and, after nodding that through, Lennon gets a listen to a work in progress, built around what he hears as some nice, twitchy sounding rhythm that comes straight off the streets of Manhattan. It was as though, working on a track that was becoming important to him, Bowie had arranged for perhaps the most famous rock star in the world to help finish it.

One of the things that he and Lennon bonded over was the tough, uncompromising managers that they both seemed to attract, tending to follow their own agenda. Lennon advised Bowie to become his own businessman, avoiding the clichéd, full-time rock and roll manager sinking his teeth into your fame, and fortune, and some of the chat turned into a song.

Bringing into the studio fame itself in the living form of Lennon, someone who'd been damaged and derailed by his success, led to the track called 'Fame', which could also be called 'Pain'. Trying to escape pain is what causes more pain.

Lennon loves the Carlos groove and, given a little encouragement – he's a little tired, a lot going on – picks up an acoustic guitar and routinely adds a small piece of his own clarification, a little musical touch which seems to transport the whole production into a different realm, and the album itself – originally a set of songs to be called *The Gouster*, pushing a new, more American-friendly, masculine Bowie – takes a post-Lennon turn, some songs falling away to let in 'Across the Universe' and the song about fame. This makes the *Young Americans* album about Bowie's American discoveries also an album about Bowie's discoveries about himself, and the doubt and fears he's feeling as America amplifies his fame and twists it tighter, as it turns into a mirage. The greater the fame, the greater the doubt. And doubt grows with knowledge.

While Lennon and Bowie have drinks and dinner in New York, doing their best to forget their secret doubts, Alomar stays in the studio and works on the arrangement, turning down the chance to join them, conscientiously following the music and the song he was helping create, and what the hell has he got to say to John Lennon anyway.

Now that Lennon is one of the guitar players on the track, with all that history he brings with him, Alomar remembers the mantra 'don't disturb the groove'. Especially when some of it got left there by John Lennon. He doesn't want to leave the studio and forget the ideas he had in mind. With Maslin, he gets on with some work, leaving Bowie and Lennon to have a conversation no one will ever know anything about, but which in a biography of fiction would have the pair of them agree never to trust someone who is never in doubt. And fame? It's a form of incomprehension. It always brings with it loneliness. It's definitely not about peace of mind. Fame is a burden, fame is a constant effort, but it's up to you to bend it to your will and make sure it doesn't end badly. Bowie could see a time coming when fame would be seen as everything, almost all that was left of the world.

Alomar finetunes the riff and it's like he captures fame as a firefly trapped in a jar.

When Bowie returns and hears what Alomar's done, he gets excited and hears something he can add, without disturbing the groove. He records a little guitar response of his own, which brings some mystery to the song – maybe some of the mystery, and the loneliness, of fame itself.

Alomar and Bowie had fulfilled the intention to make a track that was as Black as it could be, all things considered, and so Black it ended up being brazenly assimilated by James Brown himself in a track released later that year, 'Hot (I Need To Be Loved, Loved, Loved)' – he figured it sounded like Bowie and Alomar had picked his pocket, so he had the right to snatch some of it back. The rhythm of 'Fame' also shot straight onto a track by carnivalesque funk fanatic George Clinton on the future-funk 1975 Parliament album *Mothership Connection*, 'Give Up the Funk (Tear the Roof Off the Sucker)'. You don't know David Bowie if you have to ask whether he had funk, said George, which sealed the deal – Bowie's take on fame made it clear that whatever it was, it contained pure uncut funk.

Luther Vandross was convinced the first single released from the album was going to be the track he had a writing credit on, 'Fascination', originally a song he had written called 'Funky Music (Is a Part of Me)'. He'd sung it on the Philly Dogs tour with the opening act, Bowie's show band without Bowie, the Mike Garson Band, named after the touring band's pianist famous for his fearsome, atonal piano on the 'Aladdin Sane' song. The piano became a character in itself.

Both Luther and Bowie's version are about seeking salvation, but Bowie turns the original, forthright Vandross mantra about the addictive beauty of funky sound – he can't help it, he's got to move when he hears it – into a deeper, darker song about being overwhelmed by desire, addicted to his thoughts, excited and worried where they'll take him.

'Fame', not 'Fascination', was the first single from *Young Americans* to be released and Carlos, at 23, Sesame Street alumnus, had written his first number one with David Bowie and John Lennon.

Fame's a funny thing.

REACT AND REFINE

Bowie knew that Alomar was funk slick, and fast and creative in the studio, but Carlos had plenty of other tricks up his sleeve. For a start, he was fluent in the language and effects of Jimi Hendrix, which helped make him a few guitarists in one.

When Bowie decided he wanted him for the next album after *Young Americans*, which became *Station to Station*, Alomar was working in the backing band for the original Broadway production of gothic cabaret comedy *The Rocky Horror Show* at the Belasco Theatre on 44th Street, with its specialist relish for transvestism, travesty and transsexuality. It featured a manic, trashy Meatloaf doubling up as delivery boy Eddie and scientist Dr Scott, and languid, Jaggeresque Tim Curry as horny, ghoulish mad scientist alien Frank-N-Furter, the role he had originated in London in 1973.

Writer and creator Richard O'Brien was the creepy, vampiric butler Riff Raff, enjoying an incestuous relationship with his sister Magenta. This was years before the show as a forever film and endlessly performed in provincial theatres became a sexy cult sanctuary for misfits, cheery ne'er-do-wells and everyday deviants, and then a mainstream staple with participatory rituals and fun for all the genderqueer family.

The whole production was a little too immersive and unstable, too much of a blatant experience, a celebration of undefined and unfettered sexuality, for a 1975 Broadway show. The critics didn't want to party and didn't want to like it, so it didn't stick around for long, but a shapeshifting, freaky rock and roll parody show featuring a wired bisexual alien in lipstick and fishnet tights was perfect preparation for Alomar when he joined Bowie's latest troupe.

There were some crossovers between the Bowie universe and the *Rocky Horror* one. Pierre La Roche, who created the make-up for Ziggy Stardust and Aladdin Sane and the mutation from one to the other, designed the make-up for the 1975 film version.

Bowie's decision to murder Ziggy and get rid of the body is a sign that he wasn't prepared to spend the rest of his life nursing the story and the character through a decades long, *Rocky Horror*-type move into the soft, safe centre of culture, its energy dwindling as its audience grew, regularly turning up for revival after revival. He didn't want to stick with something until it was everywhere and nowhere, and he'd got nothing else to show for years of work. For Bowie, the only safe thing was taking a chance, and moving elsewhere.

The need to change and leave Ziggy behind was represented by the desolate, shadowy and malignant rock and roll of *Diamond Dogs* as it evolved into the glittering heart and soul Philly Dogs Revue. Alomar had proved he was capable of joining Bowie's mutant mobile circus by performing in *The Rocky Horror Show*, the scrawny, sing-a-long reaction to the liberating glam of Roxy and Bowie and the mock rock, sensibly wild musicals *Hair* and *Jesus Christ Superstar*. Alomar could cosmically rock as well as play the funk and cut himself loose. He could handle the theatre Bowie would use even as he started to shed the more musical-based properties of drag. He had paid his dues as both funk specialist and guitar chameleon. He was ready for all the challenges Bowie would throw his way.

When Bowie made a move, conceptually or musically, turning to the left, turning to the right, looking and finding new energy, from *Young Americans* via *Station to Station*'s plea for help to the un-American Berlin albums to the dizzy, simulated nostalgia of 'Ashes to Ashes' and beyond, Alomar was quick to follow, even to take the lead now and then, smartly racing into his own creations, reacting to an unseen new direction without flinching.

Bowie would turn his attention to a new album by asking the question – Why am I making this album? He always had an answer; usually, he was right, now and then he was less right, but some musicians followed him from album to album, answering the call, because they could help him with the answer.

Bowie said, when he was taking on America, you could always tell from listening to his albums which city, or cities, they were from. He was emotionally eclectic as well as musically eclectic, perpetually open to suggestions, so you can feel in the songs the place he was in, or the place he was attached to.

Diamond Dogs was all mixed-up, a collection of American cities he'd driven through while touring, overwhelming and astonishing him, turned imaginary. He'd prophetically sensed end times and a mad, nightmarish world crashing into fascism when responding in song to his first real visits to America, the mythical land of his dreams and influences since he was a kid.

The *Aladdin Sane* album imagined his Ziggy Stardust character – and therefore somewhere also himself – indulging and defiling himself in America – a cipher for America, like Kafka's Amerika, an ominous, alien place where everything is off-kilter, skewed and disorienting. It didn't exist in most people's imagination, but Bowie, watching from his new vantage point as star and independent traveller, could see that it could and that it probably would. The Ministry of Truth he'd read about in George Orwell's *1984* was waiting to be born.

Diamond Dogs was an attempt to create a musical of the George Orwell *1984* in time for 1984. It never happened because of a failure to get permission, and Orwell's wife Sonia, looking after the estate, took a dim view of the peculiar rock star with his pushy entourage wanting to mess with this by then sacred text, so it became a Ziggy-esque variation of Orwell's dark prophecies.

He mixed Orwellian ideas about the cities he invented for 1984, places of inequality, poverty and oppression, its surfaces used for propaganda messages to enclose the population with its Truth, with Fritz Lang's view in his film *Metropolis* that the city in the twentieth century was being increasingly represented by its tensions, its disharmony and destructive forces. Cities weren't natural; they were out of scale and we were being forced to evolve to deal with them – as we would be compelled to evolve in an increasingly virtual and disorientating twenty-first century.

Diamond Dogs is an album that takes the collapse of society and civic sanity, the cancelling of collective memory, too far; a dislocated, disenchanted entertainment containing the basic message that we are all going to die. Or, at least, glam rock was going to die, so let's have some dark fun with it, and say farewell with a sleazy, gleeful bang. Lose your mind, do it with purpose, find out who you really are beyond your thoughts and beliefs. Just the message it's great to receive from your favourite pop star.

It was pretty gloomy, anticipating the pessimistic, fatalistic and passive nihilism of the black-pilled world of *The Matrix*, the darker, bleaker side of the red pill for confronting harsh truths about reality and the blue pill for blissful ignorance and surrendering control of your life.

Young Americans brought some light and life into proceedings, an endpoint that was also a beginning, and delayed the inevitable. It was the East Coast; it was Philadelphia and New York. And then – leading to the completion of a kind of American trilogy, after the London trilogy of *Hunky Dory*, *Ziggy Stardust* and *Pin Ups* – Bowie moved to Los Angeles, where everybody is from somewhere else and everyone seemed to find even love difficult.

A move, he admitted, which didn't help.

He'd forgotten Kerouac's warning. Kerouac had never felt sadder than when he was in LA; it was lonely and brutal, it didn't have the 'wacky comradeship' of New York when things get bad.

LA is a jungle, a regular hell.

CHER AND ALIKE

Young Americans has been out for a few months by the time he appears on another TV show in an era when American television could be as experimental as it was tightly restrained. This was when the scattergun comedy sketch show *Saturday Night Live* began, taking on the experimental and getting rid of the restraints, often letting things rely on chance.

If nothing else, this looser approach suited the presentation of live music. The freedom Bowie had found on *The Dick Cavett Show* show to perform his music in the purest, most unshackled way is extended on his *Saturday Night Live* appearances and Bowie would find the space amidst the show's general wildness to deliver another of his most mesmerising and unique performance pieces in 1980 alongside the extraordinary non-binary German counter tenor Klaus Nomi. In 1975, he bends showbusiness time appearing with Cher on her television show, just to prove how the TV studio can be a great laboratory for experimenting with outrageousness,

The history-scanning 'Young Americans' title track, possibly because it seems to flatter a potential audience and give them a diversity anthem, had recently been his second Billboard top 30 hit in America, reaching number 28. The album had made the top ten. 'Fame' had elevated his fame. 'Young Americans' seemed to drag him further into the perversions and decadence of America, all the better to dazzle you. He kept repeating the word 'American', the rhythm adopting that clever illusion that Motown and other labels like Stax and Philadelphia International pulled off where, in a racially divided country, Black grooves were American grooves. This helped erase the idea that he was a red-headed freakoid in clown's clothing invading America from somewhere else, where they did things differently.

After the twitchy, frantic and wiped-out Bowie of *The Dick Cavett Show* show, hanging onto himself by the skin of his teeth, needing a walking stick for balance even when sitting down, he is perhaps beginning to decide there might be a way to push back, to come out of actually living the outsider life, living not like but as an outlaw, and recover his balance. He could experiment and create life in his music, not by operating on himself in the real world, which was pulling him apart.

Bowie's trying to steady himself and then, because he never stops working, he's in showbiz, or is making an art out of showbiz, and the drugs he'd been taking somehow don't upset his timing or trip up his singing, he's doing a duet with Cher on a voluptuous and sometimes deviant variety show she hosted at the time, with flickering hints of the more unhinged, liberated television of *Saturday Night Live*. The show, for a couple of seasons after her split from Sonny and the end of their Sonny and Cher comedy hour, was Cher's own way of trying to organise what the hell it meant to be Cher. She needed a little steadying herself.

She was 29, six months older than Bowie, but could have been around for a thousand years. At the time, for a pop singer, or any kind of post rock and roll entertainer, 29 was old and Cher, who'd turned famous much younger than Bowie did, faced years of decline, or at least had passed her peak period and was doomed to spend the rest of her time as a performer living in the past, repeating the hits, rapidly losing the edge that had made them hits in the first place. There was no clear path how to develop as a performing artist and also sustain celebrity status as you aged, and younger, ravenous others quickly took your place.

Cher's fiery divorce from Sonny gave off rock and roll, Taylor and Burton energy, and even though she had made an album called *Stars* with the revered composer and musician Jimmy Webb, and was one of the most famous people on the planet, it was her worst selling record. It didn't even make the Billboard Top 100 album charts – for Cher, a kind of death. She had fought her way out of belonging to a no-man's-land because of her Cherokee ancestry, overcoming an appearance apparently unsettling to the mainstream national imagination, and now it seemed she was being dumped back there.

Her record company, bewildered by the album's total failure, having assumed her illuminated brand name would be enough, said it seemed that no one could take Cher seriously as a recording artist. Making a serious record backfired. Maybe Cher didn't fit in after all and the white privileges afforded her as part of the palatably edgy mavericks Sonny and Cher were temporary. She was finding out it was all temporary. The only thing that was permanent was the fact that there was no safety.

As would be clear in one of her comebacks in the late 1990s – her life was a series of comebacks until she reached the safe shore of iconic late life – Cher should be no one but what an audience expected Cher to be: fun, excessive and a little daring and mysterious in those areas that don't involve subversive ideas. She must simply be famous, so her audience could share her eternal aura, feel comforted by her immunity from daily trials and tribulations, and any music must lightly reflect her fame, never question or doubt it.

SERIOUS AND IMMINENT

As part of her failed artistic seriousness in the mid-seventies, Cher had done a smartly chosen cover on the *Stars* album of 'Mr. Soul', a song Neil Young had written in 1966 at 21 when he was in the psychedelic folk rock group Buffalo Springfield. It was about the classic pressures of fame, how it changes you, and the depression of the tortured artist. It's got more than a hint of the Rolling Stones' 'Satisfaction', released a year or so before, Young already acknowledging what a difference the song's dirtied, distorted riff was making to the elementary sound and style of rock.

'Mr. Soul' was about how sudden fame limits your ability to move in those areas and places that gave you your original inspiration. You've made it and now to some extent you've lost sight of yourself. Fame has hit so hard you think you're going to die, and if you're not careful, the more fame you get, the more you want – it's like sea water, the more you drink, the thirstier you become. 'Mr. Soul' could have been about Bowie's situation at the time he did the Cher show, doing his best not to lose his artistic 'soul' and maybe actually his soul, and fighting to keep his artistic focus. Young wrote it when he wasn't ready for the suffocating, frightening impact of sudden fame.

Bowie was in the early stages of the same kind of whirlwind, which would end up with his making a real attempt to leap through unheard of, unnameable things and reach for the unknown.

His songs about stardom and the life-and-death hysteria that comes with it were written as if he was some kind of expert, but he lost control when the songs gave him for real the kind of rock star powers that were originally a fantasy.

Young's 'Mr. Soul' is an early template for the kind of raucous, reflective and evocative songs Bowie would write about becoming a rock and roll star in your early twenties, when, as Young would write, just a small glimpse of your face, your hands, your smile could trigger mass hysteria.

Like many of Bowie's songs, Young's 'Mr. Soul' is a song about the physical and psychological nature of change; Young himself had recently gone through a fundamental change in his life with the onset of epilepsy and the song connects the disconcerting effects of an epileptic fit, which felt like a near-death episode, with the experience of being on stage in front of adoring fans. It's going to change you and your behaviour, the world around you, and the way people deal with you.

Bowie also modified and ecstatically rewired other familiar rock riffs and rhythms as part of his commentary on the new realities of rock music, as Young did, borrowing the already famous Rolling Stones riff, an original source, one with its own sense of desperation and confusion.

Maybe Bowie accepted the Cher show invitation because she might give him some clues as to how to navigate American-level fame and the closeness an audience was beginning to get, but Bowie also couldn't resist a collaboration, especially an unlikely one. He could have been drawn to the idea because he identified with her irreverence, remembering how much she looked like a bold, challenging outsider in 1965, when Bowie was 18, quick to pick up wonderful, brand-new pop signals. He'd been struck by how Sonny and Cher were astounding England with their proto-hippy clothes, a fiery cartoon image of the sexual revolution. Cher wore the pants as much as Sonny, never seemed to be seen in dresses or skirts, and her appearance was fluid and unfixed, soft and tough at the same time.

The post-Ziggy persona that we see going crazy all over Sonny and Cher's 'I Got You Babe' in Bowie's '1980 Floor Show' created chaos and caused problems that needed a lot of cleaning up, but even as he was dealing with the fallout, Bowie always felt some kind of obligation to do his job, to get out into the world and promote himself – with that sense he had that, eventually, we would all have access to where he was and what he was thinking at any given time.

If his life itself was a work of art, and it had already dawned on him it might be, some instinct allowed him to understand that unusual events and unexpected alliances would eventually make more sense in a different future world. It was like writing entries in a diary – although, in his case, he preferred to do something theatrical rather than jot down a few brief, descriptive lines. Duetting and dancing with Cher – the real Cher – struck him as being a fine chance to produce some startling theatre, a sequel to his Sonny and Cher at the end of the world duet with Marianne.

Bowie was at the time of his collaboration with Cher in the middle of the kind of turbulent, overwhelming excitement, all directed towards him, that he had been turning into the pop songs, thinking he was safely hiding behind the fantasy, playing a role, wearing armour. He'd assumed he would escape unscathed when he'd finished that particular stage of his life. He'd take off the costume and he would be himself once more. It turned out not to be that simple.

He'd once said he'd sell his soul to be famous and this was a classic case of be careful what you wish for. He hadn't yet finalised a deal on his soul but there was an offer on the table. Cher herself had maybe already made the deal but was facing some kind of betrayal, facing up to the possible agony of fading from the headlines, drifting into obscurity, suffering a kind of death which would lead to a series of afterlives.

Appearing with Cher, the physical embodiment of the strangeness of fame, seeing his own dazed strangeness mirrored in her, Bowie is processing the idea that he is now the rock and roll star he once only dreamed of being, and then wrote about because it was such thrilling, inspiring material, thinking he was making art and therefore keeping his distance.

If Cher and Bowie were to interview each other, perhaps the first question would be – for each to answer – how seriously do you take yourself?

Answer: in some ways, very. On the other hand, it is also a game we play.

We watch in real time right in front of our eyes two unplaceable, implacable creatures slightly surprised by the other, dressed for action in loose, heavenly clothing, each somewhere in their own world, almost trying to work out how to move, how to sing, how to dance and, ultimately, how to communicate with other people, and of course each other. Are they playing a romantic couple, sister and brother – maybe a stepbrother – a couple who've just slept together, a couple who've fallen out with each other? Are they allowed to touch each other? One can only imagine what is going on in their minds, which becomes part of the uncanny, unplanned greatness of the performance. The performance is a collision between two singers each having their own out-of-body experiences.

They perform together on a round stage, faceless musicians in a big band doing their thing in the shadows, and fall from a great height into an absurd six-and-a-half minute medley that seemed flown in from Elvis-branded Las Vegas, bringing the blues to middle America, rather than this by then ancient-seeming rock and roll.

It's another example of Bowie placing himself one way or another inside his own reading of pop history, using a selection of mournful, cosily nostalgic songs that perhaps feature some chosen by Bowie and some by Cher. Or maybe someone drew various songs about loneliness out of a hat and the pair of them did what they were told.

Bowie's own American top 30 hit, the desperate ode to American highs and lows, desires and despairs, 'Young Americans', with its yearning cry about the one damned song that can give wings to the mind and flight to the imagination, quickly becomes a restless sequence of other songs, as if he's looking for that one damned song that will give soul to the universe and save his life. One day, there would be such things as Spotify and this would be a playlist – David and Cher's Music for the Soul, an American Fever Dream.

There's more to it than at first seems possible. Everything happens out of the blue. On 'Young Americans', Cher seems to be hearing it for the first time, stunned by all the words, arms flapping as she tries to find its centre. The song becomes, in this exaggerated showbusiness setting, an instant American classic, changing shape in a bizarre moment – losing a lot of weight, as it happens – to become a quick trip through Neil Diamond's slight and airy 'Song Sung Blue', a worldwide number one.

It's a melodic, melodramatic song about how sad songs can be a protection against depression, so Bowie and Cher could handle that in their sleep. They knew the beauty of sad songs, unlike Diamond, who sang it as though it was a cheerful song and he had never known sadness, and despite singing it from some kind of hazy, airless TV heaven, they sing it like they're feeling something.

After what Bowie's been through the previous few weeks, including 24-hour studio sessions in harsh, darkened rooms in Los Angeles tearing the brittle, battling grandeur and swooning ballads of *Station to Station* out from his debauched soul while also tearing his heart out, he gratefully sinks into its cushioning softness, losing his place with a giggle. And then it's gone.

It melts into a version of the more famous Three Dog Night version of Beatles' favourite Harry Nilsson's 'One', the sad, melancholy 'one is the loneliest number' song about the ache of solitude. You can also be lonely when you're with someone else – so two is the loneliest number since the number one.

That must have been a Bowie choice, so the Crystals' boy-meets-girl 'Da Doo Ron Ron' is from Cher with love – or vice versa. It's the earliest example of Phil Spector's Wall of Sound using multitrack recording to build a song layer by layer – an innocent, throwaway song of teen lust, played by a parade of American greats – Glen Campbell, Leon Russell and Jack Nitzsche, with Spector throwing in the giddy da doo ron ron for structural reasons. It comes from the very dawn of modern pop music.

Laura Nyro's silky, sublime song of unrequited love 'Wedding Bell Blues' – written in 1966 at age 18 – was an American number one for R&B easy listening and Nyro specialists 5th Dimension.

Pre-1960s identically dressed girl-group pioneers the Chantels prefigured Motown's the Supremes and Phil Spector's the Shirelles, infusing sweet, charming gospel pop songs with intense religious energy. Bowie drops to his knees for the Chantels echoey, angelic 'Maybe', a song that uses the word 'pray' as much as it does its title. 'Maybe' isolates the influence of religious music – and choir practice in Black churches – on rock and roll, or skip and jump as 1950s American Catholic nuns would call it. It's the kind of hybrid of compact pop song and soaring hymn that had such an impact on the musical mind of Bowie. You can hear that on the anguished *Station to Station*, which, in its own derelict, defiant way, is a form of religious music – a performance of recovery, of belief, blues to get rid of the blues.

Written when Bowie was ten, and when he was staring in wonder at those American 45s with their intoxicating labels, Buddy Holly's 'Maybe Baby' sets the stage for the classic rock and roll line-up, bass, drums, voice and all-important guitar, when it was a rare thing that a musician wrote, played and performed songs. Holly was beginning to experiment with the form and structure of pop songs – as the band he most influenced, the Beatles, would – when he died in 1959, aged 22.

You could hear the progress made in the sixties in rock and roll excitement as Bowie and Cher move on from Buddy to the

'Day Tripper' of the Beatles, with its John Lennon riff rooted in the liberating simplicity of 'Maybe Baby' nine years earlier, but sonically, conceptually and psychedelically elsewhere.

'Day Tripper' trips into 'Blue Moon' – originally called 'Prayer' written for a 1933 film called *Hollywood Party* – which Elvis reduced to a sublime next-to-nothing on his debut album, which becomes the Platters' song of devotion and longing 'Only You', then Bing Crosby's 'Temptation', which still seems haunted by Crosby, Bill Withers' unusually structured melancholic masterpiece 'Ain't No Sunshine', first made a hit by the Jackson 5, with 13-year-old Michael singing a song inspired by the toxic relationship between an alcoholic couple. Cher and Bowie make it through a reference to the comedy styling of the Coasters on 'Young Blood', an insistent Leiber and Stoller song they wrote over a Doc Pomus song.

The rapid medley is an improbable, unrepeatable, middle-of-the-road insight into Bowie's enduring fascination with songs that are about isolation and distance, about not being entirely understood, about chasing love and certainty, and with catchy songs that assume different, often ominous dimensions when viewed from different angles. Songs that are pre-rock, when musical strands were forming, or that have pre-rock influences, but feel the pull of rock, which when mixed up, creates a heady, affecting brew. Sad songs that can make you remember happy times. Sad songs that get the hurt out into the light. On *Station to Station*, he found the healing properties there are in singing, and hearing, a sad song, after just crying the whole night through.

The temporary Cher–Bowie coupling becomes a complete 'chapter' in an imaginary multimedia autobiography.

DISEASE AND SHADOWS

Before his short, dizzying break in Cherland, he's been making the *Station to Station* album, the expansive, high-minded soul music of *Young Americans* now being heightened and broken up under fervid, unrepeatable circumstances. It's perhaps his most visceral and violent album, and yet one of his most sensitive and ecstatic, and he forgets making it – or most of the details – as he goes along.

He's recording it in the Los Angeles he's escaped to that turns out to be a soulless pit, a vast, amorphous city of incredible proportions but without space or dimension. He's finding a different kind of funk in the strangest places, something other than the kind of agility that James Brown and George Clinton would be respecting and appropriating, letting the insistent, mesmerising electronic music he's hearing in Kraftwerk's 'folk music of the factories' and Tangerine Dream's Edgar Froese get all mixed up with radiant, undimmed DAM remnants of the saturated *Young American* soul sound.

German music was inspiring him to look longingly towards Europe – the depth of its history, culture and art, the beauty of its architecture, the splendour of its statues and churches that he'd been separated from in Los Angeles. The music was refreshingly unsunny as well in a place that seemed all sun, as if it was burning away everyone's souls.

It wasn't so much the electronic precision and intricate arrangements of Kraftwerk and Froese that he was thinking of taking into his music – Dennis Davis's drumming was too moving, in all senses of the word, to work with the very fixed percussion of German studio music, and the impromptu spirit Bowie wanted. It was his memory of Europe – a kind of desire – that he'd lost – its alluring strangeness and the rolling vastness of its history. He didn't want to lose the American grooves and hustle, but to merge the two sensibilities, in the same way he wanted to merge yesterday and tomorrow.

In the middle of the furies he was experiencing he was also drawn to the driving, calming rhythmic patterns of Philip Glass and Steve Reich, with their own roots in medieval and experimental European moods and systems. It sounded like soul music to him, with its own internal cryptic funk.

No one else was thinking like this – in a few years' time, a similar clash of sensibilities will mutate into synth pop, hip hop and house – and it seemed he'd reached the point where madness is the loftiest intelligence.

He was writing about himself, looking deep into himself to see what's left as he beats some kind of retreat from fame and glam, as he counts down his darkest and most degenerate days. He's only a few blocks north of suburban Santa Monica on a really busy street but he could have been on the dark side of the moon.

He'd left the streets behind, he said. He didn't know how to buy his own clothes – they just turn up from somewhere, miraculously in his size – and he didn't know how to book his own airline tickets. He was living a cocooned life, more or less needing to be looked after. He's looking into the mirror, scared of what's staring back, who the hell goes around with a face like that. It was like he had already become a ghost.

Sometimes, it's as though the final chapter of his life, his final album, might be in Los Angeles, so something inside of him, as he loses touch with reality and haunts his own dreams as a fragile, broken wraith, knows it has to be one last great hurrah.

The character he inhabits, or inhabits him, the Thin White Duke, suspended between existence and the afterlife, combining a sense of arrival and departure, is there to express at the dreadful end of his days all the wisdom and experience in his last appearance. He throws down his cloak; his revels are now ended. The angel of death keeps flying over his head.

Bowie had been a Nietzsche reader and it seemed Nietzsche had created a brief for the Thin White Duke. He is colder, harder, less hesitating and without fear of 'opinion'; a self-styled creative genius, he lacks the virtues that accompany respect and 'respectability' and opposes everything that is Nietzsche's 'virtue of the herd', an eager-to-please morality embraced by the conformist and mediocre majority, dedicated to comfort and security. If he cannot lead, he goes alone as a higher human being . . . He knows he is incommunicable; he finds it tasteless to be familiar. When not speaking of himself, he wears a mask. There is a solitude within him that is inaccessible to praise or blame.

People did tend to misinterpret Nietzsche and do things they shouldn't have done.

Bowie is looking into America, and himself, and seeing nothing but a blank void. He feels himself surrounded by a vulgar, pushing mob whose passions are easily mobilised by demagogues, journalists, religious quacks, agitators and conmen. Everyone in LA seems to want something from you. There was too much sun. Nothing seemed real. Every day seemed like five days. Everyone smiled but no one did really. It was hard to keep track of time. He'd only been there for a few months but it seemed like forever and still not enough time to prepare for eternity. He'd been told it was a good place to go to reinvent yourself. Outcasts and wanderers turn up every day in search of a new life, a new dream, a new self. But he had been pretty good at that recently and in LA, it was the city reinventing him and it was out of his control.

It's why the occult in Los Angeles finds an endless number of guises and, most of the time, it felt like he was surrounded by the fucked-up psychedelic folkies of the Charles Manson gang, by shamans he meets at a bus stop who convince him they know the secret of manipulating space and time, by the former anthropologist Carlos Castaneda, godfather of the New Age movement, showing him the paths to ancient knowledge.

He's in the city where Aldous Huxley wrote *The Doors of Perception* in the early 1950s, suggesting that the perceptual altering of hallucinogenic drugs did not distort or disorder reality, but revealed 'how one ought to see, how things really are.' Huxley didn't see psychedelics as a way of generating a demented mind, but a way of attaining a spiritual and philosophical experience of incredible importance, not just for doctors, but also for artists, writers and intellectuals constantly curious about the secrets of existence.

You'd think Bowie had found his city.

He's looking for some high level of awe and, even as his life crashes around him, he's still convinced that it's writing and singing songs and his artistic vision that help him find his place in the seeming insanity of it all. He's sure the signs will take him somewhere.

He takes some time out of working on a set of songs that presents him as an utterly alienated man so that he can appear on a middle of the road television show. He could pretend a little bit, or at least pretend he was pretending, because everything to do with the making of *Station to Station*, what could very well contain his perplexed last words, was deadly serious.

'Madness need not be all breakdown,' said the influential Scottish psychiatrist RD Laing, who was committed to revolutionising the treatment of mental illness and was once described as 'the Mick Jagger of psychiatry'. 'It may also be breakthrough.' His book *The Divided Self* was in a list of 100 favourite books Bowie once compiled. 'It is possible liberation and renewal as well as enslavement and existential death.'

PAST AND PRESENT

Angie was still married to Bowie, but not for long because the 'family' that had helped construct his stardom in the early 1970s – which included his wife, a reminder of frantic, psychedelic rock star chaos he was now determined to unload, for the sake of staying sane, and his ruthlessly efficient, star-making manager Tony Defries – made no sense to him. He seemed to be receding from his own story.

The halcyon days of their gothic looking Haddon Hall home and artistic headquarters in Beckenham, south London as the sixties became the seventies; the free-flowing creative community, a court of musicians, mavericks and bohemian drifters, that they were at the centre of; a giddy, tumultuous hippy marriage to Angie, the pair acting like kooks; the close collaboration with Angie and the team of hairdressers, stylists, designers and supporters she helped bring together for the creation of the Ziggy Stardust look. It was all becoming a half-formed dream, fading away fast in the heat and horror of Los Angeles.

Bowie, so the legend goes, always fascinated by satanic discourse, the aesthetics of the demonic, the idea of the devil as romantic rebel, is now in the capital city of satanism, where if you take enough cocaine you enter the underworld. He slips through the cracks in LA's reality into a world where he feels the impact of the Edwardian occultist Aleister Crowley, the Great Beast, the wickedest man in the world, 666, on the city's spirit. He experiments with trance, telepathy and mirror-gazing, staring into reflective surfaces in an attempt to conjure up a spirit vision.

Bowie painted some tarot cards that were inspired by Crowley's Thoth Tarot deck, a five-year conceptual attempt begun in the late 1930s to introduce deeper, darker new imagery into the cards taken from a variety of scientific, philosophical and occult sources. Crowley's cards were painted by the well-connected English artist Lady Frieda Harris, the wife of the Liberal politician Sir Percy Harris, under Crowley's sometimes exasperated, single-minded guidance. Somehow, forced on by his 'damned cleverness', she produced a deck where each card was its own masterpiece.

The deck gets its name from Thoth, the ancient Egyptian God of writing, wisdom, moon and interpreting. Crowley combined the secret attributes of tarot with a hotch-potch of magic, alchemy, astrology, numerology and the Jewish mystical system of Kabbalah – itself a mishmash of various religious beliefs. Believing the tarot had been corrupted by religion, he wanted to update the Renaissance Kabbalistic tarot system for encoding forbidden information using pictures, believing in the tarot as a tool to access the unconscious mind and explain the whole of existence.

Crowley wrote an essay guide to the use of his tarot deck, including an analysis of the tarot system itself, reflecting his belief that it can transform an individual into a magic being and reveal the structure of the universe. The cards, and Bowie's interpretation through his own paintings, reflect a state of mind that entered the sound and content of *Station to Station*.

Bowie, like many a sixties rock star, in a way members of their own bohemian secret society which gave them considerable licentious freedom, had been entranced by Crowley as a beguiling showman and drug fiend, expert at creating his own myth and courting controversy. Crowley would use the spelling 'magick' and never magic to separate his spiritual endeavours from trivial stage conjuring. He was a self-promoter with the exciting slogan 'do what thou wilt shall be the whole of the law' – imagine ourselves as we wish – committed to raising human consciousness to a higher level, a new state of being, which would lead to a whole LA onslaught of self-help gurus,

New Age cults, reality television celebrities, social media nano, micro and macro influencers and the seekers who need and follow them. The Thin White Duke was the leader of his own cult, half reckless, half recluse, urging his followers to stay with him, even if sometimes he seems to let them down.

Combined with the astonishing amounts of cocaine Bowie was consuming – cocaine being mostly good for making you want to take more cocaine, it was for a while the only thing he was interested in – this casual flirtation with the philosophy of Crowley, mysticism and the supernatural erupts into a classic psychotic mania. His constant hunger for intense experience was leading to danger. His determination to increase his knowledge come what may necessarily indicated a lack of knowledge about where it will all end. He's seeing and hearing things and developing unusual beliefs. He's drawing pentagrams and inverted crosses on every surface and a chalk circle on the floor in his house, collecting arcane books on witchcraft, concentrating on his tarot card paintings, increasingly convinced other worlds are lurking just out of sight.

Look at the wild look in his eyes.

Hear him tell the interviewer a little bit of the truth:

A lot of what he did in the early 1970s was trying to function as a shy person who suddenly became very famous. He thought the drugs were helping him break out of his inhibitions but they were actually flinging him into a quagmire of psychic and emotional hell. It brought out the worst in you, it was total trauma, and he had no idea what he was doing or what he was putting people through. It cost him a lot of years. The work was somehow good and represented the mind he then had, trying to make sense of where and who he was, trying to stay interested in reading and listening to music, which makes for good songs and good art. He didn't know what he might have been doing if he was actually healthy. Did he lose something or gain something, artistically? He didn't think it was the drugs or the experiences he was having that made the songs good because a lot of it was when he had cleaned up, and they were an early part of the recovery.

Angie Bowie is elsewhere; her day-to-day involvement now reduced to a kind of emergency contact; she remains on call. It makes for explosive pages in her autobiography. She wrote about times when Bowie's days seriously seemed numbered and his on/off girlfriends were passing through faster and faster. She was feeling like nurse, cook, staying at her post out of some sense of duty.

Bowie's moving fast even if he's sitting still or half asleep, vampirically sucking the life out of everyone around him.

In his imaginary autobiography, he remembers feeling untypically divorced from enthusiasm, becoming an automaton, disappearing into a vacuum and needing to be looked after full time. His management arranges it so that he has difficulty getting access to his own money, as though he's not capable of looking after his own affairs.

He realised that the beginning of losing control over more and more parts of his life was when he stopped choosing his own clothes to wear. At first, it was because he was climbing the ladder of success and at each step, those around him felt it was their job to look after him. Small changes, small nervous attacks become big shadows. Suddenly, you are no longer going to the shops and you even travel a few yards down the street in an enormous limousine with the windows blacked out. It was like being in a luxurious mental hospital, living inside a padded cell where meals are brought to you. You are only let out on a lead when money needs to be made to finance the operation. The money doesn't seem to be for you but for everyone else around you.

He never wanted to be a rock and roll star in the first place, not for real. It was part of the theatre he had built around him because he wanted to portray characters in a theatrical way, and rock and roll seemed the best way to achieve it. At some point, the fiction became the reality.

The characters he had created over the past three or four years started to exist outside him. They were becoming obsessed with each other, and whatever the 'original' was – Bowie or Jones – was fading away. People would talk to him as if he was Ziggy or Aladdin Sane or Jack because no one had David Jones as any kind of reference for who he was. Even Bowie now didn't exist for them. Even if they did think he was David Bowie – which he wasn't, even that was an alias – at least it was closer than being Ziggy. He had different, weird conversations with different people, depending on who they thought they were talking to.

He was pretty placid a lot of the time and in LA, where they expected everyone to be a little out there, he could see the disappointment on some people's faces, who had been expecting some green-skinned oddball shooting up on a leopard skin rug. There was a brief period, he admitted, when things did get a bit heavy, so if that was the Bowie you wanted, it was best to come in contact with him then.

You desperately need nourishment but it's the last thing on your mind. He finds himself spending time in sinister locations, unable to remember how he got there and how he got out of there. If you get any sleep it's the sort of sleep where you wake up every hour and think you haven't been asleep at all. He lays there in the dark with his heart pumping like a trapped, terrified animal. He needs the emptiness that sleep brings where sooner or later, energies flow.

Another nightly brush with annihilation.

He just about makes another day.

Angie feels he's living with a devil he's summoned up for himself out of himself, or he's mistaking his latest dealer for the devil. He's frightened because he's losing what had been central for him over the past years: her counsel, even her constant energy, however increasingly irrelevant it became, and the aggressively protective influence of Tony Defries. You could, perhaps, see slivers of Defries inside the fabricated Thin White

Duke, managing to bring some showbusiness organisation and administrative control into Bowie's chaotic if riveting world, but ending up adding to the chaos.

However disappointed he was with their presence and however tangled up in them both he had become, losing Defries and Angie didn't calm his mind – what would happen to him without them, as much as he wanted a life without them? The anxiety turns to dread turns to panic.

Angie watches him become a paranoid, abusive, irrational, out-of-control addict reduced to speaking gibberish about semen, covens, spells, witches, insemination, storing his own urine to keep Led Zeppelin's house Crowleyite Jimmy Page and a coven of witches from conjuring up the antichrist, mixing with the worst sort of people who take advantage of his fame, cravings, vulnerability.

He knew that his friends, lovers, ex-lovers and acquaintances were trying to shake him out of it, fearing for his safety, but, in his defiance, what he saw as their nagging sent him even deeper inside his isolation. You react against help when you're in such a state, see it as another sign the world has got it in for you. Why won't they let me be? If you don't step into the unknown you don't know what you're made of.

You have to find out for yourself in the end. If you do then you do. If you don't then you don't.

ACTING AND BEING

Bowie is still at the same time an actor, an entertainer. He's still, somehow, David Bowie, still on the quest to know everything that was ever known. There's an extreme narcissism but somehow he's still very likeable.

So while he's drowning in the same waters the mystic takes delight in, following secret orders, scaring the hell out of everyone close to him, he's acting in *The Man Who Fell to Earth*. Movie magic seems more sensible to him than black magic, and maybe all of this LA madness was preparation for his role as the super-intelligent, hypersensitive, ultra-paranoid Thomas Newton. He would be a character who wasn't a human being at all played by a character who was only one of many characters.

He's recording *Station to Station* and piecing together the look and demeanour of the album's anti-hero with his cool, gnarled pessimism, the Thin White Duke. It is to become in one sense a great cocaine album but also a great LA album, a great album from a lost year, a great album of mood disorder, where madness is on the mind – maybe one of a few Bowie made – and a great 'art brut' album, where the art comes directly from the psyche, and, in such pure form touches a raw nerve.

It's an album that shows how isolation can lead to greater emotion and stronger, stranger songs – the isolated person creates a micro world and – wishing they were somewhere else, finding it difficult to trust even familiar things – they start to build something solid out of their chronic uncertainty.

Yes, all that was happening. He could be in two places – or more – at the same time. He could be in a trance-like state and remembering his lines, turning his secret sorrows into glorious melody. There might be no way out but let's stick to the work. He had a sense that he was becoming one of those geniuses who, when not working, never feel completely alive.

In a way, putting your heart and soul into your work is another way of losing your mind, but at least along the way you accomplish something. He who seeks work finds rest. Your work in life is the ultimate seduction.

He needed to keep trying to find calmness at the centre of the storms. Something outside him was going to have to pull him out of it. You don't drown by falling into water. You drown by staying there.

It's someone so close to him, yet so private she is rarely part of the usual mythology swirling around Bowie that pulls him out. Coco Schwab had worked and travelled with him since the early seventies, part of an inner circle within an inner circle, unattached to any particular camp or organisation, only attached to Bowie, even more, to Jones. She would remain his closest, most faithful friend, always on call and there to help him through, standing guard over his solitude.

Rumours that might have begun simply as speculation talk of her holding a mirror to his face during some of those extreme LA mornings, just to check he's still breathing. It's poignant that if and when Bowie does mention the one who reached him at the time, he talks of how it was Coco who was always trying to hold a mirror up to make him take a good look at what he was doing to himself. A mirror, he would say, with nothing on it. She gave him a push, perhaps the only person who could, the only one who had the nerve to express it in a way that could reach him, one of the very few who could tell him the truth however much it hurt him. It was complicated and contained its own conflict, but it came down to: stop destroying yourself and go home.

Sort yourself out.

It eventually sunk in and he began to clean up his act.

But where, what, was home?

Time to consider some options.

Bowie was perhaps more human as the strange, fragile, alien genius from another planet Thomas Newton than he was in his shattered, shattering LA life. In other ways, it was difficult to separate the two. It was like the Ziggy story all over again – the character that dropped down on Earth from outer space who became influenced by our way of thinking, which ended up destroying his soul.

What Bowie didn't see coming was how the press mixed up Ziggy and him, treating him as though he was Ziggy; this was still happening in 1975, and to some extent would happen for the rest of his life. Here he was, suffering the consequences of the fame that spread from Ziggy, now mixed up with another alien manifestation, another invented character. He hadn't made it clear enough that he was intending to change character all the time. There wasn't anyone then who played characters like Bowie did, apart from the more cartoon Alice Cooper and Kiss. The rock star made you believe he was the same off stage as he was on stage. He had wanted to do the opposite but that backfired. In his mind, he separated the two: the one who writes and the character who performs.

In any other artform, it would have been interpreted as a commentary on the state of the world, on the state of truth and reality, but because it was rock, it was assumed he was the alien rock star. He was visiting from another planet. You didn't assume the writer of *Crash* or *Dune* or *Naked Lunch* was the character he was writing about. Francis Bacon isn't his paintings.

The unfortunate side effect was that for a while, Bowie also believed that he was the character. In a way, it was like Rimbaud was his poetry, which is at the root of all rock tragedies and all celebrity addictions.

He started to live the rock and roll life and flirted with the so-called early romantic death, the derangement of the senses, that he had been caricaturing and turning into albums. You can write about addiction and psychosis but it helps not to become the addict entering a relationship with the devil and following him into a black hole.

Both Bowie and Newton face new kinds of temptation in the new world they find themselves, which makes them lose sight of the life they've left behind. Both are reclusive and excruciatingly self-conscious, seemingly both extremely adaptive at synthesising disparate thoughts – they see things that others don't see. They both have the sort of will power that the most complete collection of virtues and talents are worthless without. Both consume knowledge as fuel for change and adaptation. Knowledge is power, and the true method of knowledge is experiment. According to a glimpse we get of a British passport when Newton sells his gold ring at a pawnshop near his landing place in New Mexico, to the sound of Louis Armstrong, they share the same birthday, January 8th, although Newton is a year older.

Newton, the alien, had no ears, no hair, no eyebrows, no nipples, no navel, no genitals, no fingernails and no toenails. He had cats eyes. Every character around him aged and he didn't. Time jumps years into the future, but around him it's always 1975.

Bowie could effortlessly take this otherness. He's up for anything, even if it was difficult to deal with – the discomfort and stress of having a lens being fitted to his 'difficult' eye, let alone his unaffected eye – because it all enhanced his feeling of alienation, which added to the fact he was properly alien, ill at ease at best, and otherwise frightened, freaked out and unearthly.

Director Nic Roeg had cast Bowie as Newton, adding one more mystery to the mystery, after seeing him in a startling BBC documentary, *Cracked Actor*, where he was in his nervy, detached limousine period and truly having trouble settling into the reality of being a rock star, or just a social being – or he was doing a wonderful job of playing being displaced and disorientated, and a wonderful job of sounding and looking beautifully like no other human being on Earth. He was the very image of someone suffering from what he called 'the catastrophe of success'. Roeg was transfixed and when he met him for the first time – a complicated, detached mix of nerves and intensity, struggling for words but weirdly gallant – he wondered what it must be like to see the world through his eyes. Bowie was extremely pleasant and unassuming, but he also seemed to make coming from Earth seem like he came from a strange, far away land.

Roeg had been having trouble finding the right actor for this tricky, other-worldly role, one you could see right through, see everything and nothing; a more conventional actor like Peter O'Toole, of *Lawrence of Arabia*, briefly in consideration for his height and piercing blue eyes, would have brought his other roles into the film and always seem obviously an actor from Earth, however efficiently he faked being an alien.

Bowie was not an actor as such but he had been performing almost full time as an alien, or a human pretending to be alien, for a few years. And at that point, there was no one on the planet more suited to playing a humanoid alien erratically learning to be human. He brought a certain behaviour to the film, a unique combination of awkward and graceful, polite and delicate, and he was completely uncomfortable in his own skin, which was perfect for the role.

Roeg's explosively impressionistic and transformative films were epic studies of how identity is structured where time is constantly unstable. Time is usually all over the place. Time to him was a genre, along with fear and hope and sadness.

Roeg's films included the disturbed and disturbing *Don't Look Now*, set in off-season Venice, featuring real-life couple Donald Sutherland and Julie Christie playing a real-life couple, which was both obvious and mesmeric, and co-directing the transgressive *Performance*, where he'd used rock star Mick Jagger to play a rock star, which was both obvious and strange.

'Film,' Roeg would say later in his career, 'remains mysterious and mystical to me.' Bowie called him 'an old warlock. You come out winded from the experience of working with him.' He was never sure if and when he was being directed, not sure what being directed actually meant, or if he was being left alone to work it out for himself on purpose, to keep him detached and distant, all at sea – which, if true, was a great piece of direction.

Bowie described the film as a very sad, tender love story that evolves over a long period of time, 'the furthest thing from a science fiction film really'.

Bowie's limo driver – who also played his limo driver in the film – followed him about, on set, or wherever they were staying on location, not only providing the security deemed mandatory for a rock star but also delivering his most important supply – his books, an impressive mobile library that he needed beside him wherever he was, getting special delivery status, just in case in the face of the unknown he needed a quick fix of language, some readily available company, or a reminder of what it means to be human, or not. Bowie also had a wind-up record player because as well as his regular daily doses of self-medication necessary at the time, he couldn't do without listening to music, even when sat in the middle of the desert, keeping himself to himself. None of which harmed his characterisation in the slightest.

He needed stimulation, points of reference. The shot of Newton watching numerous television screens at the same time, absorbing information from all of them simultaneously, which seemed abnormal at the time but turned out to be prophetic, was a symbol of Bowie's own insatiable need for intelligence, knowledge, any sort of tips and orientation.

The film seemed as much a documentary about the usually hidden and mostly rumoured, estimated unusualness of actually being a rock star as *Performance* did. It was also as much a documentary as *Cracked Actor*, about where Bowie was in that time between 1974 and 1976, as the red-headed pop alien Ziggy was bent by America into the tortured, withdrawn Thin White Duke.

Newton is somehow the missing link between one and the other; the carefully shaped hair he had as Thomas Newton was now orange with a discreet blonde streak, and as usual based on a specific brief from Bowie, referencing a very particular hair dye by Schwarzkopf. The hair lasted as the Man Who Fell to Earth became the cold, calculating Thin White Duke, who became the cover for the *Low* album, where parts of original pieces for a Bowie soundtrack to the film that never worked out – ultimately made for a different film in Bowie's head – filtered through to the instrumental tracks on the record.

In a science fiction film where there was only one sighting of a space suit, Bowie's clothes were made to give the illusion of a certain weightless nonchalance. Because his neck was so slender, the shirts he wore came from the boys department of Macy's on the high street in Albuquerque. When he was wearing very normal, down-to-earth, striped and shapeless cotton pyjamas, buttoned up to his neck, there was still something alien about him.

Newton falls to Earth wearing a modified olive brown coarse woollen duffel coat, charcoal trousers and black laced work boots. Roeg suggested the very English duffel coat and the only one costume designer May Ralph could find in America was not the beige colour she was hoping for, creating another unintended visual glitch.

The coat would appear on the cover of *Low* in 1977, where a photo taken by Steve Schapiro on the set of the film showcases an enigmatic, pensive, even academic album at the other extreme from the riotous, hyperbolic glam futures of Ziggy and *Aladdin Sane* and the appropriated and manipulated historic Hollywood glamour of *Hunky Dory* and *Young Americans*.

The contemplative, stoical *Low* Bowie seems quite ordinary, until you take in the orange hair, the incendiary abstract background reminding you of a Mark Rothko painting that's all light but one step away from the abyss, the luminous energy that can occasionally bloom in your final years as you wonder where you have come from and where you are going. A prophet wanders in the wilderness.

The Man Who Fell to Earth script was written by ex-film critic Paul Mayersberg, after an early version failed to be turned into a long-running series resembling *The Fugitive* TV show, where each week, the alien would be on the run and hunted, getting into all kind of scrapes. Mayersberg had inserted some lines from 'Space Oddity', 'Life on Mars' and 'Changes' in his original draft, not so much for the spaceman connection but because of what he called the 'uneasy ecstasy' in Bowie's voice. Mayersberg described the film as 'playing a game with time, and it has dozens of scenes that go together like circus acts following one another; the funny, the violent, the sad, the horrific, the spectacular, the romantic.'

It was Roeg's first film made in America, with an almost completely all-British crew adding to its appropriately off-kilter rhythms, filmed in the New Mexico desert rather than the book's original Kentucky setting to ensure the British visitors didn't break any American work regulations – New Mexico was a 'right to work' state where anyone could work as long as they didn't cause any trouble.

The first edition of the Walter Tevis novel the film was based on was published in 1963 as a pulp paperback. The introductory description of Thomas Newton on his bewildering first day on Earth, swooning over his first sips of water, seemed already to lead towards David Bowie; in particular, the way Newton found himself distracted and knocked off course by America – he was not a man, yet he was very much like a man. His frame was improbably slight, his features delicate, his fingers long and thin, and the skin almost translucent, hairless. He weighed very little, about 90 pounds. Bowie would admit he was the perfect choice to play Newton because at that particular time, he wasn't of this planet.

The drought-stricken planet Newton has 'fallen' from – Anthea in Tevis's book – is facing the kind of environmental disaster that seemed science fiction centuries in the future in the mid-1970s. The idea that Earth was decaying for manmade reasons wasn't on most people's minds. Man was making other, more obvious messes – on the planet rather than to it.

Newton's planet had wasted its water; its population was dying from thirst and Newton is sent on a scouting mission to Earth to find a new source. On his world, planet Earth is known as the planet of water, and Newton, especially after developing an addiction to alcohol – along with television and sex – is soon indifferent to how much the people of Earth take for granted the preciousness of their water and other essential finite resources.

The character Mary-Lou falls head over heels for Newton and inadvertently lures him into her alcoholic world. She's played by Candy Clark, who also plays the wife he's left behind on his home planet with their children, seen in flashback. 'You're a freak,' Mary-Lou says to Newton. 'I don't mean that unkindly. I like freaks. And that's why I like you.'

EGO AND CONTROL

In Los Angeles, he became totally confused about his own identity, which started to interfere with his writing. It was like he was losing his memory, his sense of himself. His writing wasn't fulfilling him. You could say the characters were taking over. They were becoming too assertive. This was the point when the alter egos were taking over.

He'd needed them, these second selves and distinct personas, and then it started to get out of control. They had been like secret superhero costumes he could wear at will and then take off, but it got to a stage where it was difficult to take them off. The alter egos, the other worldly characters, had enabled him to do things plain old Davy Jones could not do.

Being the androgynous, other worldly Ziggy and subsequent company enabled him to explore artistic boundaries and challenge the status quo in ways he couldn't do as Davy Jones or even as David Bowie. Using the alter egos enabled him to push the boundaries of gender, fashion and music. The introverted him became literally the life and soul of the party, a rock and roll legend, a visitor from outer space. He could unleash the inner extrovert. The alter egos gave him the confidence to embrace the extraordinary. They became a ticket to self-expression and personal growth, a form of empowerment, a series of secret identities, where he could embrace different elements of his personality and empower himself.

The alter egos started to take on a life of their own. The alter ego can empower you but it can also lead to recklessness. Dr Jekyll had created Mr Hyde – David Bowie, or maybe one of the characters he had played, became the Thin White Duke, a way of indulging his darker desires, but things quickly got out of hand. The Thin White Duke took him down a path of recklessness. The alter ego went from being helpful sidekick enabling him to be whatever he wanted to be to being his archnemesis.

Bowie as the Thin White Duke was constructing an entire metaphysical system around his sickness, entering the realm of the mystic via his disease.

SHOW AND HIDE

The cover of *Station to Station* was an abstract still of Bowie as Thomas Newton inside his mysterious spaceship, perhaps landing, perhaps taking off, taken by Steve Schapiro, who had photographed Brando, De Niro and Hoffman on the sets of *The Godfather*, *Taxi Driver* and *Midnight Cowboy*.

He'd begun his career as a political photojournalist working for *Life* magazine, photographing important events in the fight for civil rights, including Martin Luther King's march from Selma to Montgomery in 1965 demanding Black Americans be allowed to vote, where they faced violence from local law enforcers and state troopers. In 1967, he was photographing Janis Joplin, Jerry Garcia of the Grateful Dead and influential Indian sitar player Ravi Shankar in Haight Ashbury, named after the intersection of San Francisco streets where a bohemian haven became known as the birthplace of the counterculture dream of peace and equality, and a certain amount of anarchy.

When *People* magazine began in 1974, Schapiro took the photo of Mia Farrow biting a string of pearls on its first cover, shot on the set of *The Great Gatsby*, in which she played Daisy Buchanan opposite Robert Redford's golden Gatsby.

Schapiro brought immense experience, giving perceptive and iconic power to history and celebrity when it came to photographing Bowie; his work with Bowie absorbs his history and combines it with Bowie's own sense of the importance of an image, a pose, a decisive moment that would then become part of the very essence of the subject.

They bonded almost instantly when they first met, as Bowie learnt Schapiro had photographed silent movie star, ingenious film maker and supreme physical comedian Buster Keaton in 1964. It was many years after his imperious heyday. The Great Stone Face Keaton, the king of stunts made for a camera, the originator of what would become Hollywood clichés, appeared in Samuel Beckett's only film screenplay, 1965's dialogue-free *Film*, the constant sound of a projector forming its soundtrack. Beckett was inspired by the disruptive eighteenth-century philosopher George Berkeley's observation that 'to be is to be perceived'. Keaton spends the bleak 20-minute short desperately trying to avoid a camera that is chasing him – Keaton himself baffled by Beckett and the director Alan Schneider's insistence that he try and keep his face hidden at all times. He was meant to be someone who doesn't want to be seen.

Keaton, with his beautifully elastic body and beautiful head, was a hero of Bowie the mime artist, Bowie the artful dodger and living artwork. Keaton's thoughts on Beckett's film perhaps lead to the moody, shifty Thin White Duke and the LA Bowie – 'a man may keep away from everybody but he can't get away from himself.'

Mime educated Bowie in the art of illusion, in physical precision and eloquence, and most importantly, about all-body awareness. It taught him how to be himself. In a world where all artistes seemed androgynous, the yin and yang perfectly balanced, it all fed into an androgynous energy. As Virginia Woolf said, all writers must be androgynous. Bowie could say anything in mime, encouraging the kind of risks and wildest inventions into his music and characters, those improbable beings, and even his voice. Mime is a very loose word. His voice, never conventionally the voice of a singer, was the voice of a mime who had studied emotional power and felt he could do anything and go anywhere when he sang. Mime perversely freed him as a singer. It also became something he would use when he was being photographed.

Traditionally seen as the most pretentious, silly and outdated of art forms, mime was also the most mocked and derided – the striped T-shirt, the white face, the walking against the wind, hiding behind a wall or carrying a safe, the Bip of Marcel Marceau, mime's one famous name, often perpetrated by untrained and clumsy street mimes. It can feel embarrassing simply seeing a mime perform on the streets. It could be a mistake even now to suggest that Bowie is a keeper of the flame of pure mime because it might undermine his elevated status as artist and performer, as superior performing artist.

With a theoretical interest in the human body and movement, Bowie performed the great illusion of turning mime into a vital part of his own aesthetic. He was always ready for every photo session with a look, a gesture, a movement, a sudden revelation, especially when he sensed the photographer had connected with how he was acting, how he was telling an overall story that the one particular photograph and image, one particular idea, the creation of a wider tableau made up of overlapping pieces, was a part of.

Bowie would work many times with Schapiro, one of a significant international group of photographers Bowie built a relationship with starting from the early 1970s. Some were the new breed of photographers specialising in rock music, working for the counterculture music papers of the time; others came from more mainstream journalism, from portraiture, fashion, fine art, photojournalism, looking into his eyes from outside of music and the rock business, bringing in other energy and perspectives. They became an equivalent to the guitarists, bassists, drummers, stylists, designers and producers he worked and played with, an evolving group of inventive, imaginative collaborators generating the sound and vision of Bowie that becomes part of how we remember him, the different, overlapping eras and personas, and how he moved into the future and our collective mind.

The photographers, circling Bowie from all angles across the decades, doing his bidding and adding their own viewpoint, would become more than anything a kind of orchestra, even one bringing something different to what was ultimately Bowie's own composition.

SECRET AND CERTAIN

The Japanese photographer Masayoshi Sukita was an integral part of Bowie's photographic orchestra, another artistic collaborator who became a friend and would work with him at different stages over 40 years.

The first time he photographed him was a week before Bowie's two shows at the Rainbow Theatre on 19 August 1972, supported by Roxy Music, then high in the charts with their debut single, 'Virginia Plain', a three-minute glam anthem without a chorus but in every sense plenty of action, telling its own far-fetched story of music business shenanigans.

Sukita had just come from photographing Marc Bolan of T. Rex holding the electric guitar that had become his magic wand, helping him create a series of effervescent number-one singles. The theatre of glam was officially running amok amongst the nation, looking so fine. It was just in time for the spread of colour television, and the more conceptual version was led by elite avant-garde explorers like Bowie and Roxy. They were serious, sincere artists, but they decided they could flip that on its head and become showmen as well.

It was the start of the second leg of the Ziggy tour that had taken Bowie from pubs, colleges and small clubs in front of hundreds, sometimes fewer, the audience feeling they were in on a big secret, to sold-out theatres and a more extravagant show, with its eyes and ears on joyful overkill, a celebration of having made it. The secret was a secret no longer, but there were other secrets to keep, especially the guilty ones.

The lights were arranged by Angie Bowie and choreography by his mentor Lindsay Kemp, credited as special guest, for an ensemble named the Astronettes, which Bowie later used for his '1980 Floor Show' backing singers. Fans were beginning to turn up at Bowie shows dressed as Ziggy, or some valiant approximation. Many of those copying Ziggy seemed straight out of a fancy dress shop, in the way that Bowie's rhythm section tended to once they had been dolled up against their better, rough-and-ready nature as the Spiders from Mars, not quite taking to the illusion as naturally as Bowie, who had already stepped outside time.

He had the knack of looking like he fully understood how style was a matter of being curious about yourself. Then again, when the Spiders from Mars got their ragged Space Age look, when guitarist Mick Ronson got his blonde feather cut and the tight satin trousers and chest-baring waist coat, it made a hell of a difference to the sound.

Sukita photographed Bowie at his most certain and divine – it had taken him years to look this young and sensational – capturing some vivid stillness amongst the manic preparations for the important Rainbow shows.

The session featured one black and white shot in particular of Bowie as pure star seduction staring straight at the camera, hand close to mouth, one finger on lower lip, bangles hanging limp on his wrist. He had it blown up and shown in the Rainbow Theatre foyer, revealing that he was in full control of himself, at the apotheosis of being young and thinking you are immortal, and knew exactly what it was that his fans were seeing in him.

He was meant to be always changing. As soon as a system or process works, it's out of date. The David Bowie of today must never be the David Bowie of tomorrow. He never knows which way he's going, but he doesn't care. He lives from feeling to feeling. Today, he's full of ideas. Tomorrow, they will be completely different.

As his fans passed through into the theatre, barely able to contain themselves, they would look into his eyes and the show would already be beginning.

He was very photogenic, noted Sukita, not yet imagining he would spend decades taking his photo. Sukita took some photographs the next year in New York before a show at the Radio City Hall – Bowie seeming so much older, even as he hadn't aged at all – in which Bowie shows how he would use photo sessions to fill out the essence of his characters, create back stories, plan ahead.

The shoot was in New York but with Sukita taking the photos, and the Japanese stylist Yasuko 'Yacco' Takahashi bringing a spectacular Kansai Yamamoto samurai/Bauhaus inspired jumpsuit and other costumes from Japan with her, they bring out the Japanese qualities embedded in Ziggy. He said he'd borrowed from Dada, but an enormous amount was also borrowed from his knowledge of Japanese culture, the more extreme, the more believable. He loved the friction there was in Japan, how the balance between the old and the new, between Shinto temples and tea ceremonies and hi-tech conveniences was always very precarious. He found the integration of ancient and modern cultures a compelling, successful vision of the idea of a constantly evolving future.

Bowie knew his 'Basara' – a transgressive, excess beauty containing a rebellious spirit based on Japanese fourteenth-century social trends where people wore ornate and innovative clothing – and his kabuki theatre – traditional, complex performance art rooted in Japanese comic dances of the seventeenth century.

Creativity is often just a matter of making connections between things. The Japan of Kansai Yamamoto, the wearable art that he revealed at a London fashion show in 1971, flowed straight via Beckenham into Ziggy, including the short, spiky red hair, which was both Vidal Sassoon copy and make-do hair colouring and stiffener. The most dramatic of Ziggy and then Aladdin Sane costumes were all Kansai ingeniously imprinting Basara on his greatest model – knitted jumpsuit shorts and unitards, glitter yarn, grand flowing robes with giant kanji characters on the back spelling out David Bowie phonetically and apparently saying 'fiery vomiting and venting in a menacing manner'. Even if the clothes weren't made for Bowie and were constructed to smaller Japanese proportions, they fitted him perfectly, as long as he eschewed underwear, which would have ruined the effect.

The Sukita-captured Bowie, stretching his mind and body in the meta-samurai jumpsuit against a blood red background, the clothes becoming him and him becoming the clothes, contains hints of an anonymous persona existing in the same space and time as Ziggy and Aladdin Sane, waiting in eternity for Bowie to bring it to life, perhaps brought to life in songs, part of some mystery always with him, even if he never found a direct use for it.

Sukita was beginning to think he could, and would, take many photos of Bowie.

When Bowie was in Japan in 1977 to promote *The Idiot* with Iggy Pop, Sukita asked for a session with them both. Bowie was the other side of the Thin White Duke, an experience with a performative character so demanding and even vile that he had withdrawn from the need for the costume, make-up and hair colour – almost too far, almost cutting himself back to Davy Jones, catching the train from the suburbs, where no one would look twice, wouldn't even catch his eye. He was wearing the disguise of himself, cleaning out the last residue of the Duke, and the hair colour was, perhaps, absolutely natural, the least vivid it would ever be.

He'd turned his back on the theatre, on the shock rock, because of the way it had led to his internment in Los Angeles. The characters had been replaced by experimenting with sound, and with Iggy he had the greatest, most extreme rock and roll character to work with, even if he was also needing a little bit of down time. He didn't have to invent an Iggy, a rock star regarded by the mainstream as nonsensical or absurd; he had one of his own now and a very different kind of artistic exchange.

As he entered the late 1970s, Bowie was just a writer, a composer, a musician and a painter using the studio to build up shapes and sounds and rhythms, textures and shadows and flesh. The characters in the first six years of the seventies measured the atmosphere of the time; by 1977, he was starting to use purely music to do that.

The songs could become the characters – something he'd learnt from 'Fame', his American number one, from the extreme, hurting ballads on *Station to Station*, reaching its most intense peak with the song 'Heroes', which manifested itself as he cut himself off from playing heroes, or anti-heroes, and perhaps saving his soul. The song itself, the environment it represented, emerging from his state of mind at the time, was the character, with a life of its own, containing multitudes of stories and interpretations.

There was just 'him' to photograph in Japan and he told Sukita he didn't need any sets – no Basara, no racks of clothing, no cosmic shoes – just get Yacco to bring a few leather jackets for him and Iggy to at least have something to wear, something neutral. This was the time when he seemed faintly embarrassed by the costumes he had worn and the elaborate, mythological scaffolding he had erected around him between Ziggy and *Diamond Dogs*.

Sukita had an hour with each of them. Even stripped of all the characters and clothing, Bowie was still the consummate performer, using his hands, his face to make some shapes, to send out some signals and secrets. He didn't want a picture of himself in character, as part of some story, but he did want a photograph of himself as a traveller, an observer, someone in between places, with something troubling on his mind.

From his time in Berlin, he was thinking about German expressionism, and the paintings and jagged woodcuts of Erich Heckel, a founder member and secretary of the avant-garde The Bridge movement, an artistic style intended to form a bridge between the past and the present – the past being represented by the centuries-long German tradition of wood prints, the present where painting was shapeshifting at the edge of modernism.

Heckel's lost soul self-portraits after the traumas of the First World War had a physical and spiritual weariness that Bowie identified with, building himself back up after his own more personal battles, but still from a war with a terrible enemy. That we had to remove ourselves was clear, said Heckel – what was less clear was where we were going.

Bowie was particularly taken with how Heckel placed his hands in his paintings, to reflect oppressiveness, hinting at religious poses, and at the same time pointing towards the future, to breaking away from where things are. He played with the position of his head and hands in some of the photographs taken by Sukita, as if posing but also acting natural, careful about the direction he was looking in but also being spontaneous. He chose one of the shots, with an apparent explicit reference to Heckel's placement of hands, for the cover of the *Heroes* album – one of his numerous black and white album covers, showing his love of photography. It captures a certain atmosphere as well as a face and hands, and something that wasn't deliberately intended as the album cover at point of conception becomes the only imaginable cover for the *Heroes* album.

Even as he was being photographed by a series of photographers with their own skills, approach and perception, each album sleeve became a kind of self-generated self-portrait, part of a wider series of self-portraits he created. He was always in control of setting, pose, face, eyes, time and timing, and aware of how they would all be part of his future.

For the penultimate studio album, *The Next Day* in 2013, his first album for ten years, when there seemed to be no more space left for another Bowie album and there was a general acceptance of that, the now-classic *Heroes* cover had a clean white panel placed over the top, covering up Bowie.

During the 36 years between *Heroes* and *The Next Day*, the *Heroes* cover with its photo of a 30-year-old Bowie at a certain point in his life had become one of his most distinctive and recognisable. The blanking out, the taking away of one iconic sleeve when Bowie was at his most alive, almost an act of resurrection after profound recent stresses and strains, creating an absence, seemed charged with meaning. It was both a return and a kind of warning,

The *David Bowie Is* exhibition was about to open, a parade of his history, of just about all his yesterdays, and here was Bowie saying, well, the past doesn't mean that much to me. The next day always means more. I can have control over that, to an extent; I can change myself – and by doing so, maybe make changes to my past, make corrections, connections and adjustments, and even put things in a different order, shake up the timeline and shift the emphasis about why things happened the way they did.

There was a hint of Bowie – an erased Bowie – on the cover of *The Next Day* but it was close to being the first album by David Bowie that didn't feature his image, even if, as with original editions of *Lodger*, it was his splayed legs, with his broken upper half on the back.

For his final studio album, there was no Bowie on the cover, not even a stray body part or two. The final pose, the final character, the final adventure was complete absence. There was no title. There was a black star, charting a new course, marking out a new direction, a new day, one that was beyond Bowie, but all about him.

COSMIC AND EARTH

Another significant member of Bowie's photographer orchestra was Brian Duffy, who he first met in Duffy's studios in Swiss Cottage, northwest London in July 1972, days before Bowie performed 'Starman' on BBC's *Top of the Pops*.

Bowie brought to Duffy's studios the same shiny red boots and Freddie Burretti-designed quilted jumpsuit that would soon become famous after he wore them for his aroused, arousing 'Starman' performance. He also brought with him a Vox 12-string guitar, the instrument from which his stardom-making songs had come, for something to hold and touch and pose with, to prove he was now a rock star, and the guitar deserved some credit too. He was Ziggy Stardust, who played guitar. As Duffy saw it, he was shifting between dimensions.

Duffy was effectively photographing Ziggy Stardust as much as if not more than he was photographing David Bowie. To some extent, he was photographing both of them at the same time, sharing some kind of aura, urging each other on, relying on each other for their existence.

When choosing his key collaborators, David Bowie liked to work with people possessing their own lively, original mind, one that could take him by surprise. He quickly bonded with the no-nonsense and experienced Duffy, a kind of father figure with a hell of a temper who had his own idiosyncratic and irreverent way of seeing things. He was down to earth, blunt and belligerent, but on the sly, a fancier of the cosmic. They would talk philosophy but in an earthy, demotic way.

Duffy was the more cerebral and revolutionary member of an elite trio of uncompromising, working-class fashion and celebrity photographers in their late twenties and early thirties nicknamed the Black Trinity, usually known by their surnames.

With (David) Bailey and (Terence) Donovan, described by sixties' model Patti Boyd as 'rock and rollers without the music', Duffy helped locate the subversive freewheeling attitude, visceral and free, of what was defined as the Swinging Sixties.

Rejecting traditional fashion photography, seeing it as too quaintly camp, the Black Trinity mixed off-the-cuff energy with observational street savvy and cool abstract precision. 'We didn't do what we were told,' Duffy once remarked.

When he started work with Bowie in 1972, as famous in his own world as Bowie was in his, he was still not keen on doing as he was told. Bowie didn't tell him what to do but he showed him somewhere new to look, and another place to explore. Duffy, 13 years older, showed Bowie a thing or two in return.

Between August 1972 and April 1980, Brian Duffy and David Bowie worked on five different photographic shoots. These resulted in images that we now associate with Ziggy Stardust, Aladdin Sane, the Thin White Duke, *Lodger* and 'Ashes to Ashes' – a series of dramas that illuminate and infuse pop culture history.

Five times as David Bowie changed from one sort of performing artist to another, addicted to trying out different things, the equally restless Brian Duffy was there to take the photographs that confirmed and projected the changes forward. Duffy became a trusted co-conspirator as Bowie experimented with the imagery of pop stardom, captured the spirit of the times and left ever-changing traces of a legend.

If Bowie, the performer in this production, was always looking for attention, Duffy, the photographer, could give it to him in the most effective way possible. He looked carefully at David Bowie, clearly there to be looked at. He sized him up, took him in, studied him, chatted with him, shadowed him, advised him, interpreted him and, in his own way, embraced him.

He had taken the magnetic photograph that appeared on the cover of *Aladdin Sane*, which eventually took on a life of its own. Bowie imagined Ziggy becoming an 'electric boy', thoughts flashing in his mind like lightning. This led to Duffy mischievously increasing the size of the modest bolt of electricity that make-up artist Pierre La Roche had outlined on Bowie's face at Bowie's request, turning a discreet, almost throwaway symbol into significant culture-rupturing statement. La Roche quickly filled in the exaggerated flash with red lipstick, the monster beauty mark representing membership of a particular tribe, a symbol of the exciting, risk-taking outsiders to which Bowie belonged, even led.

Duffy had one more idea. He had met renowned illustrator and airbrush magician Philip Castle while working on the 1973 Pirelli calendar with the provocative pop artist Allen Jones. The calendars were first produced in 1964 by the UK subsidiary of the tyre company as a risqué corporate gift for important clients. By the 1970s, each annual edition would showcase the leading models, actresses and photographers of the time, and symbolise an era's style. Castle added to the naked 'electric boy' image an elemental post-human glow and at Duffy's suggestion, a molten pool of liquid dripping over Bowie's clavicle. This mysterious teardrop on the skin La Roche had painted milky white implied that the alienated character, Bowie as Ziggy as Aladdin Sane as Bowie, had been through some kind of trauma to come into being. Bowie's eyes were shut, allowing his stardom to explode around him, sending shockwaves into the future.

Decades later, for the image that represented the V&A *David Bowie Is* exhibition, in a different take of the same photograph, his eyes would open, as if to take in that future where he had now landed. As Duffy saw it, he was photographing a different form of energy and capturing the moment inspiration strikes.

Three years after they had designed Aladdin Sane in 1973, between them, Duffy, now a friend, was commissioned by the *Sunday Times* to photograph Bowie on the New Mexico set of

The Man Who Fell to Earth. Duffy persuaded Bowie to come out to the nearby 3,200-square-mile White Sands National Park for the shoot – an endless barren wonderland of surreal white sand dunes often rising to over 60 feet high, left over from an ancient dried-out lake, 60 miles from the site of the detonation of the first atom bomb in 1945.

Bowie arrived late from the film set as the sun was rapidly disappearing. He wore a wide-brimmed hat, a tieless white shirt and priestly loose-fitting suit, shimmering between his lost, disorganised self, Newton the estranged visitor and the nihilistic, corrupt and corrupting Thin White Duke, all as real as each other. Bowie's clothes as Newton intersected with the functional yet futuristic Thin White Duke look he adopted after the film, an expressionist modification of transsexual Weimar Republic clothing and noirish 1940s jazzman suits.

Time was running out. Highly skilled at solving technical challenges, Duffy took a few chances with the fading light, with a combination of Bowie's moving arms, darting eyes and physical stillness. He saw a man falling apart, a performance at the edge of time, an actor deep in thought and a freaky pop star spinning outside glamour. He couldn't put it into words, so he pointed his camera.

Because the shoot happened late in the day, Duffy riskily shot Bowie in dim light with no autofocus, with a one-second triple exposure, while Bowie kept his body still and moved his arms so that Duffy could get the blurred action he was looking for. There was no Polaroid taken and limited time, and only one chance to get the shot. Duffy would not see the processed film until he returned to the UK to see if his gamble had paid off.

The photo is of Bowie as a ghostly figure belonging nowhere, an isolated, increasingly powerless alien, an otherworldly traveller and mysterious, adrift and troubled pop star somehow still making things happen around him, taken under time pressure in the hushed and lonely desert as the Earth rotates away from the sun, the white sand casting a strange, soft, eerie glow, reflecting and scattering the light upward and out.

SENSE AND FORCE

Once upon a time, in his mind, Bowie opened a wardrobe door and mentally put all his characters, his painful memories and recent traumas into the wardrobe and closed the door.

He had created a visual image of a safe, secure place and thought of the characters and the traumatic memories as items that could be packed away. It was a very LA way of storing difficult feelings until he was ready to process them – an LA way of dealing with an extreme LA situation.

He locked the 'wardrobe' and left Los Angeles after about a year living there. After that, he avoided LA as much as he could and definitely wouldn't want to stay there for any length of time. He still had the key, he said, just in case – you never know when he might need those characters again, or, at least, when he could face up to them and deal with them in a healthy, recovered way. Throwing away the key would be a way of losing control, of throwing everything over to fate or chance.

Any unwanted thought or feeling, any person – ex-manager, ex-wife, drug dealer – that intruded into your consciousness, you could learn to put away into the wardrobe until you were ready to deal with it.

He was in control of the wardrobe, and it was up to him when to open it and when to close it. Freud said 'feelings buried never die', but Bowie wasn't burying them, as if out of sight out of mind. The feelings were accessible, but only if and when he decided to unlock them.

The wardrobe was a temporary placeholder. He needed time and space to work through the sleazy, threatening LA digression without being overwhelmed by it. The container was a way of putting away a chaotic jumble of incidents, reminders and associations until he was ready to talk or think about them.

One of the tools he used to process all the feelings and work through his fears, through the rush of elation and depressions that had led him to LA and seemingly trapped him there, was writing songs and making albums – a form of journaling, in the jargon of recovery from the self-abuse, a method of building up resilience where affirmative difference replaced negative difference. It was a way of replacing the unnatural, unhealthy numbness and indifference he was enveloped by in LA with the kind of energy and unabashed idealism he had in the early seventies.

Station to Station was the cry from within for him to get back to Europe – as rendered in his imagination, another potential safe space – and rediscover why he had started writing in the first place. Before he found Bowie, he needed to find David Jones again, quickly, before he lost sense of any of the Davids and one of those alter egos took over and he, as he put it, depending on who he was talking to, 'went completely off my rocker'. At that point, it seemed as though it would be the Thin White Duke, but none of them taking over would have been a good thing.

Each character had his own point of view, his own strength of character, and he let it be that way. This meant having to believe in them wholeheartedly for a short period of time, and then suddenly changing horses in mid-stream to ensure they didn't take over. He became his own paintings for a while. He had to stop that. He'd been seven, eight paintings and, as he went along, he didn't completely erase the paintings he hoped he had left behind.

He thought of himself as a performance artist, a post-Duchamp painter dealing in ideas, events and, once he had broken into the mainstream, spectacles, rather than creating straightforward optical art.

Music and the imagery that came with it was 'painting' for Bowie, a form of producing various interpretations and elucidations of the reality he found himself part of – it was his lack of success as a painter that made him think of music as his oils or his acrylics.

He would explain that he never loved rock and roll as a lifestyle. He wanted to use rock and roll as a medium as one would use paint. He felt outside it. And after Los Angeles, he tried to keep himself away from the circus elements of rock and roll – the socialising, the clubs, the nightlife, the drugs, the various systems you enter when you take drugs so industrially. He had to take himself out of it.

He had to get as far away from the disconnected sprawl of Los Angeles, the lack of focus, as possible – or at least go somewhere that suited his temperament more, a place where he could luxuriate in anonymity. A portal into other worlds rather than a dead end creating a mirror-lined portal back into itself.

DREAM AND LOGIC

Before deciding where, he needed to discover a new way of writing, a way of approaching songs more abstractly and impressionistically without losing the rhythmic force Alomar and his core rhythm section had introduced. He needed a new kind of person, a new kind of musician or unit to bounce off, not necessarily Kraftwerk, who he originally wanted as an opening act for the 1976 *Station to Station* tour, retrospectively called the Isolar Tour, a.k.a. The 1976 World Tour and also On Stage.

When they politely declined, even while appreciating that Bowie's patronage in interviews had accelerated their admission into the Anglo-American pop music world, Bowie had turned to another formidably European aesthetic model for his opening act, the 1929 silent film *Un Chien Andalou*. A collaboration between 28-year-old Spanish-Mexican director – and Buster Keaton fan – Luis Buñuel and set designer and painter Salvador Dalí, it became their golden ticket to acceptance in André Breton's new deliberately evasive anti-fascist surrealist movement. See anew, think anew. Bowie fans coming for, perhaps, some Ziggy, some electric Aladdin Sane, some plastic soul, maybe even a sign of 'Space Oddity' and 'Life on Mars' were greeted with a different sort of dream logic and an immediate insight into his dark, scrambled state of mind at the time.

The opening to their evening was made up of the opening to *Un Chien Andalou*, where a title card says 'Once Upon a Time', a smoking man nonchalantly tests the sharpness of a straight-razor and then slices open a woman's eyeball, soon to be followed by dead, rotting donkeys on a piano, ants emerging out of the palm of a hand and a cross-dressing man falling off a bicycle.

'Open the way to the irrational,' was the intention of the surrealist pair riffing off each other in the way Bowie was looking for from a new artistic comrade. 'Include everything that strikes us regardless of its meaning.' It was made as an attempt to film a dream and in many ways, it's a dream of death, and Bowie had just come close to death, going deeper than just letting it hang around in some of his songs, sometimes at the edge, sometimes embedded inside.

The show would start a few minutes after the vision of death with the ten or so minutes of 'Station to Station', Bowie crooning the interior obsessions of his mind as if his life depended on it, and a dream of the Thin White Duke, proving how reality might change but the logic of dreams never does. A dream in 1929, a dream in 1975 never loses its power as supremely rendered as by Bowie and by Buñuel and Dalí.

See him tell an interviewer how seriously affected he was by his dreams. When he was young, he found the 'dream state' far more effective at catching his attention than what was outside his school window. There seemed so much imagery and stimuli inside him. When he saw *Un Chien Andalou*, it was exactly how his dreams felt to him and it gave him ideas about how he wanted to write, represent the power of the sub-conscious, make the leap from false, everyday 'reality' to the super-reality where the impossible opposites – dream and vigil, politics and morality, good and evil, saint and demon, man and woman – can be united.

The show would be the technically ambitious, arena-sized spectacle befitting his fame, but the stage would be empty of props, give or take a packet of Gitanes in his back pocket, and he would be exposed in all his new, vulnerable alert state by relentlessly forensic white spotlights, giving the tour another name, The White Light Tour. He could walk across a relatively empty stage with none of the extravagant accessories of *Diamond Dogs* and as long as he was being looked at by others, it became a theatrical act.

Any costume was stripped back to almost mime simplicity – white shirt, black waistcoat, black trousers, the Thomas Newton hair he shared with the Thin White Duke swept back to create an almost hostile silhouette. The minimalist setting was a blatant sign he was enacting a new beginning

FAST AND SLOW

He was jumping in the opposite direction from the active, frustrated punk-rock beginning to take hold in New York and Britain, flirting with strange forces, claiming to be King Arthur reincarnated, taking daily the amount of cocaine that when you take that much in Los Angeles you see the devil and the devil sees you, you cut lines and spin circles until it feels like you're floating. Swastikas float in front of your flickering eyes. Punk was pathetic-sounding next to what he was dealing with.

The Sex Pistols had played their first London date in February 1976 – as Bowie begins the American part of his *Station to Station*/Isolar tour – with their guitarist Steve Jones casually noting that they're not into music, they're into chaos – three years after Bowie had famously noted on *Diamond Dogs* that this was genocide, not rock and roll. The Pistols' singer Johnny Rotten, with his spiky red hair and theatrical menace, cavorts and cajoles like the deranged bastard offspring of Ziggy Stardust.

In May 1976, after a few gigs turned into fights, interviews that promised more chaos and with a manager dedicated to creating spectacle, the Sex Pistols played a short weekly residency at the 100 Club in London, building up their splenetic attack on what they saw as rock's aristocratic complacency.

The same month, Britain got a shocking glimpse of the Thin White Duke and his irrational visions as he arrived at Victoria Station, London for the beginning of the European section of the *Station to Station* tour, looking less like Ziggy and more interwar Weimar Republic Germany with a severe, robotic twist of Kraftwerk.

Bowie's recent interviews had created their own controversies as, out of practice with some of the dark arts of British tabloid journalism, and in many ways out of his mind, he suggested Britain could benefit from a Fascist leader to make some changes to a nation stuck in its past, unable to contemplate a world without an Empire. A pop star was always going to run into trouble channelling Walter Benjamin's thoughts on fascism, and the Führer cult, appearing to give the masses a chance to express themselves, and how the logical result of fascism is the introduction of aesthetics into political life.

Less unfocused, less fascinated with the relationship between Nazism and the occult, less tangled up in the mind of his latest and most obsessed character, Bowie might have explained better how what he saw as the weakened state of the nation was leading to a strong, uncompromising new kind of right-wing leader, as it did within three years with Margaret Thatcher.

Talking politics was a sign he was either at the end of his method tether as the Thin White Duke, or the cocaine was causing loose lips and a loose mind, and he really had become so self-important he thought people would care about his views. Or stardom was going to his head, all that praise for his intelligence, wit, charisma and principles leading to a frustration that he hadn't extended himself into politics, or maybe literature or film directing, more grown-up pursuits.

He got trapped trying to explain through a veil of intoxication the parallels he saw between Nazi rallies and the increasingly big rock concerts. It didn't help when what appeared to be some kind of austere version of a black Nazi uniform was hanging from his 100-pound frame and, with slicked back blonde-ish hair and a grim expression, he was caught in a photograph as he waved to his fans at Victoria station from the back of his open-topped car throwing what appeared to be a Nazi salute.

He was far away from punk, which, considering the nihilistic state he was in, might have contaminated him and his music. The one thing he had in common with those early punks was a provocative aesthetic fascination with the swastika as a direct method of causing shock. There was also an attempt to restore the swastika's benign ancient meaning as a sign of good fortune, utterly destroyed when the Nazis made it their sinister logo.

What the hell was that about, braver souls would later ask, when the quote about Britain needing a Hitler, the apparent admiration for right-wing tyranny and the fascist salute were mentioned, this rotten stain on his image. It's no excuse, he sighed, but he wasn't himself – and playing a character who wasn't himself – and even as he was crawling out of the heavy darkness hanging over LA, he was still beholden to cocaine. It was the cocaine that was into fascism and loved Hitler's style.

He always acted as though punk meant little to him, not least because he had Iggy Pop in his camp. Iggy was there more or less first and then, working with Bowie on *The Idiot*, he got to post-punk first – the kind of post-punk that added adventure and the sonically eclectic to punk basics, using *Station to Station*, *Low* and *The Idiot* as a blueprint because of how they were so weirdly and desolately the absolute opposite of punk, a marvellous blending of reality and imagination just as punk was happening.

It's what drew Bowie to Brian Eno as another metaphysical therapist alongside Iggy; another busy, resolute conceptualist who believed that inaction saps the mind and who had plenty of things on his mind other than punk. The trends Eno were spotting and following were not what was being written about in the music press, and certainly not what was being promoted by mainstream record companies. In his own, more scientific, analytical way, Eno was as heretical as Iggy.

SONG AND TRANCE

Experimentally minded art student Eno had left Roxy Music in 1973 after their first two albums, as soon as he had made his obtuse, randomised marks on their luxurious, beautifully played and sung pop songs. He'd released a series of solo albums at Bowie-like pace – both were in a hurry in the seventies – that initially contained disruptive, wonky pop songs, imagining a veiled, convivial Velvet Underground. They were gradually losing the words and singing, drifting towards disciplined, sensuous instrumental formlessness made of sound that didn't appear to be produced using any known musical instruments. Removing the lyrics and voice from his songs was, he would say as an artist, like removing a figure from a landscape. The landscape remained. And then he could do more with this landscape.

During downtime on the *Station to Station* tour, Bowie had been listening to Eno's *Discreet Music*, his contribution of treated and manipulated synthesiser sequencing and tape looping and echo to Obscure Records, a label he had formed releasing mid- to late-twentieth-century avant-garde classical music by composers from the immensely influential John Cage to so-called minimalists Steve Reich, Michael Nyman and Gavin Bryars and the post-minimalist Harold Budd.

Discreet Music was his fourth solo studio album after leaving Roxy Music and the first to be released as being by Brian Eno instead of simply Eno; Eno was the deviant pop singer, Brian Eno the analytical theorist using the primitive tools of early electronic music.

He was still 'Eno' on an album he made in 1973 with his friend and King Crimson guitarist Robert Fripp, whom he'd met during sessions for an album by Robert Wyatt's Matching

Mole. They found they were on the same wavelength, pursuing the same goals, and fascinated by experimental, musical and technological processes.

One was intensely almost diabolically musical, his guitar playing dense, convoluted, at times intimidating; the other a happily self-confessed non-musician, producing sound as something that would delight him, using machines, noise-makers and tape delay.

Agreeing to pool resources, to see what would happen when opposites attract, although they both loved tinkering, Fripp turned up at Eno's home studio with his guitar and 'jammed' with Eno's tape delay system and elementary looping system. They created selectively manipulated loops; improvisations and meandering solos filtered through an ever-shifting time lapse that became a sublime, gently fierce undulating, overlapping drone driven by a subtly erotic charge.

The piece they made, 'The Heavenly Music Corporation I', found its title by taking a brand name for marijuana cigarettes from the classic counter-factual 1962 Philip K Dick novel *The Man In The High Castle* which imagined a world, and more specifically an America, where German and Japan won the Second World War.

'The Heavenly Music Corporation I' was somewhere between an elegiac slow-motion tribute to Jimi Hendrix and an attempt to glimpse inside his soul, which was also the soul of the guitar, and for all its single-minded abstract detachment was an intimate insight into two musicians finding each other and finding something new about themselves. It was a friendship linked to a way of life, two musicians going in pairs like artists often did – Picasso–Braque, Duchamp–Picabia, Gilbert and George – a curious marriage, a questioning artistic togetherness.

'The Heavenly Music Corporation I' continually teases the possibility it might last forever but finds itself at an end, for no particular reason, after 21 minutes. The second side, the spikier, fizzier, more energetically fractured 'Swastika Girls', seems sometimes to break into a fleeting preview of the transcendent guitar Fripp would contribute to 'Heroes', with a title more to do with a photograph Eno had pinned up in his studio than the music, which didn't as such need a title.

On a Fripp and Eno sequel to *No Pussyfooting* in 1975, *Evening Star*, the surprising, deceptively deadpan double act were sifting detail and various distractions out of their music as though removing dust and grit, drifting between intentionality and accident towards what was the emergence of a new genre. The sparser, spacier and discreet consequences of the experiments on *No Pussyfooting* made its original exploratory minimalism sound positively frolicsome.

Eno admitted in the sleeve notes to *Discreet Music* that he preferred making plans to executing them, gravitating towards situations and systems that, once set into operation, could create music with little or no intervention on his part. He would set up his carefully chosen soundmaking equipment – in this case, the tape machine as a compositional tool – prepare a set of compositional parameters and then leave things to chance, with just enough room left for some additional corrections and effects. He would become an audience as much as a creator.

One side of *Discreet Music* was the 30-minute title piece, played at half speed. Unlike most of the processed electronic and music systems and phasing techniques that inspired Eno, it was produced like a pop album. The three pieces on side two had more formal reference points and different compositional methods, but were still given pop power and ultimately also achieved their own lonely, lovely sonic existence.

Bowie was transfixed by this quiet, unhurried and calming music, on the verge of vanishing, made to be listened to or ignored, like an object in a room you sometimes used and sometimes didn't need to use, but was always there.

It was made using machines which rendered it to some extent detached, but it also was emotional and poignant, and didn't seem averse to melody, which, as an arch melodist, Bowie found completely intoxicating.

Eno had discovered ambient music, as he liked to say, planting a flag with his face on it into this new territory, which he clarified and perfected on 1978's *Music for Airports*, but it was always there.

Others could make claims to have made ambient music before – John Cage, La Monte Young, Morton Feldman, John Cale with Tony Conrad, Terry Riley, Miles Davis – but they weren't the assertive, talkative types to think of naming it and leaving proof, nor compile instructions for its use as a kind of modern utility. Naming something is the same as inventing it, Eno would say.

The original source of this kind of background/foreground music, turn-of-the-twentieth-century French pianist Erik Satie, had given it a name – 'furniture music' – and promoted it through his own image-building antics, but the passing of time had put that in the back of a dusty cupboard, where cultural treasure hunters like Cage and Eno would eventually find it.

Eno made a more detailed map, and would spend the next few decades perfecting the idea and producing music for other places and moods, eventually producing a generative music app where sound composes itself according to a variety of environmental factors theoretically forever. It was sound where the centre was everywhere and the circumference was nowhere.

As a painter, Bowie recognised how the music was more painted into existence than played, and the human on a recently ruptured, ever-evolving spiritual quest connected with someone else also unabashed about making some kind of affirmation of existence, without sentiment or dryness, without relinquishing a definite sense of irony about his position. Listening to *Discreet Music*, Bowie felt pulled towards the Europe he was dreaming of that did and didn't exist, the shifting, tantalising place he had been yearning for. He was hearing fragile sound that seemed static and peaceful, but that was always changing, and he became more interested in its scene-setting quality, and how that could work in a song, in a more concise setting, brief and to the point but offering hints of eternity.

Eno's ambience became a new, more wholesome, enlightening and soulful addiction than the cocaine and the affiliated occult forces. It was only four years since Eno and Bowie had both played at the Rainbow Theatre in London as bright, speeding, nouveau pop stars, but Eno seemed to have moved elsewhere, into a different dimension, connecting with the work of the German musicians Bowie was fascinated by, including Cluster and Harmonia who both collaborated with Eno. Bowie and Eno, as celebrated symbols of glam, had known each other for years but never worked together, and in Eno, here was someone who could make the world more interesting, who cared as much as Bowie did about how things work, how reality is designed, and what he wanted to hear and feel.

COULD AND SHOULD

Wedded to *Discreet Music*, not least because it helped diffuse all sorts of LA-mounted anxiety and tension, Bowie decided to get in touch with Eno, who possessed what he called the brightest, keenest mind in modern music.

Eno's collaborations in the studio so far had been for his niche Obscure label, where he assembled ten albums of research and development music, and with other inscrutable, self-conscious English mavericks, fused art and pop. There was a brief cameo on the erratically epic Genesis concept album, *The Lamb Lies Down on Broadway*, feeding some of Peter Gabriel's vocals through one of his synthesisers. His contributions were credited as 'Enosofication'.

He was still feeling his way into becoming a record producer, initially with Talking Heads and U2, and Bowie liked how Eno was an idiosyncratic expert in the studio, a versatile, open-minded collaborator not yet familiar to a wider audience or in any way overused.

He imagined Eno was just the person he needed to help him reconnect with himself, to let come what comes, to let go what goes, and see what remains. He was fed up with trying out personalities. He wanted someone to tell him how to be himself. He needed some simplicity in his life.

Bowie and Eno talked about getting together, and found that they had similar ideas about what music could and should do, apart from just being listened or danced to. It could do many other things as well and it could be made in ways that Bowie hadn't considered. Eno talked about different methods and processes of writing music, and Bowie talked about a possible hybrid of electronic music and Black American music that he had constructed on *Young Americans* and then deconstructed on *Station to Station*. Eno hadn't considered that, but as a fan of Sly and the Family Stone's funk minimalism, sensed a compelling possible fusion of tone and temperament, of voice and space. Each found a new sidekick, where they didn't necessarily share tastes but where there was an intellectual and artistic harmony.

What linked them most closely was a love of change and impermanence. They were compulsive changers, do something, move on, do something else, move on again.

They also enjoyed each other's company. On the first day that they started working together, Bowie, wanting to impress the brainy cultural auditor and, a little nervous, told Eno he had just written a song that Bob Dylan had covered called 'Always Crashing in the Same Car'. Did he want to hear it? Yes please.

When Eno heard it, he thought it was the best song Dylan had done in years. Dylan at his very best! Bowie then admitted it was him singing it. It was a perfect Dylan impression. He could do a great Ethel Merman as well.

When Iggy and Bowie as a couple met Eno for the first time, big fans of *No Pussyfooting*, they hummed it for him. He was very touched.

For *The Idiot* and *Low* – at the same time Eno was beginning work on his ambient masterpiece *Music for Airports* – core contacts and complicities were arranged around a shapeshifting, interconnecting set of double acts and trios: Bowie and Iggy, Bowie and Eno, Fripp and Eno, Bowie, Eno and Visconti, and the DAM Trio of Davis, Alomar and Murray, all these super-sensitised brains mixing and matching. Aesthetic companionship was embodied in constant collaboration.

He'd played at being temporary rock star, suffered for his art, and now he just wanted to make music with people whose company he liked. 'Bowie' was a choral effort as well as one man's odyssey.

FIXED AND FITTING

Alomar would get rightly bugged how when the 'Berlin' albums would get sorted, rated, analysed and mythologised as the trilogy, the absolute centre of everything Bowie, the essential contribution of DAM around which everything fitted and floated got relegated beneath, say, the exalted guitar of Robert Fripp on 'Heroes', the studio reinforcements of Tony Visconti and the synthesiser manoeuvres, art games, self-regarding ambience and incidental abstractions of Brian Eno – all those jolts and digressions giving realism an extra twist.

Who the hell gave them the space, the structure, in the songs so that they could do all that? Something needed to be fixed, something needed to be focused. Yeah, he'd say, Bowie may have been depressed during the making of *Low*, and that was part of the legend, but DAM were pretty happy making that music, and don't forget the groove on some of those laments, the life in some of those songs of misery and despair.

As he was making it, Bowie might have sometimes been thinking of *Low* as his last album – he couldn't take all of *this* anymore. He might be basing the traumatised 'Always Crashing in the Same Car' on a real, but unreal, experience of deliberately smashing his car into a wall in an underground car park – because life is not an easy matter and sometimes the mind rebels against itself – or ramming a drug dealer's vehicle after an abortive meeting, or both. Whatever the source, the motivation, it needs to work as a self-contained song, so that the power of the music, as well as the power of the memory and the singing lifts it up into its own world.

And then think of the pre-Eno and pre-Berlin *Station to Station*; Bowie had a house band, and the DAM band within a band, that was able to perform music of fused contrasts borrowed from everywhere and nowhere, past, present and future Bowies colliding in one place, so that it was at once aggressive and meditative, numb and noisy, funky and delicate, good and evil, ethereal and scary, avant-garde and Broadway, raw and glam, pop and complex, sombre and sensational, spacey and noisy, soulful and desolate, linear and atmospheric, embedded in America's urban decay and floating over a scorched, apocalyptic wasteland.

With the DAM module, Bowie had found the centre for an extra-sensory, otherwise interchangeable ensemble, the equivalent of the feisty, febrile bands Miles Davis hung his 1970s connecting of jazz with funk, rock, electronics and the avant-garde around.

In the autumn of 1976, for *Low*, a necessary experimental switch from one state of mind to another, which still required isolation and commitment from everyone to the cause, his musicians settled into the Château d'Hérouville residential studios in Normandy, ten miles south of the English Channel in northwest France. The majority of the album that became the first part of the Berlin Trilogy was recorded there.

A rundown, rambling former eighteenth-century country house in the village of Hérouville, once the home of Frédéric Chopin, in the late 1960s it had been turned into a 16-track recording studio by French film composer Michel Magne. The Grateful Dead spent time there in 1971 when a local festival was rained off and invited the local village to watch an impromptu performance, temporarily transferring San Francisco psychedelia into the French countryside. The next year, underground darlings Gong set the trend for disappearing into the French countryside and used the isolation to produce induced fantasies. They were quickly followed by Jethro Tull, whose wasted time there and the dazed music they produced would be released more than 40 years later as the 'Chateau D'Isaster tapes'.

Bowie had recorded his *Pin Ups* album of favourite sixties songs there in 1973, not as disappointed as Jethro Tull by the chaos of the place, the year after Elton John had christened it as an elevated bohemian space for estranged rock stars with his *Honky Château* album, to return for his next two albums.

The Bee Gees weren't living a New York life when they recorded the majority of *Saturday Night Fever*; they were in the château, dreaming up disco drama. It was a long way from Gong, but it followed the same principle. In the recording studio, wherever it was, you could travel anywhere and be anything you wanted.

As much as it was a creative decision to use the premises, there was also the attractive proposition it presented as an 'offshore' opportunity for some tax avoidance at a time of 83 per cent income tax for high earners.

After a drop in studio standards and some necessary restoration and fumigating, and the arrival of a more rock and roll new owner, Laurent Thibault, a former bassist for French progressive rock group Magma, who also engineered, Bowie would use the château in his year of recovery from perilous times in Los Angeles.

He loved the atmosphere, the light and remote setting, feeling its quintessential Europeanness was the perfect backdrop for some low-profile self-help, which began with working out the sound and style of the album he was producing for Iggy Pop, his first post-Stooges solo album, both men in urgent need of a spiritual clean. He hadn't worked for a couple of years and needed emotional support as much as anything.

Bowie was as under the radar as he needed to be given the circumstances, an unstable, reluctant rock star who had just crash landed, accompanied by a living character who needed some direction, rather than one he had to invent. Both of them dragging with them some of the skeletons, scandals, manias and shadows they had tried to leave behind in America.

Because he cared, or because he was stealing energy, or searching for inspiration, Bowie sorted out and celebrated the gloriously demented Iggy Pop when he produced the third Stooges album, 1973's *Raw Power*. Iggy was on the verge of total collapse and his group were all over the fractured place. Maybe Bowie as some sort of conceptual impresario was playing the role of manipulative, star-spotting puppet master, promoting the obscure, manic but exciting idea of Iggy and allowing a short, brutal avant-rock masterpiece to materialize years ahead of its time.

Bowie said he wanted to get involved because he didn't think Iggy was being taken seriously as the 'Great American Writer' Bowie thought he was. The animalistic, physically extravagant way he behaved on stage and off was getting in the way. The media was doing a similar thing to James Osterberg – who played Iggy with excessive relish – as they had done to Bowie and Ziggy. Bowie considered him a musical underdog, which he'd been since starting the Stooges in 1967, and he loved this kind of underdog.

Bowie shrivelled the Stooges' traditional place-shattering distortion to singed skin and bone, and Iggy sweats, bleeds and issues threats on the rim of destruction. He was a cult artist before and remained one after, but he and Bowie were now partners. 'He'd like to be me,' laughed Iggy. In a way, he could be, without having to take off the costume and make-up. He could live through him a little bit, live with him for a while. They could be each other's therapist with their very own social code and a whole host of unconventional psychological techniques.

Both arrived in France damaged and determined. Bowie recharged Iggy Pop there on some of the early work for *The Idiot* and worked on experiments for a new kind of music that would reflect a reawakening from a weird clash of stupor and hyper-awareness.

The Idiot as a reflective, portentous resetting of the sound and sensibility of Iggy Pop was a testing ground for the otherness of *Low*, which for a while was to be titled *New Music Night and Day*, and was actually released in January 1977, three months before *The Idiot*. There was plenty of night on *The Idiot*, and the light, what there was of it, was low.

The album used the highly efficient and eloquent, funky as hell Davis, Alomar and Murray rhythm section as it moved forward into a music that used atmospheric electronics but not as comprehensively as Bowie would later. Because this was Iggy, even though he was in a very different, more weathered place than he had been on *Raw Power*, the guitars needed to make an impression, as fractured and messed up as they were.

DIRECTION AND MISDIRECTION

Stuck in the country house with nothing to do, and nothing around them for miles, close but not close enough to Paris, the musicians, with Bowie, his new artistic partner Brian Eno and Tony Visconti – who'd completed the mixes for *The Idiot* in Berlin, grumbling how much work was needed to make them into a record – were forced to hit deadlines and satisfy artistic requirements.

The muse, Bowie admitted, had deserted him and, for the first time in a decade, he had no particular statement he wanted to make. He explained the strange thing was that by not making any specific statement but by just floating towards a position, a direction, *Low* ended up having a kind of point of view, even if you couldn't quite put your finger on it.

A position, a point of view he might not have had if at the beginning of making the record he knew exactly what he wanted to do. *Low* wasn't a theatrically based concept album like the ones he'd made since Ziggy; it was a series of experiments. When he didn't have anything he wanted to say with words, Eno gave Bowie the courage to make an instrumental piece, immersed in his own appreciation of sounds without words. It was good to shut up sometimes but still be saying something – saying a lot.

He'd always wanted to write some instrumentals and whereas before, there was always someone or something to say, and, well, you're known as a singer, that would be a bit obtuse, but with Eno, there was no reason why not. The famous and beloved singer not singing on some songs was exactly the reason to do it. The influences on the music tended to come from emotions and feelings, from ecstasy to deep depression, from his new social environment, rather than other music, and other writing.

In that period between 1976 and 1979 when they made *Low*, *Heroes* and *Lodger*, it was as though Bowie and Eno were twin poles – there were other coordinates and feedback loops between individuals and within duos and trios, between the studio team and the musicians, but the relationship between Bowie as the 'author' and Eno, as the 'adviser' was at the core of it all. Had they been doing something individually, fewer things would have happened inside them. Two minds ended up creating a third mind.

Eno was keen on approaching music from different angles. He would think of a statement he wanted to make musically and Bowie would think of a statement he wanted to make musically, and neither would tell the other what that statement was. They'd come up with a theme, or a chord sequence, or a number of bars to represent that statement in one key and another number of bars in another key, and then they'd both go away and write about their individual statements. Then they'd return and record what they were doing and listen back to what they had come up with. And by putting together the two statements, they ended up with a third piece of information, which neither of them would have found on their own and which neither of them expected. Eno would write some music in defence of melancholy. Bowie would put together some chords imagining a magical mirror. Bowie would ask Eno to write a very sad song with an almost religious feel and Bowie would respond with his own feelings.

The music was always a surprise to them – sometimes very pleasant, sometimes not so much. They'd rarely tell each other what they were doing, looking for that moment when the two statements somehow existed in the same place as part of the same world. It was a way of avoiding musical clichés and their own clichés as writers and music makers.

When the two sets of ideas were put together, they could then take this third piece of information somewhere else altogether. It was a means of channelling unconscious thoughts and it suited Bowie, whose methods of writing lyrics were developing the same way in an attempt to break away from various forms of cultural and social conditioning.

Bowie found that getting to that third thing as exciting and stimulating as any of the sensations and illuminations he had been frantically chasing in LA. Songs started to become something, fighting free of any reference points, representing how, as artists and musicians, Bowie and Eno didn't want to make any specific style of music. Together, they found a way to compose music that was free of enclosed, established forms and open ended, a system of free association that was adequate to the range of Bowie's imaginative needs.

In a way, working with Eno echoed how he had worked with his mime mentor, Lindsay Kemp. Eno taught him how to do with music what Kemp had taught him he could do with his body. The characters could stop coming, and the music could now take their place.

ART AND COMMERCE

Sometimes, even with an album as contemplative, remote and tactful as *Low*, where Bowie seemed to want to turn himself into a stranger, unknown to a wider audience, there were occasional moments when the energy shifted. The concentration switched from the experiments and the personal distillations of dreams to assembling something deliberately made for a wider public that would seem to the record company, the financiers, a potentially significant revenue-collecting single. One that could be played on the radio, in the daytime, as an advert for itself.

During the making of *Low*, the low part was taken care of, especially on the opening track and the second side where Bowie withdrew into himself so much that there were limited, often only abstract, textural vocals. The profile part came with the song Bowie offered to the record company to calm their anxious feelings that he had perhaps gone rogue, or, worse, gone classical.

Side two was mostly instrumental, windblown and barren, as though Eno, with his attitude that absence was suggestive and emptiness makes room for form, was a cult leader and had convinced Bowie to join his esoteric coterie. Bowie was still in an LA trance, susceptible to cults and their possible answers to life's problems.

The label's attitude was, where was 'Space Oddity', where was 'Life on Mars', where was 'Starman', where was 'The Jean Genie', where was 'Fame'? Where were the hits? They were where he'd left them and what they'd now become. Bowie's thinking was this record wasn't going be about singles, about hit records. It was a record about experiments, because, he was thinking, all life was an experiment, and the more you experiment, the better.

Eno, as teleological cult leader, had also brought with him the Oblique Strategies cards he had recently developed with his friend, the artist Peter Schmidt, 110 or so cards each with an idea, thought, prompt, inspiration, aphorism, action or suggestion – some whimsical, some cryptic, some benign, some matter of fact. They were designed to overcome indecision and lack of clarity when creating something, of particular use when working inside a recording studio, with its time pressure and high studio costs. If your mind went blank or you needed some direction, pick a card, do what it says and discover a way of moving forward and overcoming a sticky patch by doing something you wouldn't ordinarily think of. They were like little jolts of electricity to the imagination.

Eno had carefully written the original self-help instructions on small pieces of card himself, before they became increasingly designed, printed and housed in a special box, and 35 years later, an app.

He didn't want them to be used lightly because, as a believer, when he did use them, he would religiously follow what the card said even if that disrupted everything he had done up until that point. He took the process seriously, otherwise it wouldn't work. It required faith.

A card drawn at random could say, carry on what you are doing, or do nothing for a long time, or give way to your worst impulse, or get your neck massaged – tidy up, give the game away, be dirty, or simply water, riff or reverse. Some of the instructions became famous: emphasise differences; emphasise repetitions; honor thy error as a hidden intention.

He'd used the cards on *Discreet Music* – repetition is a form of change, listen from another room – and on the albums of songs he worked on before and during working with Bowie, with advanced and parallel hints of Bowie's *Low* and *Heroes*,

Another Green World and *Before and After Science*, where the post-Roxy, topsy turvy songs were becoming instrumental – still pop song length, but losing the words, all that interfering language, and the singing voice. Perhaps the card he picked up that inspired this drift towards ambience was 'Remove specifics and convert to ambiguities', or perhaps 'Remove ambiguities and convert to specifics'.

Oblique Strategies had their precedent in the idea-generating Lateral Thinking books of the psychologist, mental strategist and self-help pioneer Edward De Bono, conceived in 1967 to generate ideas and break habits using illogical means.

In 1969, media theorist and abstract philosopher Marshall McLuhan designed a pack of cards more obviously linked with playing cards, 'Distant Early Warning', based on a line in his monumental 1964 book *Understanding Media*, in which he explained how he thought of art as a 'distant early warning system' that can be relied upon to tell the old culture what is beginning to happen to it. More ornate and dated than Eno and Schmidt's deliberately timeless seeming cards, less solemn than De Bono's book, McLuhan's 52 cards were another means of stimulating problem solving and discovering different ways of thinking.

Some of McLuhan's cards were his own words – his famous 'the medium is the message' (ten of diamonds) and 'a man wrapped up inside himself makes a small package' – and others used quotes by other thinkers, including John Cage – 'silence is all the sounds of the environment at once.' Cage's development of chance techniques on the making of music and roots in the compelling logic of Zen Buddhism and the use of the I Ching – the Book of Changes – to reveal your own wisdom and explore and capture consciousness was another influence on Oblique Strategies and on Eno himself.

Cage, though, would try to get out of the way of how a piece of music was composed. Eno would fussily interfere and persuasively guide. If you were looking for a hit single in the middle of this instinctive experimental play, he was good to have around.

The band's musicians with Eno and Visconti followed Bowie into focusing on Bowie's studied single concept, determined to satisfy the record company's commercial needs without sacrificing the overall *Low* mood. 'Sound and Vision', a song dragged with him from days locked into his LA cell, was about the peculiar nature of the relationship between viewer and TV image, about getting your bearings when you're on your own and all of reality and the entire pattern of human life comes to you through screens, tailored only to your needs and desires. Losing a sense of the shared reality that kept him tethered to the rest of the world and able to communicate with it, he was considering the mythical dimensions of the electric age, musing on how technology is a mosaic distorting our perception of reality and making it harder to distinguish fact from fiction.

On 'Sound and Vision', Bowie is floating in a sea of solitude, feeling tough and tender, fighting hard to reach solid ground, to find a place where he belongs, even if just for a while. Maybe he's too fragile to survive in a harsh, lawless world. It is the dramatisation of various tensions in his life that make it a work of art, framed by the unhurried, unshakable rhythm of Davis, Alomar and Murray. They carry the song through time like it is an object built to outlast cultural, technological and socio-political changes.

It is a song that says in order to make plans and implement them – for instance, to compose music and make an album – we need a world that is reasonably predictable and stable. And we have to have a sense of a shared reality before we can happily escape into our own realities.

It wasn't an obvious subject for a pop song but in his own way, Bowie was writing about a love affair and if you listen to it 50 years after it was made, it's about technology as an extension of our bodies and the internet as an extension of our nervous system.

By 1976, seven furious years after 'Space Oddity', when Bowie didn't really know how to write a pop single, falling into it almost accidentally, he had learnt what a David Bowie single should consist of – as estranged as he might be and dismissive of conventional commercial considerations twisting his arm to repeat himself and stick with what people expected from him.

As varied as they were, all his singles could be considered sequels to 'Space Oddity', at least up to 'Ashes to Ashes' but also at a push to 'Lazarus' and 'Blackstar', making space where there was no space, compelling the listener to think of a life experience, transcending form through form itself; hymns, elegies, speculations and incantations carrying you into the future. Just like Little Richard on 'Tutti Frutti'.

He could pack a lot of sensation into a few words and pack those few words into a lot of melody, and that made it a pop single. His *Low* ensemble seemed to have played together for years even if made up of a temporary combination of the tough, deadly funk of DAM and the fanciful, finespun guitar of the Scottish guitarist Ricky Gardiner, one-time member of capricious, emotionally intense progressive rock group Beggars Opera, who found himself in the right place at the right time to be part of these recording sessions.

Gardiner would dream up one of modern music's most resolute guitar riffs for the Bowie produced 'The Passenger', the song Iggy wrote about touring when Bowie was the in-the-shadows keyboardist in his band. It was released on the *Lust for Life* album that Bowie somehow managed to squeeze in during early 1977, between *Low* and *Heroes* and plenty of other public and private obligations.

After being set up or unlocked by Bowie as a new kind of impulsive, sophisticated adventurer on *The Idiot*, which, apart from anything else, rescued him from being sucked into punk and getting quickly used up and spat out, Iggy took more control of songs and style on *Lust for Life*, not wanting to seem reliant on his benefactor. Bowie had picked him up but he'd helped pick Bowie up.

When they were touring together, Iggy would say he never saw anyone work as hard as David Bowie. He would listen non-stop to music, the fan never stopping being a fan, an expert in the new but also now the searcher; the sifter looking for clues, textures, ideas, new pathways. He would jump straight into interviews before the show, he would be doing the performance, and afterwards, meeting people, chatting them up, making friends and contacts, suggestions, adjustments to the set list. He'd be knocking on the guitarist's door at four in the morning after a mad brainstorming session with Iggy, saying, let's write a song, right now.

Iggy had a better idea of what he was after *The Idiot*. A little poetically introverted, a little healed, but still het up and nomadic, a feral punk hero turned depraved but perceptive existential entertainer always capable of blowing up in your face when it seemed appropriate. Bowie had located and to some extent sponsored Iggy, the raging, ragged star who from then on remained a restless, radiant icon.

'The Passenger' reflected how Iggy's own self-lacerating alienation at the time was mirrored in Cold War West Berlin's world-weary, outsider status. Gardiner would note that he had written this conjuring up of coldness and estrangement doodling on his guitar on a glorious spring morning in a field near his house in the country under a blossoming apple tree.

EAST AND WEST

By early 1977, Bowie had pulled himself out of the morass of LA, forever fixed in his mind as the gateway to hell, the end of the mind if not the doorway to death, and although not completely free of various substances and alcohol, he was looking less drawn and slaughtered; he'd left the hellhole to the skeletal remains of Ziggy Stardust, who would wander forever through an endless night.

Bowie couldn't go back to London; he'd 'killed' himself there, in all the drama of Ziggy Stardust, and his scandalous totalitarian-touting return as the Thin White Duke made him think he wouldn't be welcome.

With Iggy as roommate, he'd found his anti-LA, moving to West Berlin when the levels of comfort at the Château d'Hérouville started to drop, and necessary supplies were running out and not being replaced. Being in Berlin didn't necessarily immediately mean he'd fully regained his youthful freedoms, and on the surface the city didn't seem like a vital burst of positive energy and life. He was joining serious people living in a precarious part of the world that might collapse at any moment, surrounded by a wall covered in machine guns that sometimes seemed to close in on him until it felt like it was right outside his apartment.

You needed the kind of self-reliance and self-sufficiency he'd totally lost to survive, but the city helped him recover it by forcing him, through its utter indifference to his predicament, to be himself. As a metropolis, still with its local dangers and temptations, and dealers, and that damned wall, it seemed a secure place to be.

Scouting with Coco, he found an apartment in the Turkish quarter. It was grubby and unpromising on the outside, but inside, there was potential to turn a high-ceilinged space filled with light into a custom-built sanctuary, with carefully designed separate rooms off a long central corridor for music, art, son Zowie and his toys and bike, sleep, and food and drink in a kitchen that somehow seemed perched in the open air amidst snow-covered mountains.

There was also an anomalous, cosy living room decorated and sumptuously furnished like something he had inherited from previous German owners, but with a faint sense of otherness. He had designed it and chosen the furniture, lights and rug himself, because he was in West Germany and local people coming to visit him would be impressed by this room, as if this visiting stranger had naturalised himself, found a way to fit in as some kind of local himself.

He called Berlin a very curious and earnest city, a place of longing, an original place of origins and radical instability, of lives lived in the margins, a city like nowhere else, where different tumultuous histories and charged encounters overlapped, a city loaded with metaphors and ghosts and a mood of seen-it-all cynicism that masked a deep, constant yearning for a better world.

Perversely, Berlin was the perfect setting for the kind of progressive thinking, and nights on the town in bars and dives that he and Iggy could deal with, where you met friends fairly easily and the talk didn't go very deep, unless you wanted it to.

It had the friction he'd liked in New York and Los Angeles, before he grew too comfortable, or too uncomfortable. Being in Los Angeles had quickly felt like being nowhere; being in Berlin felt like being somewhere, surrounded by mysteries and also an ordinariness that had its own welcome dynamic.

The absurd, tragic wall that encircled a society was irresistible as a symbol of an isolated and divided condition, of a world torn apart, the split between East and West, between two different worldviews, between freedom and oppression, between absent and present.

He went to a place where he had to learn to live by and for himself again – a place where he had to walk down the road to the shops on his own and buy food himself, use money, make small talk.

He had to learn to do that again, learn how to buy a plane ticket, which felt naïve and trite – most people can do that on their own obviously, but not the rock star, which he had become, because he had managers and aides and assistants and record company people that were treating him as the rock star, the weirdo, and doing everything for him. They all had jobs because of him, but somehow they controlled him. Yet without him, they didn't exist.

There was this permanent-seeming entourage forming a barrier between him and the world and he needed to reduce it to about two or three people, to get his freedom back. The freedom to just be ordinary, in his own particular way.

That became his new character, someone who was ordinary to himself, even if the outside world considered him very much not normal and insisted on treating him as special, to satisfy their own desires. He could not treat himself as special. He wanted simply to be an artist, observing, thinking and finding and absorbing influences, not the rock star, buzzing with clichés, born only to entertain and fulfil the fantasies of others.

A city of constant changes, Berlin had a palpable weirdness about it that was all around and out of sight. It could be interpreted and imagined in so many different ways, and had become as a much a city of the imagination as a real place, everything folding back on itself.

Bowie couldn't write in a city where he was settled or, at the other extreme, too unsettled. He liked to be in a new place, somewhere he needed to get used to so he could recover a form of naivety. He could only write when he didn't know the people, their fears and desires, the nightmares in their head, how they lived, where they went at night.

The first few months in Berlin were spent first of all enjoying not being in Los Angeles and simply observing people and life as it passed him by, mingling with people going about their business who didn't recognise him, and if they did, mostly let him go about his business. He could pretend to be a real person and get away with it most of the time.

He followed in the footsteps of the novelist who best captured the soul of Berlin and its lowlife in the early 1930s, Christopher Isherwood, visiting from London in the footsteps of the poet WH Auden, seeking a dream space in the city's thriving, open gay scene. 'Berlin meant boys,' he said. Isherwood was always ready to head back to Britain if the dangers he saw growing started to take over, as freewheeling decadence and excess began warping into the rise of the Hitler's Third Reich. He famously wrote in the book containing stories that would inspire the film *Cabaret*: 'I am a camera with its shutter open, quite passive, recording, not thinking.'

Isherwood, Marlene Dietrich, Leni Riefenstahl, Günter Grass, John F Kennedy, Bertolt Brecht – all represented Berlin at various times, as would Bowie, each seeing and feeling a different place, all of which was Berlin. The city's name and fame were also rooted in Alfred Döblin's turbulent, twisted, turning, riffing and rioting 1929 novel *Berlin Alexanderplatz*, set in the hectic Weimar Berlin confluence of various avant-garde movements Isherwood had manifested between the two world wars. The lurid weirdness and whimsy of the interwar Weimar years turn sinister and Berlin's jitters become more jagged and corrosive. Rainer Fassbinder's audacious, deliriously operatic 1980 13-part television miniseries – plus fantastical epilogue – filmed what had seemed unfilmable, an avant-garde work of art about an avant-garde work of art that found even more Berlin inside Döblin's. Fassbinder made the series knowing how the story that was only just beginning in the late 1920s had 'ended.'

The brutally majestic novel used a fragmented cinematic montage technique, folding in the real in the form of newspaper stories and adverts, songs, weather reports, train timetables and political speeches to convey the modern city's swirling, futuristic density, where time is not a linear experience. It was as much the adventitious, sometimes methodical cut-up technique of William Burroughs to come as it was the amorphous, self-sustaining universe of James Joyce.

The serendipitous spirit of William Burroughs had been a factor in the writing of songs for Bowie since *Diamond Dogs*, and in Berlin, he felt the spontaneous spirit of the genuine cut-up – cut the words and see how they fall – give meaning and life back to words as images in sequence. He'd been inspired by Burroughs, who remarked as he was writing his cut-up 'trilogy' of *Nova Express*, *The Ticket That Exploded* and *The Soft Machine*, 'When you cut into the present the future leaks out.'

The rearranged texts appeared to be referring to future shifts in feeling and meaning, to worlds that hadn't yet happened. All this was of particular interest to Bowie, and Burroughs had gifted him with a method of retrieving a future and interfering with reality.

They were a kind of time machine and also, for Burroughs, not necessarily for artistic purposes, they were a weapon, a sword. 'I bring not peace but pieces.'

CHANCE AND ORDER

In 1959, Burroughs had elaborated on the idea of his friend, painter, poet, multimedia shapeshifter and techno-shaman Brion Gysin, who had stumbled into the practice whilst using a Stanley knife to cut up some paper as backgrounds for various drawings he was assembling. He was using a copy of a New York newspaper as protection for the tabletop he was working on, and cutting through to the newspaper, he accidentally ended up with some sentences and headlines – as well as images – that made him laugh when he put them together in random order.

Burroughs saw something deeper and stranger – a route to the accidents that often made writing, photography, painting and composing something other than what was intended, and an insight, even a shortcut, into the mental processes TS Eliot used in the recombined arguments of *The Wasteland* in 1922 and John Dos Passos in his radiant magnum opus 'U.S.A. Trilogy', written between 1930 and 1936. Inside both were processes previously mapped out in the linguistic collage and linguistic Cubism conceived by Gertrude Stein in 1912.

Gysin and Burroughs had, by chance, echoed the notion of the Romanian poet, playwright and cofounder of Dada, Tristan Tzara, who was perhaps inspired by Lewis Carroll, who answered the question 'How do I be a poet' with 'First you write a sentence/ and then you chop it small/ then mix the bits, and sort them out/ just as they chance to fall/ the order of the phrases makes/ no difference at all.' It was as though it was a technique lost and rediscovered by different generations – one of particular use to the more curious, more cerebral and antic writer of pop songs.

In 1920, Tzara came up with the instructions on how 'To Make a Dadaist Poem', which involved a newspaper and some scissors and cutting up a likely looking article, putting the words in a bag, taking them out one at a time and then putting them in the order that they appear. The poem will then resemble you.

This was one way of collecting and arranging words, and Gysin had another, and Burroughs another – 'images shift sense under the scissors', said Burroughs – and Bowie his own, which would become, by 1995, a sentence randomiser proto-app designed for the writing of lyrics, which he called a 'verbasizer'. This created a flurry of potential combinations of meaning, topic, slogan, vision, verb, noun. It was a systemised method of achieving in his songs the volatile blending of realism and surrealism, of real people and imaginary moments, the rejection of stable identities and meanings, where he had found he was most at home.

Life, and perception, is a cut-up and as soon as you look out the window, you're cutting up reality. You don't have to leave your apartment – you're glancing around, you see a book, or a newspaper, or a magazine, you're looking here, you're looking there, you're cutting your data up all the time. The cut-ups simply make this process that goes on all the time explicit.

Eno, extending the thinking of John Cage, collapsing all distinctions between 'high' and 'low' art, had introduced to Bowie an enhancement of the accidental moments that often happen in the environment of the recording studio as part of the to-and-fro of building a finished piece of music from an original sketch or plan, that could be nearly complete or relatively primitive. Into the sessions for *Low*, and then *Heroes* and *Lodger*, Eno brought an openness to welcoming chance into the compositional procedure. He saw how the recording studio was one immense machine for cutting up tapes into loops and randomly rearranging and editing sounds and rhythm.

At the same time, Bowie brought in his approach to finding lyrics by cutting up found words and sentences, playing games with words and sounds. The juxtaposition of one thing that didn't necessarily belong with another thing produced a new sensation, a new kind of awareness.

Bowie would try to explain it in interviews at the time, filled with excitement at this new method of making words come true, at a style of writing lyrics that suited his mind. He was eager to express how it reflected what happened to his mind when he was working on a song, taking something to help make things go faster when he needed them to, and slower when he needed them to.

He'd take a piece of paper and write three or four sentences about a character that he wanted to appear, then another three or four sentences about the environment he was in, then another set of words about some situation . . . and then a few arbitrary statements about whatever he fancied – what he had for lunch, the weather, some small talk with someone who served him in a café, it didn't matter – just some incidental colour that had absolutely nothing to do with the basic premise of the song. Then he would cut them all up into individual lines with a pair of scissors and then cut those lines into three- or four-word statements, not paying attention to where he was cutting, and then mix them up. Then he would lay them in lines so they became sentences. He would immediately use sentences that fell into the song, and others that didn't quite work he would use as an idea for a new song or a new perspective for the song. It provided a way of capturing the thought process itself and in a pop song that can be the most wonderful way of opening up another, one which resembles this one but takes you somewhere else. And then that leaks back into reality. Something randomly produced becomes part of our surroundings.

It makes you realise how astonishing it is that a mere twenty-six letters of the alphabet serve to form our words and express our thoughts.

THREE AND MORE

Low had been a liberating experience, a series of experiments that immediately proposed other potential lines of inquiry, with Berlin and its Hansa studio right by the mysterious, matter-of-fact wall becoming a more established base for the recording. Bowie and Eno decided to make another album using similar processes and personnel, eager to extend and consolidate their energising chemistry while it lasted.

Being artists, and in their own way permanent art students, they discussed making a cohesive series, a musical equivalent of the traditional triptych: three separate pieces that can tell a story across time to develop or express multiple points of view. The pictures may represent different moods or characters, but they flow into each other across liminal spaces, sharing enigmatic elements and making cryptic connections and associations.

The diptych or triptych emerged through religious paintings in the Middle Ages, mostly used as altarpieces, and by the turn of the sixteenth century, Hieronymous Bosch's enigmatic, ecstatic 'The Garden of Earthly Delights' moved from Creation to Judgement to Fall, for some a vision of the fallen state of humanity, for some a utopian version of the paradise before or without the Fall. This was closely followed in 1612–14 by Baroque artist Peter Paul Rubens' 'The Descent from the Cross' and in 1638 his dramatic and monumental 'Elevation of the Cross'.

In the twentieth century, there was a resurgence of the concept. Warhol's silvery, poignant Marilyn Monroe diptych in 1962, a different world of worship from the early Christ-based depictions, contrasted and fused her life and death, the private and the public, mortal and immortal, hero and anti-hero. Mark Rothko's 'Rothko Chapel' contains three majestic, magnetic monochrome panels as part of a sacred space, tense and still, created by an atheist. And Francis Bacon used the triptych form consistently between 1944 and 1986, inspired by Rubens, including 1965's 'Crucifixion', 1969's 'Three Studies of Lucian Freud' and 1971's 'In Memory of George Dyer', the first of his Black Triptych series, pain objectified onto a canvas, a representation of moments, reminisces, scenes and events that seem to lead to Bowie and Eno's attraction to the idea of a triptych. Bacon called them 'a balanced unit', better and more compressed than a series of five or six or even more. They should each be in their own frames, able to be perceived separately, but ultimately existing in one imaginative space.

Bowie's own Berlin triptych was very much of, about and set within the city itself, a city of the mind, and a meditation on transience and immutability.

Heroes was perhaps the central panel, with *Low* and *Lodger* on either side, a way into and out of the centre, which contained its own set of balanced units, just as the two on either side were their own centres. Some would say that *Lodger* was the centre, with 'Move On' at the centre of that, what Nabokov called nostalgia in reverse, the longing for yet another unknown land. Or it could even be *Low*, with 'Speed of Life' at its centre, a song where the original lyrics were never used as Bowie left behind the world's somewhere and purposefully headed into his own nowhere.

By *Lodger*, Bowie was patching a disintegrating world into new and inexplicably irregular forms, and beginning to leave 'Berlin', eventually heading back, and forward, to another London album, *Scary Monsters (and Super Creeps)*. *Lodger* was formed of more haunting fragments of broken memories, but the end of the world has once more been postponed and Bowie knows his place again, more aware than ever how easy it is to lose your footing, even if you are on the alert for danger.

At the centre of Bowie's Berlin, at the centre of the triptych, which overlapped with the centre of Bowie's focused mind, was 'Heroes', which became its own celebrity with its own history and a multitude of interpretations. For, as Bowie had said, a song could now be one of his characters, a 'hero' with a life of its own, a figment of a generation's imagination, and he didn't have to do interviews pretending to be that character. The song, he said, manifested itself at the time he had decided to stop playing characters. He was no longer the art object – the song was.

In one sense, the song, he said, was nothing more than a pretty love song, nothing to do with the sweeping gestures of heroes. It takes its time becoming more than 'Bowie's pretty love song' after a slow, low key beginning, possibly because of the simmering dissonance and the uneasy mood changes that suggest hidden depths. Bowie's ability to do this intrigued Eno when they worked together. These changes would come suddenly and throw the songs and stories into whole new worlds without causing any turbulence.

The music for 'Heroes' had come first, which, compared to other pieces they were working on at the time, possessed a certain triumphant glory that challenged Bowie to respond with something that had grandeur but also discretion. A stately, slightly fractious chord sequence Eno had come up with was based on their shared love of the Velvet Underground and their appreciation of the almost literary magic of a collection of chords.

Bowie directed the musicians towards an interpretation of the chords – how long each might last, perhaps play around with the chords for this number of bars – until the foundation of a song appeared, as if rising up out of a mist, lingering between uncertainty and probability. There was no clear sense of where the verse was, where a chorus might be. The near formless song existed for a while without a title.

As usual, the musicians of DAM were a little baffled by all the conceptual card playing and swapping roles. They weren't sure what the song was or what was expected, but it was that sense of vagueness Bowie and Eno encouraged, looking for the unusual, so that any meaning, any sort of sense, would only be achieved when the song was finished. Even then, nothing was fixed, nothing was absolute.

If the song was new to them, it would be an adventure for the listener, whenever they listened to it, however far into the future.

It became a song about 'heroes', with the title even placed inside inverted commas, because what was a hero and could a hero only be a hero in a heroic world?

Bowie was reinventing the idea of heroism, saying a real hero is always one by mistake. It became a song about heroes that wasn't really about being a hero, about feeling split in two, a song about lovers that wasn't about any particular lovers, a song about secrets and danger, exile and loss, withdrawal and isolation, about the difference between somewhere and nowhere, about a wall in the mind and a wall for real.

Bowie sings it like an overseer taking charge of a cosmic space and shining a light on history – ultimately the song's own history – with Eno's spectral multitracked backing voice stacking and harmonising his almost comically thin tone until the sound becomes weirdly divine. Robert Fripp's guitar was itself a kind of triptych; called in at a moment's notice to add his interpretation of what the song was and what it could be, he quickly improvised three keening, chiming performances, one after the other, hearing something immediately that made sense. When played back together, they were like brush strokes painting the same line, each one subtly different, lifting the song into an unexpected musical sphere. It was as if Fripp was suddenly telling them a precious secret of some sort, silencing Bowie, Eno and Visconti as they listened with what they wouldn't want to call awe. Eventually, the room let out its breath.

You start with an idea, maybe a great idea, maybe not, and when you start working on it and playing around with it, all sorts of wonderful things you never anticipated take over. And you finish it thinking, what an astonishing song to have ended up writing, it's so much better than what was planned.

As a pop song, a seven-inch single, edited down for convenience, 'Heroes' was released on 23 September 1977, and even though it's remembered as though it was an inevitable and immediate number one, it went no higher than 14 in the UK charts and failed to chart in America. *Heroes* the album and the single succeeded in making Bowie unheroic, which he wanted as a corrective to the years of playing 'heroes', just someone who happened to have a point of view about what a hero was and wasn't.

It would take a few years after it was dreamed up and constructed for the song itself to become a 'hero', making its way into history, accumulating meaning, stature and power. It was a soundtrack to the fall of the Wall, an inspiring moment of victory, leading to the end of the Cold War, the obsolescence of border walls, a temporary reshaping of the modern world, signifying peace and hope and triggering the collapse of other East European regimes. 'Heroes' then made sense in the new, darker era that unfolded after his death, and the erection of new symbolic walls representing political agendas, border control and societal divisions. The post-Berlin Wall evolution towards a global village was a delusion that lasted barely into the twenty-first century.

'Heroes' didn't create a better, 'heroic' world for the next generation but in times of confusion, when all the world is a hopeless jumble, underneath the sky that's falling down, it reminds us there were others before us, and they had ideas about how to help us adapt to disconcerting change and not so much the unknown but the end of the known.

Impressions chosen from another time made into art and song can help us prepare for a near future increasingly piled high with disorienting new technology, fractured communities and radical shifts in social value. 'Heroes' imagines, as if this alone can make it happen, a world where songs, and art and reason, still have worth, and still have the power to engage, transport and purge. It's a song that celebrates how songs can exist as living entities, fighting those forces which in an increasingly reductionist world actively work against the mysterious.

RISING AND FALLING

On the cover of *Lodger*, the third part of the triptych, Bowie is all over the place. And he was all over the place musically, reporting on his travels local, international and dream with a supernatural realist's eye for detail and a natural surrealist's rampant playfulness, menace constantly rippling under the surface, reflecting how the unconscious is a prime site for violence.

He had been somewhere, been nowhere, and now he was running down the edges of different countries and continents, lodging wherever he found himself, embarking on various pilgrimages, looking for something. Not knowing where he was going but knowing he would arrive.

The experiments of *Low* that led to the experiments of *Heroes* led into a rejuvenated Bowie experimenting on Bowie and an album that conjured up the ghostly hints of previous alter egos, origin stories, high concepts, rock star flourishes and science fiction fables.

The album proved how of all his peers and contemporaries, he was the least disorientated by the cultural force of punk and the subversion of post-punk. He was as post-punk and experimental as anyone and anything, and, with the singles 'Boys Keep Swinging' and 'D.J.' as pop – if still abrasive and abstract – as anyone and anything. He was ready to flaunt himself again, exhilarated at feeling unattached, from Angie, and from Defries, and from the monster he'd become.

The performer who'd been so out of step with his solo debut in 1967 was now leading the charge in 1979 – a very active, fast changing twelve years – up to speed, not out of place and usually beyond when placed next to albums of the year, as punk, dub and electronica spread through and around genres, as explored by: Talking Heads, Joy Division, Gang of Four, Buzzcocks, Wire, the Fall, Magazine, Public Image Ltd, This Heat, Throbbing Gristle, Linton Kwesi Johnson, the Human League, the Flying Lizards, the Specials, Swell Maps, the Pop Group, Popol Vuh, Augustus Pablo, Marianne Faithfull, the Raincoats, the Cure, B-52s, the Slits, Blondie, Pretenders, Elvis Costello, XTC, Siouxsie and the Banshees, Keith Hudson, the Clash, Yellow Magic Orchestra, Holger Czukay, Henry Cow. Or, coming from other directions: Michael Jackson, Prince, Chic, Earth, Wind and Fire, AC/DC, Bob Dylan, Rickie Lee Jones, Neil Young, Joni Mitchell, Philip Glass, Art Ensemble of Chicago. And from the edges of Bowie's 'Berlin' came a covert genre of its own, comprising Iggy Pop's *New Values*, Robert Fripp's *Exposure* and Michael Rother's *Katzenmusik*.

Eno's working title for *Lodger*, *Planned Accidents*, came from the studio processes, methods and procedures increasingly being used that were as much a part of 'Berlin' as the musical and technical ensembles. The concept of the cover photograph came from that title and Bowie's desire to represent himself in the image of a man falling, as though from one unexpected adventure to another, from one life to another – even as the man who fell to earth, from one planet to another.

Bowie put a lot of work and thinking into the sleeve for *Lodger*. He scrupulously assembled one of his premier creative teams, perhaps, on the quiet, thinking he had made his best ever album, and, you never know, when everything is added up and graded for eternity, his best album ever. One where he says even small things intensely, each song capturing his ideal sense of an all-at-onceness, a spirit of worldly, lonerish romantic indifference, a condition of heightened consciousness. There's propulsive logic and playful self-awareness but also a moral seriousness and loftiness of purpose.

The elaborate cover shoot, an intricate stage set in itself, was directed and photographed by Duffy, responsible for 1973's luminous Aladdin Sane image. After the minimalist portrait photography of *Low* and *Heroes*, this sleeve was going to contain extreme drama, a still-life version of a showstopping theatrical moment and a Bowie caught in the act of transformation as he changed roles, synthesised influences and presented a new series of identities, poses and movements.

The team of collaborators in the production of this image and the overall sleeve included a friend of Duffy's, the pioneering, underrated British pop artist Derek Boshier, part of a more critical generation after Richard Hamilton and his 1955 'This Is Tomorrow' collage established the pop art template, swiftly responding to the early infiltration of American pop culture into British culture.

Boshier was at the Royal College of Art between 1959 and 1962 with other significant artists from working-class backgrounds, including David Hockney, Allen Jones and Patrick Caulfield, who all used popular mediums and popular imagery in their art, as well as their own obsessions and intrigues. Boshier's mixed media collage pieces possessed Marshall McLuhan-influenced Dadaist leanings. In 1963, he appeared alongside Peter Blake and Pauline Boty in *Pop Goes the Easel*, a fizzy, fragmented documentary collage directed by rowdy visionary Ken Russell, his debut film and an early delirious sighting of British pop art.

All through the 1960s, Boshier made direct and indirect contact with sixties and seventies pop personalities from John Lennon – to whom he sold his first car, a green Triumph Herald, elsewhere both obsessed with Hieronymus Bosch – to an ex-student of his at the Central College of Art and Design who eventually went by the name Joe Strummer, of the Clash. There were connections between the interests of Bowie and Boshier, both paying attention to the trends, imagery, places and events of these two decades.

In 1962, one of Boshier's paintings, 'I Wonder What My Heroes Think of the Space Race', based around a vivid blue moon floating above a bloodied earth, featured a cast of his heroes who had died tragically young, from Admiral Nelson and Abraham Lincoln to Buddy Holly. Along with 'Space Oddity' it's one of the most compelling and allusive commentaries on the Space Race. But, like Bowie, Boshier was nothing if not inconsistent and phobic about the world's need to pigeonhole. He would soon move on, in case he was trapped forever inside one theme and one work.

In 1973, with no knowledge of Bowie's 'Changes', he had produced a monumental installation called 'Change' as part of an exhibition at the Whitechapel Gallery, a changing series of collages, film images, diagrams and small drawings morphing from blots, graphic abstractions and images of weather into Maoist stars and protest posters. It was, he said, an exploration of 'change of pace, exploration, face, alteration, variation, transformation, modulation, permutation, shift, merging or difference at different times'. The artwork evolved and parts of it could have been an abstract video for the song 'Changes' and how the inner life keeps moving on with whatever reality gives it to work with.

Boshier first came across Duffy in 1979 when he was commissioned to curate an exhibition at the Hayward Gallery in London titled *Lives (where artists use other people as the subject of their art)*, with the intention to integrate so-called 'high' and 'low art', and the well-known and the obscure. It caused controversy, as the borders were still rarely crossed, but such synthesis was entirely natural to Boshier.

There were fine artists, including Hockney, but also commercial graphic designers, including the great post-punk designer Barney Bubbles, who designed the poster and catalogue, cartoonists, video artists and photographers, including Duffy, who Boshier considered the most inventive and interesting photographer of any kind from the 1960s and '70s.

A few months after the exhibition, Duffy called Boshier and said he knew someone, a good friend, who he'd like to introduce him to. Duffy thought they would have a lot in common.

Boshier assumed it was some sort of blind date, which sounded interesting, but it turned out it was David Bowie, which was even more interesting. Bowie asked him to help design the artwork for the next record. Bowie had already done his research – when he was told about Boshier, he went into an art book shop in Covent Garden and asked for some catalogues or information about Boshier.

Before Boshier went to the meeting, before he knew it was Bowie, he'd been in the same book shop. The owner, recognising him, said, 'So you know David Bowie?' Boshier knew of him but they hadn't met. But then, a little later, he found himself in Duffy's north London studio talking with Bowie. He tried hard to keep his cool but couldn't help looking into his eyes, and felt some kind of lightning bolt shoot through his mind.

ART AND DEATH

Bowie and Boshier did find they had many things in common. Boshier had studied mime and had been offered the chance to study with Marcel Marceau in Paris, but preferred the more solitary pursuits of art and the other form of quietness inside an art studio. They both travelled to and through numerous countries, were willing to change direction and move through phases, and borrowed ideas and styles from other artists and writers, using them for random juxtapositions. They both saw that the meaning of an image or a word could only be understood in the context of what it was placed next to. They shared an interest in how an artistic object – like a song – would metamorphose into something else one step at a time.

Wherever they lived, they instantly responded to the cultural, social and physical environment, absorbing everything around them – current events, personal incidents, political situations – sometimes to a fault.

They also shared a fascination with the mythology of the falling man and the fall of Icarus, with a world that's falling. It was on Bowie's mind after his Los Angeles 'fall' into hell and the motif ran through Boshier's politically and morally charged art, all the way to 2020, aged 84 – four years before his death – and his *Icarus* exhibition, which ran concurrently with his newest fascination, the Korean *Masked Singer* show, where singers and celebrities hidden inside spectacular costumes and masks challenge a panel and the wider audience to guess who they are.

Like Bowie, Boshier loved to be up to speed with the latest cultural intrusions, especially one playing with a mass audience and mystery, and any suggesting a new, sublime juxtaposition

– in this case, Greek mythology and post-modern mainstream light entertainment.

The 'Icarus' part of the exhibition was six paintings featuring various figures, objects and creatures falling from the bright azure sky, including clothed rabbits, scrapping fighters, executives wearing demonic masks, jigsaw pieces, horses, mobile phones and video game controllers.

His first falling man materialised 60 years before. A standard project at the Royal College of Art encouraged students to base a work on a famous classic painting. Boshier chose one of William Blake's illustrations for Dante's *Inferno*, 'The Simoniac Pope', featuring a figure hanging upside down suspended in a well of fire. The Pope was falling into hell, suffering the consequences of turning his back on spirituality and being tempted by materialistic desires.

After he left college, using an isolated, sometimes fragmented outline of the hanging figure, Boshier began inserting into his work a repeating image of a solitary naked figure looking as though it was falling through space. It represented 'Everyman', and Boshier's speculation on how the vulnerable, exposed individual was dealing with the pressures of changing times amplified and distorted by mass media. Sometimes, the falling man represented the end of an empire, the end of a corrupt, powerful regime.

Boshier's 'falling man' or 'fallen man' prefigured 1975's 'Fall of Icarus' by Marc Chagall, where the falling man was Icarus, from the eighth book of Ovid's *Metamorphosis*, who dared to fly so close to the sun that his wax wings melted and he plunged to the ground, which is red as blood. Daedalus, his father, had made wings for himself and his son using feathers, beeswax and string so they could escape their imprisonment on the island of Crete. Daedalus warned his son to avoid the sea and its moisture and the sun and its heat, but Icarus 'fell in love with the sky' and, carried away with the thrill of flying and an amazing sense of freedom, soared higher and higher.

Icarus's story is typical of Greek and Roman myth where individuals who display tragic hubris against the gods, believing they are above their laws, ultimately meet Nemesis, the goddess of retribution.

Chagall was 88 when he painted his version of the myth, looking back on his life and his constant ambition to fly higher, go beyond the ordinary, break rules, always risking a tragic end.

In Pieter Bruegel's sixteenth-century 'Landscape with the Fall of Icarus', the original source of all Icarus paintings, the boy falling out of the sky is barely noticed, a small part of a greater landscape, shown as simply a small pair of legs flapping out of the sea – what William Carlos Williams in his 1962 poem of the same title called 'a splash unnoticed'. Even such an astonishing death is ignored and the masses are indifferent to his fate. Everyone is focused on their own lives. A proverb at the bottom of the painting says, 'You don't stop the plough for a man who's dying'. Life goes on.

In Chagall's 'Icarus', a crowd notice the fall; it's a kind of performance. They could be applauding, impressed by the act. They might even be able to save Icarus, give him another chance, despite his folly.

CRASH AND BURN

Bowie, with his confident, knowing sense of art history and theatrically playful sense of self, used art and music as a kind of compass, and had some ideas about how to create his own Icarus tableau – a story of a grand idea and a lack of control. The falling man could also mean falling from grace, falling standards and even falling for no reason that you know.

For him, the *Lodger* cover was more than an album sleeve, a decorative piece of packaging. It was part of a landscape he was creating, one that was part of the music on the record. When he knew what he wanted, which often involved a certain amount of uncertainty, he showed no sign of creative self-doubt.

Derek Boshier was in a design trio equivalent of the Visconti/Bowie/Eno studio group. He was the Eno – Duffy the Visconti – brought in to introduce the unthought of, some extraneous interference, that would take Bowie's original notion of identity and fragility into new areas.

For the outside of the gatefold sleeve, Bowie wanted to construct his version of an image of a falling man, with his face distorted by G-force, like a pilot breaking the sound barrier. Nylon fishing line attached to parts of his face was used to distort Bowie's face and suggest a broken nose, tugged into place for each shot by Coco Schwab and regular Bowie hair and make-up artist Antony Clavet, who'd thought of the idea.

A bandage on Bowie's hand from a minor recent burn – he'd accidentally spilled some hot coffee – was left where it was to emphasis the general sense of topsy-turviness. Clavet had said to Bowie that he needed to work on his burnt, bandaged right hand, and that it would take an hour to sort out. He was taken aback when Bowie said 'leave it on'. It went with the crumpled suit, the comb he was holding in his hand, and the fact that this was meant to be an accident site, with a feeling of real violence and unceremonious disarray. Life just happens, sometimes because you make it, deliberately directing its flow, other times because it just does and you go along with the flow.

A fabricated steel frame, designed to be obscured by his body, was built a metre off the ground to separate Bowie from the background. As part of how the illusion of Bowie falling was created, a sink was laid on the floor underneath the frame. A jet of water was shot into the sink to add an indeterminate element of disorientating energy. Duffy took the picture from high in the studio rafters to create the illusion Bowie was falling through space. At first sight, he seemed to be on the floor and then you noticed – he wasn't on the floor, he was falling, he was moving.

For the cover artwork, Bowie decided to use one of the ten test low-resolution Polaroids Duffy had taken as they went along, checking for light and positioning. Ten was the number of shots you had in a single pack of film.

The shoot was highly choreographed but the accidental, factory-efficient moment of the Polaroid photograph, taken on the highly portable, folding SX-70 instant film camera of the same type that Andy Warhol carried to all his social engagements, gave a bleached, discoloured tone to the image that Bowie preferred. The glossier, sharper, higher-resolution Kodachrome shot, in some ways more intimidating, introduced a drop in tension. It was fiercer but oddly more commercial.

The rough, off-the-cuff snapshot of a dishevelled and disfigured Bowie crashlanding onto the floor of a cold, sterile room showed how far and wide he'd travelled in the six years from the weightless, transcendent and fey beauty of *Aladdin Sane*, and how much he had remade himself, sometimes using outside forces, sometimes by sheer will, continually slipping the confines of a fixed identity, one act of reflection after another. Surprise art by surprising yourself remained one of his mantras. Push back at what you know how to do. Keep changing.

One of Boshier's roles was to add lettering and his distinctive, scratchy graphic marks to the image, the kind he would use on envelopes when he sent friends newspaper cuttings or drawings. He framed everything inside a postcard-like panel he'd used in one of his sixties pieces, turning the Duffy Polaroid into a kind of postcard – a postcard from someone always on the move, from someone who can only stop moving from one thing to another by crashing to the floor. He carefully sketched out his proposed layout, which in itself was a work of art, as a blueprint for the final image of this 'falling man'.

Before he travelled to Berlin to show Bowie and Coco the artwork, he mentioned to Bowie that they hadn't done anything for the inside gatefold. Bowie opportunistically told him to do what he wanted, as though Boshier would be supplying the visual equivalent of Eno's backing vocals on *Lodger*'s 'Boys Keep Swinging'.

The sleeve – if you didn't mind thinking Bowie must be up to something wanting to make such a statement, even if just more shiftiness – seemed to be about life and death, the beginning and the end and all points in between, including time and the suspension of time. Using the water spurting into the sink as a background, Boshier collected a series of found images: a famous photograph of Che Guevara's autopsy, the Italian Renaissance artist Andrea Mantegna's painting 'Lamentation of Christ', the image of a baby and a double image of two Omega wristwatches chosen totally at random.

Boshier used the chance presented by their meeting in Berlin to ask some of the questions he was always interested in, which he felt Bowie was interested in as well: 'Art doesn't stop time or create a space to protect us from it passing. So why do we need it in our lives? What does it give us that other things do not?'

Because it was a David Bowie album, a performer's commercial product but also a place to play, Boshier used a behind-the-scenes photograph of Bowie being carefully readied for the shoot, as though the subject of some kind of complicated surgical operation.

The arrangement of images sparks various interconnected memories, recollections and associations, and a cascade of interpretations. They are like postcards sent from a dream, a series of mysteries organised by a pop star who clearly understood however much knowledge you possess, there is always room for more wonder and mystery.

The enigmatic artwork being turned into promotional posters and full-page ads in the music papers emphasised the subversive quality of presenting a pop star as a battered, haywire figure as well as Bowie's love of resisting easy interpretation, of the fertility of uncertainty. Let them wonder about you.

BEAUTY AND BEAST

Bowie would stay in contact with Boshier for the rest of his life: as a friend sharing private moments as both moved around the world, looking out for interesting spaces and ideas; as fan, a consistent collector of his work and regular attendee at Boshier shows; and as occasional collaborator on stage sets and artwork, including the front cover of the *Let's Dance* album. Some Boshier sketches of heads and his regular walking figures motif are on the inside sleeve.

A 1980 piece by Boshier, 'A Darker Side of Houston', was projected behind a boxing Bowie on the cover – Boshier had moved to Houston to teach, one of his arbitrary relocations to unlikely places, which might have seemed especially strange at a time when, coming off 'Lives' and *Lodger*, and with the Clash, he was set up for a period of acclaim and cultural buoyancy. So, of course, he sought some far away quiet. Maybe just for a few months, although he ended up making a life there.

His sudden changes of direction and location, forcing himself to be uprooted, included moving at the end of the 1990s to Los Angeles, seeing it as the best place to hold and develop his artistic position. Boshier dealt with LA better than Bowie, avoiding – or exploiting – all its potential pitfalls and the heat of the sun. He trusted his instinct to the end, sometimes an instinct for conflict, knowing however unreasonable the decision, it would lead to art.

When they didn't see each other for a while, Bowie would find a way to communicate, slipping a mention into an interview – 'the British artist Derek Boshier was right when he said the contemporary artist is the true creator of a world that did not exist before they gave shape to it.' He trusted that Boshier would see it, or someone he knew would see it.

(Bowie was always a media addict, keeping up with everything he could, as participant and consumer. Henry Rollins tells a story of how when he first met Bowie at some event, astonished and in awe to see him in the flesh, he couldn't believe it when Bowie shouted over to him 'Rollins!' and immediately started talking to him as though they were old friends. Bowie quoted with admiration something Rollins had said in a German magazine six months before.)

Boshier would also paint a number of portraits of David Bowie as the great self-impersonator, some commissioned by Bowie, others because he had an idea, including one that was more accurately a portrait of Joseph Merrick, the Elephant Man, Bowie twisting his body and face into the shapes he used when he played the Elephant Man on Broadway. It was one of Bolshier's first paintings since he had lost patience with the medium in the late 1960s, turning to sculpture, assemblage, installation and film.

Bowie rarely if ever made himself available for a painted portrait but they were both in New York, Boshier renting a loft in a run-down, off-grid area of the Bowery, Bowie rehearsing for his Broadway debut. In unpromising circumstances and inside a hot studio with no air conditioning, both of them doing something that didn't come naturally to them, Bowie stripped to the waist and found his pose, straight out of rehearsals, blurring into his Elephant Man, and held the awkward position for a few hours. He had an incredible ability to be still whatever was happening around him.

After Bowie left, Boshier, needing some kind of background for Bowie's head, remembered reading that the Elephant Man was sometimes known as the Jungle Man. He used some plants that were in the loft as the background, Bowie's tense grimace emerging from the foliage. People said to him, it's OK, but it doesn't look like Bowie. He'd dug deep below the beauty and found another face, another aura, the real thing shimmering in the distance.

He had a wonky view of Bowie anyway, which is maybe one of the reasons Bowie liked him – everything he knew about Bowie was slightly, whimsically off, freshening his story. He thought Bowie's eyes were damaged because someone threw a stone at him. He thought his dad worked at the YMCA, not Barnado's. It was like Bowie from an imperceptibly different universe, which he put into his paintings.

Everyone knows the glamorous, protected Bowie, he said, the one everyone is looking at. There are other Bowies, less known Bowies, not surrounded by a publicity machine and hemmed in by the expectations of his fans. The Bowies that no one is looking at, the Bowies not demanding anyone's attention.

The painting is maybe not Bowie, but what is – and, in a way, there was more Bowie in Boshier's painting than at first seems obvious – Bowie stepping outside, having to be himself for a shapeless few hours with his hardworking, obsessive and disarming friend, feeling warmth and generosity waft towards him, making art for the sake of it, wandering somewhere unfamiliar.

Becoming the inexplicably broken, helpless and wounded body on the cover of *Lodger* was a form of rehearsal for playing the Elephant Man the next year. He played him as the professional freak, the medical wonder, the loneliest, most agonised and ugliest person in the world, the dignified, charming human being with a sharp mind and inner light who loved conversation, and ultimately as bona fide celebrity for whom fame became a route to a sort of establishment acceptance, superficial but better than the horrible alternative.

Merrick as the Elephant Man would become increasingly famous after his death; even more famous because David Bowie played him, David Lynch made a film about him and Michael Jackson wanted to own his remains, sealing him in modern cultural vocabulary.

Bowie used his skill as a mime artist to imply Merrick's extreme deformities, protrusions and thick, lumpy skin, rather than using prosthetics and make-up. It was his pose that made the painting, said Boshier, it was more his painting than mine. And, of course, eventually Bowie would own it.

BOWIE AND BOWIE

In late 2015, Boshier wasn't particularly thinking of producing any new Bowie paintings, but he was inspired by an email he received from Bowie expressing delight at a recent Thames and Hudson monograph about the artist, elegantly edited by the writer Paul Gorman. Bowie said that he loved it very much.

Not fully knowing how ill Bowie was, not realising Bowie was reaching out to all his friends, feeling the end was near, with one final hello and goodbye, Boshier thought he'd reply to this lovely gesture with a drawing as a thank you. Before he managed to think of something, Bowie died.

His best, most natural response was to do a painting that reflected his thoughts on his friend, collaborator, fellow traveller and image maker. He ended up making three, rich with superabundant colour, wit and flamboyance. There were a lot of Bowies to consider and to contrast, and Boshier took to the task of finding imaginative space for his Bowies to play with considerable glee and love.

In 'David Bowie Twice', he had Bowie as a fantastic white-faced Pierrot glowing with melancholy next to a smiling Bowie in his 'civilian' clothes as a local New Yorker, in what turned out to be his last years. Behind the Bowies, getting along splendidly, there's an array of Boshier-made drawings that he connects with Bowie. There's a mushroom for the drugs Bowie took, a courtly dancing couple, a musical instrument coming to life – something that always tickled Bowie – toys for home life and family, representations of theatrical figures and mime artists, and hints of something beastly, fantastical and magick with a k.

The New York Bowie figure points down to the name of his wife, Iman, inspired by a 1797 full-length portrait by the

Spanish romantic painter Francisco de Goya of his hoped-for lover, the alluring Duchess of Alba, in black mourning clothes for her recently deceased husband, pointing her softly pink-nailed finger towards the ground, where the words 'Only Goya' are faintly written – he created the fantasy that she would be doing the pointing and had written the words as if they had real life intimacy, or she yearned for him and he did for her. But in the end, it was a fantasy of a perfect love, launched into history in the painting.

For Bowie, Iman was the reality of a perfect love, with a special hold on him. And this isn't Bowie pointing at Iman's name – it's Bowie being guided by Boshier to make the gesture, the painter's loving tribute to their time together.

Another of the Boshier paintings, 'David Bowie, Jack Kerouac and David Bowie', put Halloween Jack and Ziggy Stardust, blooming glam twins ready for lift-off, in a picture with Jack Kerouac, a cool, moody-looking older brother in eyeliner checking in on them, suitcase in hand, ready for another trip to collect more vital information about the world, and maybe lose his mind now and then.

Bowie would sometimes credit Kerouac as being his first inspiration for making him leave one life and head forward into another, even into others, not really thinking where he would land or how comfortable the landing would be. One day, he would find the right words but first of all, he had to move on, everything ahead of him. It would all end in tears.

The intensely spiritual Kerouac loved the mad ones, the ones who never fade away, never say anything boring, the ones who explode like spiders across the stars. *On the Road* was like some Beat version of the Oblique Strategies for a teenager born in the 1940s – on every page a solution, a decision, a revelation, some naïve, ragged advice. He had nothing to offer anybody but his own confusion.

Whatever hyper-romantic, heartfelt elements entered Bowie's forming sensibility, that intoxicating sense of longing for something higher, the questing for some great beauty to admire, some mission to be completed, would never fully leave him.

Behind Boshier's glam Beat dreamers there was a series of dancing B-Boy poses because Boshier saw a connection between breakdancing and mime – agility, lightness, storytelling – and the sense of freedom and possibility Kerouac preached and tried to practise.

The third Bowie painting, and the first one he completed, put Bowie into pictorial space with a singer Boshier thought of as an eighteenth-century Bowie, Theresa Cornelys. He'd walked past a construction site in central London and seen a big notice in front of it saying this was the site of the greatest nightclub in the world. Intrigued, he did his research.

Known as the Empress of Pleasure – even, in one scandalous court case on a sign held by a fan, as 'Empress of the vast regions of taste and magnificence' – Cornelys was an Italian opera singer, courtesan, showman, artist and on-and-off lover of Casanova. After European work, travels and marriage, looking for somewhere that suited her, she made it to London in 1759. A year later, with the help of various lovers, subscribers and sponsors, she leased the imposing Carlisle House in Soho Square, the former mansion of the Earl of Carlisle. It was in the centre of London but had a rural appearance, still sensed even today. She turned it into a private entertainment club for dancing, gambling and refreshments, relatively innocent at first but, driven by her ambition, rapidly growing to become an early form of the nightclub, where the most fashionable, best-dressed and forward-thinking Londoners went to dance, drink, party. You could get everything you wanted for a good time without having to leave the place, a brand-new concept, making her a bold social visionary.

Members could find the kind of company, pleasure and visual distractions that weren't available anywhere else and get intoxicated in many different kinds of ways. There was a large pool filled with goldfish and an indoor park with freshly laid turf and real pine trees. Famed furniture maker Thomas Chippendale supplied mirrors and chairs, and even a bridge from which you could stare at regularly visiting royalty and the famous, elegant and notorious. You had to look the part, or know the right people, to get in. Not everyone was allowed. There was a mysterious door policy with unwritten rules, although everyone knew what they were, and who was unlikely to get past the door and break into heaven.

It was an opulent, multi-level pleasure palace with moving pillars of lights where masked balls would be thrown for 800 people and a banqueting hall could accommodate 400 people at a time. Johann Bach performed and there was a first sighting of roller skates. Cornelys became an influence on the fashion and culture of the time and her club was so busy that a new traffic system had to be created in the Square to deal with all the carriages. It was as though you could walk through one door and come out the other side in Suffragette City.

The rise and fall of Theresa Cornelys was exciting, scandalous and swift. Debts mounted, competitors were more modern and lured the hipper, flashier dressed and more divine clientele – everyone getting pickier, chasing the new until it was chased out of town. By the early 1770s, she was bankrupt, using the name Mrs Smith to escape bailiffs and selling donkey milk.

Over 200 years later, after Soho Square being the haunt of William Blake, Karl Marx, JMW Turner and sundry outsiders, mavericks and misfits, close to where modern jazz was first heard in the UK and skiffle and rock and roll soon followed, David Bowie would share a flat with Lindsay Kemp, just off the square.

It was near Trident Studios in the centre of Soho's red light district, the facilities where Bowie recorded 'Space Oddity', *The Man Who Sold the World*, *Hunky Dory* and *The Rise and Fall of Ziggy Stardust and the Spiders from Mars*, so where Bowie became Bowie.

Boshier puts 'the Empress', the original Soho clubber, bringing hedonism to London, advocating glamour every day, every hour, together with Bowie, spreading the word in the early 1970s.

He's in his best, most time-and-space shattering Japanese emperor outfit, the spectacular padded unisex satin jumpsuit which Kansai Yamamoto designed for the 1973 *Aladdin Sane* tour. Cornelys is wearing a luxurious eighteenth-century nobleman's *'habit à la française'*, made up of a wide-lapelled patterned frockcoat, waistcoat, breeches, silk stockings, decorative cuffs, gloves and velvet slippers. It was a look appropriated and exaggerated by the extravagant fashionistas known as the Maccoronis, heartily mixing Continental style with English tradition.

He's got lilac Ziggy spikes; she's got elaborate lilac Marie-Antoinette hair towering above her, with New York skyscrapers behind her. She's from the early 1760s; he's from the early 1970s. But they look like they're seductive futurists out on the town, where time doesn't matter.

They look like they gave birth to the New Romantics, somewhere in Soho, after a hell of a night out, when the time was right.

STRANGE AND DANGER

On 1 July 1980, Bowie visited Blitz, a club that had been running for a year and a half each Tuesday in a dusty wine bar on the unassuming edge of Soho. Bowie was working with Tony Visconti on his first post-Berlin album, along with the DAM Trio and Fripp and shuffled musical company, intended to wrap up his mercurial seventies epiphanies and unleash a thrilling, chilling new kind of power, his best album ever, as if the album before, *Lodger*, had been merely a place to settle scores and check for wear and tear. It was magnificent but to some extent it was maintenance. His standards were as high as ever.

Style evangelist Steve Strange ran Blitz as a dissident theatrical private party for maybe 100 regulars – dandies, artists, extremists and fashion insiders. A select few assuming *noms-de-plume*, improvising masks, took at face value Bowie's mantra that however lost you feel, anyone can be a hero, even if just for one day. Originally, the Tuesday night was even called Bowie night, before someone thought, if it really was a Bowie night, it would have its own name, it would look as though it was moving on, finding itself.

It was a place where you could avoid the mob, the drunks and the homophobes, the same old people who always want to spoil the party. You could dance a brand new dance in loud, dark places, which is sometimes all you need in life.

Remorseless electro-evangelist and in-house DJ Rusty Egan compiled the soundtrack, as many extended 12-inch mixes as he could get hold of, as if all music began with Kraftwerk, Roxy Music, Yellow Magic Orchestra and Giorgio Moroder, and pop culture as a liberating religion where you could be what you wanted happened purely because of David Bowie.

In the 1960s, David Bowie, sometimes with partner in time Marc Bolan, had prowled the Soho of mods and rockers, artists and scoundrels – and creeps and monsters – like an explorer hunting for clues and inspirational signs of life, looking for people he could trust, looking for the keys to freedom. Back in Soho in 1980, as the dust settled after all that spiralling, searching 1970s movement, he found a very different place, but one he recognised, one that could be seen as an extension of his own hectic futurist imagination.

The action had moved on but spiritually stayed where it was, taken up by people as young and fearless as he had been 15 years before, risking certain dangers for the sake of the euphoria. It had been knocked into new modern shapes, sounds, colours and spaces by glam, punk, post-punk, electro and disco, but could still be found in underground clubs and style magazines, displayed by a loose collective of precocious and free-spirited instigators and inciters doing their own exploration of self and performance.

Bowie was fascinated by the volatile spirit of this new scene, its resplendent mixture of futurism and nostalgia. He could see how it had emerged from his own experiments with the invention of personas and the way life could be changed and challenged through art; how in the twentieth century, life for many had itself become a form of art.

The Blitz partygoers were loosely linked in the press as the Blitz kids, not yet named as New Romantic, and quickly domesticated as punk had been. They reminded him of the music scenes and clubs of the 1960s, where a space was created for new, different things to happen, of disjointed, anarchic creative collectives, such as Andy Warhol's Factory, most of the members of which came from bad homes. These were the kinds of ambitious dreamers he had been when he was looking for fame, or as close as he could get to it. Swinging Sixties London had been like a test lab for the entrepreneurial inventiveness of the early 1980s and Bowie immediately connected the two.

To get inside the deafening darkness of Blitz, you had to convince sentinel Strange – the latest in a line of superior hosts and hostesses guarding their ritzy territory that stretched back to Theresa Cornelys – that your own important, self-conscious version of a fearless, well-turned-out star had been taken from Bowie and one of his inventions. It was punk and post-punk but with added Bowie as the androgynous, Dionysian cat from Japan, dressed for a subversive mission, throwing open the masquerade of masculinity, clothing as a means of resistance.

And then, one Tuesday night, out of the blue, there he was, maybe having just completed his song about what he called the grim determination and contagious frenzy of fashion, which could become depressing and counterproductive, called 'Fashion', just as 'Fame' had been called 'Fame'. In a way, just calling it 'Fashion' made it a positive anthem about fashion, however dark and troubled the lyrics.

It became pure fashion itself, with its all-embracing mechanical disco stomp, Fripp's piercing guitar driven by unseen forces, Bowie's unhinged, come all ye faithful, all who are weary holler, the joyous, pomposity-puncturing beep beep – just as the injured, unsettling 'Fame' had become an uplifting insider insight into fame. A few notes and there was the sound of fame, of fashion – and nearby, of fascination.

In central London, as he put his finishing touches to *Scary Monsters (and Super Creeps)*, his twelfth album in ten years, an image-saturated finale to Bowie's transformations, rearranging his own mythic history, steadying himself for a new decade, fashion was in the air, more than usual, setting the stage for the 1980s of MTV and the digital futures and celebrity commotion beyond.

PAGEANTRY AND OFFSPRING

Arriving without prior notice, Bowie slipped in through the back door with appropriate entourage, including, of course, Coco Schwab. Here was the chameleonic man/icon himself, the singer of the Blitz irrational anthem 'Heroes', which made audible a new world that gradually became visible, the one who taught those inside how to pose and provoke. He was checking out a scene, a whole theatre of pretension that couldn't have existed without him, observing his 'children' close up in their natural habitat. The regulars there on the night, having had no idea who would be walking amongst them, suddenly found that David Bowie was stood behind them or sat next to them. Close enough to write a love letter and hand it over to him, close enough to look into his eyes, which was too much to deal with.

Bowie being there had a weird way of making them feel they were floating and bringing them down to earth at the same time. He was the least fashionable-looking person in the place – his hair was an ordinary mess, he might not have passed the Strange barrier if he had been anyone else – but it was David fucking Bowie.

Always hyper-sensitive to new trends, and potential new collaborators, Bowie drew on the protean post-Ziggy visual language he found at the Blitz club, its inhabitants with their disposable identities. He reacted to how they have reacted to him, inheriting his view of how the body can be the best work of art and how influences from outside music, from art, theatre, film and literature, add deviant, crusading power to performance.

A select group of individualists, including Strange himself, were paid £50 to appear in the 'Ashes to Ashes' video for the first single from the new album, a song that in the beginning was called 'People Are Turning to Gold', reflecting how, as a piece of autobiography, as well as some sort of pageant, the song was a sunset and a sunrise. A haunted celebration between history and hallucination dense with clues and messages of how pop music can cast a magic spell, and in all sorts of ways take over a life, it formed the end credits to his 1970s, where he'd opened impossible spaces in people's minds.

Bowie was more than ready for the video age. It was the most expensive pop video ever at the time, with a budget of £35,000, co-directed by Bowie, who drew the detailed frame-by-frame storyboard, and the already experienced David Mallet. He'd made all the early Blondie videos and two of the videos for singles from the *Lodger* album, the girls will be girls meets boys will be boys meets boys will be girls 'Boys Keep Swinging' and song about fallen angels, 'Look Back in Anger'.

Bowie, scanning ahead to what few others could see, wanted the video to be an entity in itself, not just a straight performance. He would use this new model, the pop video, to play with time, blur past and present, spin between several worlds at once and blow people's minds in the way he had with 'Starman' on *Top of the Pops*.

He could even bring in ghosts of his old characters – none of them ever completely left behind, especially Major Tom, who was now swinging above Earth on some endless orbit in his graveyard, his padded cell in the sky, a glimmer of deja vu whispering at the edge of perception, a ghost that wants something. Major Tom was reminding people that however much pleasure they might be having, there was always a shadow hanging over them. And, as much as he breaks free of his past, the shadows follow Bowie.

Strange was preparing his own visually conscious electronic group, Visage, and, as much as Bowie was using him to gain instant access to some exotic and unstable private new energy, to his precious list of contacts, he couldn't resist the call. It was a form of support for his own project, an irresistible endorsement. Hell, it was David fucking Bowie. He'd have paid to be in the video.

Pop music, not least because of Bowie, had become a wonderful circus of misfits, dreamers and outcasts finding ways to survive in a cruel world, and why not put that into a pop video set in multiple time dimensions that takes us down to the seashore near some crashing waves to watch a spooky farce?

Bowie asked his regular designer Natasha Korniloff to make him 'the most beautiful clown in the circus' and his brief for co-director David Mallet was 'a clown on a beach with a bonfire'. He asked him, not knowing what was technically possible, can you make the sky black? Mallett gravely replied without turning a hair, yes. If no one grown up was looking, if you had the vision and the right kind of colleagues, you could do anything in a pop video.

The video includes some footage representing the endless absurdity of human behaviour. Bowie leads a small procession of clubbers recovering from a night of revelries, dressed for a funeral, a wedding or a visit to a club with a dark romantic theme, none of them seeing the world the same way, paying close attention to their lord and master as he performs certain rituals. The video age was emerging from the solarised mist.

Maybe in the end he was just taking the opportunity to throw people off the scent; he was nothing more or less than a poet of sensation looking to capture some excitability, writing out of compulsions, seizures, preoccupations.

FACE AND FACT

For the covers to 'Ashes to Ashes' and *Scary Monsters*, Bowie wanted to work with Duffy again, who had quit photography in 1979 feeling fed up with the lies and repetition of fashion – burning his archive in an act of finality, looking to reinvent himself as Bowie always did and find another voice outside photography.

He couldn't resist the call from Bowie for a kind of encore before he turned to furniture restoration and occasional directing and producing – a quiet life, mostly released from the tyranny of images. The 1980 session with Bowie was his last with Bowie and his final one in general.

Duffy photographed David Bowie for the fifth time becoming or playing a character, the Pierrot, another 'I' in the storm. Duffy was not as in control as he had been of the *Scary Monsters* session and the general cultural direction of travel. These were different times, very different from the sixties he helped conceive and how it spilled into the seventies, and there were new breeds of artists, designers and fabulists appearing, and different social settings.

The visual artist and Chelsea School of Art student Edward Bell became part of the team working on the Pierrot shoot after Duffy and Bowie had visited a private view of his first exhibition, called *Larger Than Life*, at the Neal Street Gallery in Covent Garden.

Duffy believed Bell would choose one of his images as the basis for a cover painting but Bell used one of his own photos from the session, and the album sleeve features only a tantalising shadow from one of Duffy's photographs, reflecting how Duffy himself was withdrawing from photography, knowing his time was up.

In his portraits of Bowie in costume, Duffy brought to life Bowie as Pierrot, playing the archetype of the self-dramatising artist, presenting to the world a stylised mask both to symbolise and veil artistic ferment, to distinguish the creative artist from the human being.

Duffy's photographs of the Pierrot are magical and melancholy, on the dream edge between photographically still and eerily spectacular. They are not only the final collaboration between Bowie and Duffy but the end of a series that most specifically defined Bowie's intense, reflective desire in the 1970s to constantly make himself new. They represent the last time Bowie would play with his form and appearance as David Bowie in such a visible, fantastical way, until the last years of his life, over a quarter of a century later.

Bell wasn't so keen on the pristine, poignant whiter than white Pierrot, reflecting the tension between Duffy and Bell. He had other ideas. During the shoot, this perfectly achieved version of the iconic loner, the Romantic darling, the socially elusive subversive, always watching and learning, trying to make sense of nonsense, was slowly distressed and stripped of its clothing. Bowie's make-up was smeared, his clown hat removed, his hair messed up and he started to smoke a cigarette, a mere echo of a man as he passes from one state to another, staring the ambiguities of illusion and reality in the face.

It was as though Bowie was making sure he was not trapped inside another character that might want to take him over and drag him back into the shadows. He was playing a role and then taking off the costume. He replaced this facetious scoundrel with himself – maybe the artist, the poet, the exalted entertainer – before he found himself forced to by circumstances beyond his control.

Bowie was on the cover of edition number seven of *The Face* magazine, November 1980. *The Face* was launched in May 1980 by Nick Logan, previously editor of *NME* and *Smash Hits*, establishing an influential new type of style magazine. It flamboyantly defied the reactionary grip of Margaret Thatcher's assault on the nation's imagination and updated for an antic post-punk world the energy and adventure of the Swinging Sixties and any advancements made by the counterculture. It covered music through a filter of fashion, design, film, photography and culture. The image of Bowie as lavish, capsized clown is for a piece inside the magazine about the Blitz scene, 'the cult with no name', which was also a cult of the self, characterised by a burning need to create for oneself a personal originality, even create yourself as an art object.

The cover anoints Bowie as contemporary participator in the cult as well as a figurehead and main inspiration. It was published three months after the release of 'Ashes to Ashes' and in the same month Steve Strange's own Visage, with Rusty Egan, Midge Ure and Billy Currie of Ultravox, and members of the literate post-punk stylists Magazine, released their most successful single, 'Fade to Grey', which reached number eight in the UK and, for a New Romantic equivalent of 15 minutes, gave Strange a brief glimpse inside the worlds where Bowie was permanent, even immortal.

The images of Bowie in a mysterious new form immediately became a powerful and provocative part of the marketing for the music, which Bowie would sometimes lightly brush off as a fairy tale, for all its sophisticated artistic logic, even if one created by an apocalyptic mind.

The three 'Ashes to Ashes' seven-inch-single sleeves feature Bowie holding, looking at and listening to a silver shoe. In fairy tales, shoes can sometimes render you invisible. In a dream, holding a shoe can symbolise that you are seeking self-improvement. Shoes are the physical and symbolic embodiments of the past, present and future paths we walk. Shoes can represent endurance, protection from the environment, sometimes even subjugation and struggle, but also ambition, determination and direction.

The single cover came with a border of soft, pastel-coloured images energetically manipulated by Bowie using a marker pen and then turned into postage stamps. The first 100,000 copies of the single came in three different coloured sleeves, each containing one of four sheets of the stamps, creating numerous combinations of sleeve and stamps to collect.

The marketing helped the complex, cryptic single, a kind of shattered farewell, an ode to addiction, surprisingly become his first UK number one since a 1975 re-release of 1969's 'Space Oddity', to which 'Ashes to Ashes' could be interpreted as a sequel. It poetically continued the story of Major Tom, who also appeared to return in 1995 in a Pet Shop Boys remix of 'Hallo Spaceboy'. And, more obliquely, he was still orbiting in 2015's elegy for himself, *Blackstar*. Sometimes you need to end where you begin.

Bowie had opened strange doors that would never be closed again, helping his many followers cast their own spells. The soon-to-be somehow officially christened New Romantics and their vaporous Goth step-cousins were the last great exclusive and distinctive British fashion tribes: Bowie disciples helping spread the gospel of the spectacular, influencing the capricious, all-encompassing visual language of pop culture ever since, as it moved into a new digital age. A weird, ever-present streaming where strange things started happening to time and space, pressing in on truth and human intelligence, just as Bowie always knew would happen, just as he always planned for, leaving traces everywhere he could. Hoping people would never lose their willingness to be moved, mesmerised and changed by songs that are somehow more perfect than the world can ever be, even as they deal with life's aching, agonising imperfections.

THEN AND NOW

Bowie landed at the right time in the right space to operate and negotiate as the world moved on from the World War and teenagers took on some of the responsibility to create a new reality. They even had a new kind of power to reject the wrecked past they were handed. You could hear the new realities they were creating in the songs they wrote, sang, listened and danced to, and see them in the clothes they wore. It's a period that started to fade in the twenty-first century, as it lost its hold on reality, and lost its power to be anything other than available, everywhere and entertaining, an accumulation of legacies and legends, of superstars and sensations.

Bowie was right there, growing up and responding to an environment full of tension and generational challenges, but also full of possibility. In between the end of rationing and national service, and so the end of a gloomy, difficult wartime hangover, and the beginning of social media when everyone could design and distribute their own image; between the Cold War and the end of the Berlin Wall; between a television in everyone's home and the deeply problematic emergence of AI on everyone's phone and therefore inside their lives, which they might have to permanently share with another presence.

New Worlds and worlds within worlds with their new situations and complications were being rapidly generated, and Bowie was ready to respond. Under the circumstances, he had the right mind, the right drive and determination, and the ability to transform societal and cultural turbulence into art and entertainment. Bowie was blessed, if that's the right word, with a vast, early source of sounds, songs, images, traumas and experiences that produced a distinctive aesthetic and worldview. He found himself in the middle of an explosion of energies, good and bad, that created the sixties.

He was also exactly where he needed to be as fan and performer during the rise and fall of the record – the vinyl album and the vinyl single which gave him a canvas to work on. Art students weaned on Dada, surrealism, abstract expressionism and minimalism were increasingly likely to use music as their medium, and modern artists were using performance, film, parody, dance, conceptual events and commercial advertising as coordinates in their work.

The brand new, post-war formats and methods of transmitting songs and images were all but gone as viable creative vessels by the time he died. Peak vinyl activity was during the 1970s, as the sophistication of the recording studio exponentially progressed, and this was Bowie's peak period as pop star, moving faster than any of his peers by continuing to listen to the music of the day, keep up with it, even ahead of it.

When the vinyl age began to come to an end in the early 1980s, and the compact disc slowly replaced the record album, and the seven-inch single as an object began to gradually disappear, he lost his way a little – there were still songs and there were still 'albums', but the pressure was on for him now to be trapped inside the hits and costumes of the 1970s, and trail off into endless elder statesman nostalgia – the end of risk, singing the same old songs, draining them of meaning and vitality.

DRUM AND DANCE

Ready for the hyper visual MTV era he helped shape, Bowie had his biggest hit single in 1983 with 'Let's Dance', from his biggest selling album with the same, let's-get-down-to-basics title.

It was ingeniously produced by Nile Rodgers of swinging disco maestros Chic in the exact image of a sublime international pop hit called 'Let's Dance' by a bronzed, parading golden-haired millionaire David Bowie. Initially, Rodgers was alarmed by the idea he was expected to produce a track called 'Let's Dance', which seemed a little unsubtle, even a little corny coming from a prime mover behind Chic, but he soon got into the meta-swing of Bowie's world and its unusual processes, which included taking a cliché and turning it on its head.

Bowie – on the other side of 'Berlin' and now acknowledged as a kind of wizened, ancient master, the imperial influencer, though still in shock after the 1980 assassination of his friend John Lennon – was in the mood to try something different. He still wanted to confound people, which, oddly enough, meant actually selling records like the international superstar he had become, whilst still, in the eyes of the rapacious music industry, selling like a cult, their worst four-letter word for someone who also expected luxury budgets for his 'experiments', which occasionally meant even not singing.

Before he danced with Nile, he had something to get out of his system. He had fallen out with, and away, from the label that he was with throughout the seventies, RCA. They had not liked his recent albums, especially hating his gleefully devious and offensive 1980 single 'Alabama Song', a cover of the debauched Brecht/Weill song made famous by the Doors, each verse ending with the same message of impending death.

It was perhaps the most uncommercial record RCA had ever released, apart from Lou Reed's brain-splitting four sides of nasty resentful noise, *Metal Machine Music*.

Bowie's one final gift for RCA made even 'Alabama Song' and *Low* seem glossy. The last record Bowie would release on the label was a five-track EP on which he performed songs he originally sang in a 1982 BBC TV production of *Baal*, Bertolt Brecht's earliest full-length play written in 1918 when he was twenty. The story explored the effects of a tormented genius/artist and cursed, amoral poet living outside a society that would eventually destroy him.

Bowie got the part after the director Alan Clarke saw him inhabit the Elephant Man on Broadway. The Elephant Man made Bowie realise how much he liked playing 'characters with a mental limp', and the chance to play Baal, a conniving, drunken monster and an incorrigible, lazy charmer, was an irresistible way of finishing the Berlin period – and his time at RCA – with an immaculately conceived, satisfying oblique encore dedicated to jarring audiences from the comfort of a fantasy world.

In some ways, the Berlin Trilogy had become a tetralogy, except that RCA marketed it as though they had been handed a snappy, stinking stray dog, and the record was allowed to slink off into the margins of Bowie's discography.

He could have proudly presented it to RCA with a little note, explaining that when something seems the most obvious thing in the world, it means any attempt to understand the world has been given up. Alienation is necessary to all understanding! Something artificial is needed to represent reality! Ironically, Baal is always hell-bent on destroying relationships with the people he knows.

Baal saw Bowie at his most unwashed and withered, just the right side of crude, an arrogant, self-conscious and nihilistic poet wearing unglam braces, plucking a dirty, rattling banjo and relishing more contact with Bertolt Brecht, who knew exactly how to make a work of art that would help an artist, a performer, enter the world anew.

The record was made as a sly, pointed way to release himself from his RCA contract, as he owed them one more piece of product, but he also made sure it reeked of formidable Brechtian style and confrontation, Brecht and Weill's own reputation given a careening, modern sonic elevation, and Bowie making damned sure he sang the songs as well as he had ever sung anything.

He recorded it in Berlin at the Hansa Studios – by the Wall – with Tony Visconti who fastidiously rounded up a small orchestra, some of whom not only knew how to authentically recreate the tattered, teetering, supremely addictive 1930s Weimar sound but had played in original 1930s productions of Brecht and Weill musicals.

Bowie hated RCA so much he gave them a set of anti-pop songs about an abusive, anti-establishment character with intense, animalistic energy backed by frightening, raucous sounding music, but with supreme, fantastically persuasive vocals tantalisingly reminding the label of his glory days. The starman voice lingered, but any pop star personality had, it seemed, totally and deliberately disintegrated.

RCA wished he would reprise the 'jauntier' Philly song and dance routines – we weren't recognising each other's qualities, Bowie drily admitted, not used to a record company trying to influence his musical direction.

He was also free of his glam-rock-era manager Tony Defries's hold over his finances. He had a new record deal with EMI Manhattan, Bowie retaining ownership of his records, which brought in a rush of welcome enthusiasm and more of a sense from the label that he could be trusted. Trusted with being David Bowie.

Once he was free of being told what to do, he did, naturally, what RCA had been in their abrasive, impatient way encouraging him to do – agreeing, in his own way, that all the experimenting was actually eradicating the content. He got out his dancing shoes.

While on holiday in the South Pacific, walking a beach with blue water and blue sky and white sand, the music he was listening to tended towards R&B and blues, from James Brown to Albert King, very much music about pleasure rather than pain, music filled with enthusiasm and optimism. Why had he chosen this music to listen to and what would happen if he took another approach to the American rhythm and blues and funk that led to *Young Americans* and then to the diseased soul music of *Station to Station*? What would happen if David Bowie had Chic, or near offer, as his backing band and drew from soul its positive, transformative power less abstractly?

At the time, suffering from the prejudice that had built up from the white rock world because of the perceived trivialities of disco – introduced in the first place as white rockers, and sundry novelty acts, chased fashion and went disco – Rodgers was also looking for a new start.

Bowie, a fan of the Chic and Sister Sledge songs, met Rodgers in New York and already knew that he was more than just a disco guy, and that anyway his disco was a sophisticated distillation of jazz, blues and pop. He envisaged a kind of sequel to *Young Americans*, this time more explicitly about how a certain European music sensibility was influenced by the blues. It would mean losing Carlos for the record, as having Rodgers meant there was no place for Alomar to work.

Bowie the blues connoisseur heard another great guitar stylist at the Montreux Jazz Festival in 1982, the then little-known ferocious Texan Stevie Ray Vaughan of blues rock group Double Trouble, who, Bowie said, seemed to consider Jimmy Page a modernist but knew why Hendrix was a blues player. Vaughan had the hard-edged, uncompromising blues flow and incredible timing Bowie wanted for his new sound, which needed some voodoo as well as the gloss. Vaughan got it, especially on the title track of 'Let's Dance'. There was nothing cute about it at all – old fashioned but not old.

Alomar was back as band leader for the grand Serious Moonlight Tour supporting 'Let's Dance' – still getting his album fee – but Stevie Ray never made it, because he and Carlos were completely incompatible, or because Carlos decided his sound wasn't right – old fashioned *and* old – playing some of the most loved 1970s Bowie songs. For 'Let's Dance', he was as perfect as Fripp had been for the trilogy and *Scary Monsters (and Super Creeps)*.

When Rodgers heard Bowie's sparse acoustic demo of 'Let's Dance', it sounded to him like a folk song. By the time it had passed through the shrewd, populist and optimistic mentality of someone who knew how to make music fit into the commercial world, and the desperation of Stevie Ray Vaughan, playing guitar for a reason, spilling his own secrets, it might not have sounded like art – Bowie's surrealist instincts were a little muted and there was a certain amount of applied business theory – but it sounded *historical*.

The drum sound – which was art – was historical on its own, elevated using pioneering effects and delay. For those who are counting, it was the classic 1980s gated snare reverb that Visconti had previewed through the altered drums on *The Idiot* and *Low* taken further, as studio engineers and technicians searched for better ways to capture the sound of the snare drum as it was hit. They were looking for emphatic new methods of organising the snare drum so it could compete with the electronic drum machines marching their way into the mainstream. The 'Let's Dance' drum was as seductively clean and alien-sounding as a drum machine but with more human contact and force, a mix of precision and poetry.

Bowie had to some extent regretted the 'depressive' *Low* drum sound, which then became fashionable and over-used. For 'Let's Dance', there was a different, harder clap – which he then had to suffer hearing again and again as that also became the 1980s fashion. The new drum punch initially helped the record match the picture Bowie had shown Rodgers when he was explaining what he wanted his new record to sound like – Little Richard getting into a red Cadillac that looked like a spaceship.

If Bowie was now crowded out by those inspired by him, those that imitated him, and a whole new breed of rivals and competitors, if the avant-garde sounds and progressive beats were coming out of New York and Chicago scenes mixing funk and Kraftwerk like he once tried, this cut through the noise and interference. He could still stand out, and knew how to play himself owning this new sound in the video.

And where on, say, *Station to Station* or *Low* and *Heroes*, it might take a few minutes of a song for Bowie to turn up and start singing – if at all, which caused the rolling eyes at RCA – Rodgers used a producer's trick from his hit-making years with Chic and Sister Sledge, a trick that came from understanding how people listened to music on juke boxes, looking for a quick fix, easily bored and without necessarily the commitment Bowie tended to expect from his audience. As a Black artist, it was difficult to get radio play on the kind of stations that would carry their music to a wider, white audience. In response, he would cut to the chase and always start his songs with the chorus – aaah, freak out, we are family – so a DJ and an audience were grabbed before they had time to work out if the song was 'Black' – funk, soul, disco, something that might usually trouble them and, so they said, their audience. It was pop music, it was a story, it was a moment that sucked you in and you stuck around for more of those moments.

This was as revelatory to Bowie as Eno encouraging him to not sing – it was the exact opposite and he was happy to still be himself on both sides of the argument. Bowie would always marvel that Rodgers was the only man who could make him start a song with a chorus.

Rodgers also brought with him the innovative mixing engineer he had used on the impeccable Chic and Sister Sledge records, Bob Clearmountain, who had also mixed recent records by Roxy Music, Chic's abstract mentors, Bruce Springsteen and the Rolling Stones. Rodgers and Clearmountain's combined mastery and speed, and Bowie's fast, precise, one-take singing, recorded by Clearmountain – also responsible for the alchemic drum sound and the American bigness of the overall sound – meant the album was completed in 17 days. It was done, and shined, before Bowie could second-guess this hi-tech, compact, deliriously commercial big band sound, which in the end was what he asked for.

The consequences were Bowie's biggest hit single, 'Let's Dance', a number one in the UK and America, and the album his first platinum seller. Before he knew it, his new, more calculated, scrubbed up rendition of 'the pop star' had sent him into an international Space Race with the likes of Michael Jackson, though not necessarily one he wanted to take part in. A year later, Nile Rodgers would be producing Madonna's breakthrough album *Like A Virgin*. Bowie was still opening doors, still influencing pop's direction, sometimes without setting out to do so.

SUIT AND TIE

Bowie wanted to step gracefully out of his 1970s personas, provocations and reinventions, determined to come down to earth and live the dream. Though in doing so, he apparently violated some of his own rules of engagement.

As he navigated the 1980s, he left behind the slippery, shape-shifting characters in the 1970s, and gradually revealed a charming, easy-going star personality, with palatable residues of enigma and mystique and a light coating of pop idol craziness. This was his '80s Bowie character, above the rest even as he had to compete. After a final flourish of costume and explicitly symbolic presentation with the Pierrot of 'Ashes to Ashes', having passed on the dressing-up baton to his slavish godchildren, the New Romantics, and their MTV nurtured descendants, leading all the way to the everyday, everywhere pop stars of the mid-2020s, his preferred choice of public and stage costume was in the guise of no costume at all. He adopted the gentleman's suit, what he called his 'armour'.

With occasional detours into the casual, smart casual and near-weird casual, the suit would be his choice for the rest of his life. He wasn't so much sentimentally returning to a sixties mod style, consciously inverting values associated smart dress, as following the neutral, natural style decision of one of his writing heroes William Burroughs, with his own particular, inscrutable public presence. It was still a costume, still making a statement about status and social position. The well-chosen suit and tie put you somewhere between discreet and available for consultation. It didn't need to be an expensive suit; it simply needed to fit well.

William Burroughs had taught him that the public treat you differently if you wore a suit. Your creative language might be radical or even disturbing, but if you wear a suit, you seem reasonable, and if you're up to no good, it's ultimately in the service of pretending you are helping people in some way. If you wore a suit, in the middle of all the trends and fashions, some of which you set off, you were hard to place.

DOWN AND OUT

Let's Dance seemed to set him up perfectly for a period as a revered but irrelevant elder statesman, heading off on regular tours, cashing in on what he had achieved – performing shows featuring numerous costume changes and a revived array of the old familiar characters, wiping out what he would do next if he was independent of normal expectations.

As if confused by the success, or deliberately continuing the commercial line of attack, the downward spiral all pop stars must endure as originality drifts into the average, he seemed to lose his timing, his strategic shrewdness. It led to a run of albums, *Tonight* and *Never Let Me Down,* that were amongst his least favourites, despite him still being inside them, occasionally as astonishing, as exquisitely self-conscious, as ever. It was as though the conceptual drive was mid-range commercialism, or distracted genius, where being David Bowie was getting in the way of being himself.

By the late 1980s, Bowie was seen as a former pop idol, a shipwrecked star and, most of all, perhaps worst of all, an ageing rock star expected to stick to rigid retrospectively minded patterns. Replacements for his position as Britain's favourite pop singer, like George Michael, of all commercially minded, hit-making people, were commenting that 'Let's Dance' had signalled the beginning of the end of the David Bowie we all knew.

The general view was that he'd seen better days and it wouldn't get any better in a world where the new kept coming, meaning that what was once new was quickly old, which contradicted the essential, forward-looking spirit of pop. At the time, as he headed towards his forties, 30 seemed old for any relevant pop and rock musician, and 40 a kind of madness. But

Bowie wasn't really a pop or rock musician. He played at being one, made some of it part of what he did, but mostly got that out of his system, even at the risk of losing fans and critics.

Some people are good at repeating themselves and giving people exactly what they want, wrapped up in a showbusiness bow to satisfy the audience's needs. He just happened to not be one of them. He found it stressful writing for an audience. It's foolish to just try to be popular, he would say. He'd learnt that with 'Space Oddity' and in the years after, when it seemed he couldn't follow it with another hit, that it gives you short-lived satisfaction.

After the smart, commercial hits co-designed with Nile Rodgers, with occasional intuitive interference from the off-beat poetry of Iggy Pop, he became more conscious of the audience – now one that didn't seem to be the kind that might follow him from place to place and concept to concept as the fans in the 1970s did. Those fans had moved in five years from the transformative highs of *Ziggy Stardust* and *Aladdin Sane* to the nervy, knowing lows of *Low* via the traumas of *Diamond Dogs*, the Americanised hype-funk of *Young Americans* and the desolate, dissociative post-funk of *Station to Station*, where he seemed so low. They were deep, driven fans; they were drawn to the shifting visions and stylistic distortions. They went along even when their favourite singer didn't sing. But those who bought *Let's Dance* and singles from the album were casual fans, shoppers, passing through, with no real attachment to Bowie. The music was just another product on the shelf.

In the post *Let's Dance* period, falling into a different kind of wilderness from ten years before, he was no longer finding it uncomfortable to call himself an actor, an entertainer without an overriding need to have something to say. It was temporary; the avant-garde was his favourite home, even as he took with him the entertainment, the need for attention,

He avoided having to continue going through the motions and losing his direction by forming a band, Tin Machine, one way of clearing his head, of starting again and shedding narratives that uncomfortably clung to him. He deliberately returned to what he called the embryonic fundamentals of rock, back to ground zero, before setting out on new travels. He returned to his dream of the gang of his teenage years that revolved around the music but was also about the friendship, the community he built around him.

He needed to breathe life back into his music. He was looking for a way out after becoming the compliant, mainstream rock star he had always avoided becoming in the seventies. Back then, he'd escaped the pull of fame, either through indulging in the rock-star excesses that began as theatre, as a controlled experiment, or trying something incongruous to prevent his music from becoming a formula. He'd developed strategies for absorbing new sensations and searching for himself in others.

His Phil Collins period, he called it. (Collins was besotted with the gated snare drum.) The success of 'Let's Dance' took him by surprise – he never realised he would have that kind of popularity and he didn't know what to do with it. He was playing stadiums and it was heady but kind of scary. How could he follow it up? He tried to meet the audiences' expectations, to be engaging, even cuddly and uncomplicatedly bright, but it felt artistically and emotionally unsatisfying. He was not the only one to have blundered, he noted. There were two or three others, not to name names. Apart from Phil Collins.

TENSION AND ATTENTION

As an artist, he wasn't here to please others, only to please himself. If a byproduct of pleasing himself was pleasing others, then he was right all along to only be concerned with pleasing himself.

At the end of the 1980s, he deliberately avoided his glittery Starman and Stardust hits, and his other fondly remembered travels, perversely escaping what on the surface seemed a safe space but for him was a dangerous place to be. Or vice versa. He went to war with his more sentimental audience and to some extent himself. He didn't want to be completely defined by his past. The work he did had to be new for him again and again, so that it was always an adventure.

In 1990, making a pact with his audience, or breaking a pact, for his Sound + Vision tour – another dutiful, money raising venture after his difficult, disappointing eighties – he decided to ask his fans around the world to vote for their favourite songs of his they wanted him to play, possibly for the last time.

It was rooted in an idea he'd had when high on the experiments around his 'Berlin' period, when he imagined fans collaborating each night on the tracks he would play live, what they would be, and the order they were played, every night a surprise for audience and band.

Nothing came of that, but as he aged increasingly feeling the pressure to simply play his most crowd pleasing hits, he handed the responsibility over to his fans, and let them make the decision, as if it put himself at a distance from having to simply go through the motions. There was some play involved, which kept him engaged.

He could treat it as an artistic exercise. The process made the whole reality of being expected to stick to his greatest hits a little more interesting – who would vote for what song in what country?

He wasn't interested so much in the obvious songs that would be chosen – those were to be expected. He worked out maybe the obvious fifteen or so: 'Life on Mars', 'Changes', 'Fame', Let's Dance', 'Starman', 'Heroes', 'Fashion', 'Rock 'n' roll Suicide', 'Drive in Saturday', 'Space Oddity', 'Golden Years', 'Ashes to Ashes', 'Modern Love,' 'Heroes', 'Suffragette City', 'Rebel Rebel'.

He was intrigued more about what the next layer would consist of; the not-so-obvious ones – 'Time', perhaps, 'The Secret Life of Arabia', 'Be My Wife', 'Stay', 'Speed of Life', 'Repetition', 'TVC15', 'Wild is the Wind', 'Subterraneans', 'Memory of a Free Festival'?

And what was beyond that? Whatever was beyond, the roads rarely travelled, the open spaces, that was where he wanted to go next, making music that for him had a more mysterious hold over his inner life.

His past was part of who he was but most of what he was consisted of always becoming himself. For him, the past was work done, like parts an actor had played. You couldn't take an old role into a new film or play. You had to leave them behind, so they didn't interfere with where you found yourself later. You'd glance back, try different arrangements of certain songs, put them in a different context, but you wouldn't drag them with you, weighing you down. In the end, he was never hung up on keeping an audience. To truly satisfy an audience meant never doing anything with an audience in mind.

New songs, new art, new theatre, new collaborations, the transitions in between, the dialectic between order and disorder, were always the rivers that took him to where he wanted to go.

Once he got the eighties out of the way, he had other ideas about what a lifetime of comebacks, of new reveals, would look and sound like, whilst still seeing into the future – towards the end of an era, potentially the end of everything, and the beginning of something else altogether, where there were always more mysteries to solve and shadow selves to find. He was always in the midst of being formed. He understood that his prodigious energy to create and his potential for originality were inseparable from the unresolved and likely unresolvable unconscious turmoil that dogged him.

Eventually, as if the way forward was to retrace steps, he would find himself back with Nile Rodgers, not so much making a 'Let's Dance 2' with *Black Tie White Noise* but correcting something that had been nagging at him, remaking it with more of himself. His collaboration with Rodgers was this time a coupling of the alienated avant-garde Renaissance man and the immaculate, supersonic hit man, and he bent and warped it more in his direction.

He would find himself back with Brian Eno, touching base again with process and concept, with potential trilogies and cryptic quests, ready for the final few years, ending with art not entertainment, but art that recognised the artistic qualities of some entertainment. He didn't claim to be the trailblazer, he didn't claim to be where you'd look for the now, the moment, but on the other hand, he was extending his range and still imagining a future, which was now a sighting of a future where he was no longer here, at least, not in person.

He would find himself back, stirring up personal dust, indulging in a little light nostalgia, putting together powerful bands, wildly, wonderfully contradictory, controlling his mythology, losing his way, groping for self-understanding, finding his sense of humour, still alert to changes happening around him, metabolising everything he knew about art and form into his new albums, the avant-nostalgic *Buddha of Suburbia* soundtrack, *Outside*, *Earthling* – the transgressive sixties Newley fan transformed into an enthralled nineties Nine Inch Nails admirer – *Heathen* and *Hours*. The latter, in 1999, another one of his occasional trippy 'debuts', as if re-imagining a first album was where he corrected some thoughts and remade his mind. It was his assured, unflustered way of leaving the fancy, ferocious twentieth century he so ingeniously plundered.

He realised that thoughts and ideas don't age even as the body does; the mind and body get older but not necessarily at the same speed. In his case, unless the mind was playing tricks, his consciousness stayed young.

A question is asked, and he has the answer. He's 50 years old and it's the middle of the 1990s.

He always knew what to say, and he more or less said:

It's good to keep asking questions. Finding the answers, if they exist, is less good. Thinking there are answers is probably the road to madness, and I can see a stretch of that behind me and I now know I don't need to run down it so fast anymore. The idea that everything will remain unclear until the very, very end is very beautiful, and actually quite comforting.

IMAN AND DAVID

As the 1980s turned into the 1990s, and Bowie turned to the comradeship of being in Tin Machine, seeking a way out of feeling he was adrift from the collaborative energies he'd enjoyed with Visconti, Eno and the DAM Trio, he was also lacking steadiness in his private life.

The demons weren't as extreme as they had been but they still lurked. He was still drinking and was nowhere near what his parents' generation might have called 'settling down'. In some ways, he felt like an endangered species and there was no guidance that he could find, in all those books he read about art and artists, thinking and dreaming, regarding what to do and be next.

He was introduced to Iman, a model fluent in five languages, by a mutual friend, the hairdresser Teddy Antolin, who asked him over to LA for a dinner party to celebrate his birthday, also inviting Iman. The friend felt the pair made sense when Bowie turned up to the party dressed in all white driving a white Mustang, and Iman also arrived wearing all white. Both seem to float above the air like mysterious beings. Bowie looked into her eyes and felt a new kind of calmness. A calmness he'd never experienced anywhere before, let alone in the sprawling abyss of Los Angeles.

They talked all night – it sounded like they swore and laughed all night, as bawdy, fascinating and chatty as each other. He was worried she might find him a bit bonkers, which he was liable to become, especially when he was excited. She didn't turn a hair. Maybe this time, love wasn't going to be so much trouble.

Together, they looked like world experts in how to have a good time. They'd found each other at the right time in terms of where they were with their lives and with their work, and their own mysteries. He felt like he had known her for aeons.

Within months they were engaged, following a proposal, backed by a love-smitten song, 'April in Paris', on the River Seine. By 1992 they had been married twice – the first time in April, in Lausanne, Switzerland, where Bowie then lived. This was a modest, relatively secret registry with two witnesses in the humble local civic centre, Bowie sweeping Iman off her feet when it was over. He was thinking in that moment: this is the cleverest thing I have ever done.

The second time was in June. This was the society wedding, in Florence, the city where they had spent their first summer holiday together. It was one of Bowie's favourite places, where the Italian Renaissance began, an optimistic hub of humanist scholarship and the artistic, the bridge between the medieval and modern ages, elevating the importance of the free-thinking, inquisitive individual and secularism to the level of the wealthy and the church. This was a time when Europe was evolving from a collection of medieval feudal states into concentrated town centres and cities, filled with palaces and villas, creating a new demand amongst the newly wealthy for unique furniture, ceramic bowls and domestic and consequently secular art.

The newly wealthy, as well as the usual church patrons, started to become supporters of the arts as classical and literary Greek and Roman ideals, the solid foundation of civilisation, mingled with new ways of seeing and interpreting the universe along with new forms of architectural space.

A significant turning point was pioneering sculptor and Renaissance cofounder Donatello's intimate, costly mid-fifteenth-century bronze statue of a youthful, beautiful and androgynous looking David, radically separating sculpture from architecture, giving sculpture its own space. Donatello's David is shown with an enigmatic, knowing smile, a relaxed, contemplative pose and performative hat and boots. The legendary Old Testament biblical king is represented almost as an idealised and highly stylised teenage sex symbol, captured having just heroically slayed the giant, bearded Goliath with nothing but a sling shot, liberating his people, the Israelites, from the tyranny of the Philistines. He stands almost languidly with his foot resting on Goliath's severed head, symbolising how heroes can emerge in the unlikeliest circumstances. Willpower – or the grace of God – and seductive wiles and cleverness can triumph over physical strength.

The shepherd's hat in particular was a then modern novelty, a humble item on a figure traditionally represented as a king, which makes it seem contemporary to this day, drawing attention to David's provocative nakedness, with the laurel leaves of victory on top suggesting David as a poet or musician.

Look into his eyes. There's something going on. Some suggest that one eye is open and the other almost closed, representing the mind's ability to perceive both the external world and internal insight.

It is the first known unsupported standing nude statue produced for over a thousand years, so it could be seen from all directions. Viewed from behind, it was difficult to see what gender or sex the figure was.

Sixty years later, Michaelangelo's more famous, muscular and monumental 17-foot marble David is a kind of prequel to Donatello's, even as it absorbs some of his style. His David is represented before the battle, nervous and tense, but confident and hopeful, rather than relaxed and triumphant. His pupils are mysteriously heart shaped, creating shadow, carrying the weight of the future, years before the heart shape was a symbol of love. There is a slight squint when viewed from some metres below, but once the sculpture is on a plinth, the eyes look correctly proportioned.

Placed in front of the city's government building, it came to symbolise the strength, independence and civil liberties of Florence, and its defiance in resisting the power of surrounding states, the Florentines identifying with David's underdog spirit.

Bowie saw his roots in the innovations, discoveries and stylistic transformations of the Renaissance, its belief in humanity's capacity to achieve greatness through knowledge and free will, as much as in jazz, cabaret and vaudeville, or German expressionism and surrealism, or Brecht, blues, Bromley and Burroughs – and Berlin. Renaissance Florence and Cold War Berlin were both centres of significant cultural and political change, on the edge of a new era, at the crossroad of historical forces.

It was no surprise his marriage to Iman took place in the city of Davids, where Donatello's David had announced the rebirth of humanism.

The ceremony was held in the St James Episcopal Church, with circling helicopters, siren-whining police escorts and a thousand bystanders, but still for close friends and family only, including his mother, Margaret Jones, and son Joe, just turned 21, soon to use the name Duncan Jones, as best man

This ceremonial sealing of the marriage generated a little more attention than the official Lausanne service. For one, it was featured in *Hello!* magazine, then the popular home of awed, superficial celebrity mania. The piece now looks very quaint and restrained compared to the social media fuss such an event would have created 30 years later. There is a brief interview with the couple, dealing professionally with having just multiplied their fame wattage, as if this soft interview and pages of neutral, happy wedding photographs might help promote future protection from intruding media tentacles.

In the interview, Bowie said he saw no problems at all that they were of different religions. He wasn't a religious person. Neither was Iman. He was a spiritual person. He had his own relationship with God. Iman as well. Hervé Leger designed her dress. Thierry Mugler designed Bowie's suit. No frills, no gimmicks.

There was also no 'Here Comes the Bride', which they both loathed, so Iman walked down the aisle to 'Evening Gathering', an exquisite Bulgarian folk song sung by a Bulgarian female folk choir, Le Mystère des Voix Bulgares. Bowie wrote music for the rest of the service – tender, cossetted dream music, lush music, a little piece of enchantment, with exaggerated decorum and his own saxophone playing, the sound of someone feeling on the cusp of a new, promising life.

OLD AND NEW

Not long into his marriage, having broken up the ultimate politeness of the Tin Machine band, tipped into action by returning from holiday to Los Angeles airport and driving through the aftermath of the 1992 LA riots, he made his first solo album since 1987 and all that self-doubt. *Black Tie White Noise* is a collection of wedding songs and commentaries on the idea of partnerships, collaborators and various aesthetic and personnel mergers, creating conflicts, frictions and difficulties to see what he had inside him, what he had to say.

One thing he had to say was the unabashed confession in 'Wedding Song' – the wedding music that he wrote for Iman, the opening piece on the record, with added words – that he was going to change his ways, he was going to be a good boy.

The album begins and ends with wedding bells, and Bowie doesn't give a damn who thinks that might be corny, in the same way he doesn't give a damn whether the album sounds fashionable or fully understands the fashions of the time. It didn't matter whether he was behind or ahead of the times. For him, it exists in its own zone of self-discovery, pursuing for him what felt the right combinations of past, present and future.

From now on, Bowie will make music by laying out his own stepping stones. His voice is everywhere, protean and amalgam, but he'll follow his own instincts, to an extent withholding his identity whilst leaping over it into otherness, even if it means competing with himself and the timelessness of his past.

The partnerships and interactions on *Black Tie White Noise* included reacquainting himself with the saxophone, returning to instrumentals, to the covers of *Pin Ups*, and processing the gruelling death of his half-brother Terry, who had died eight years before, reaching the sputtering depths of his mania. The album is a fundamental, unorthodox celebration of collaboration, a way of remembering how it was before Tin Machine, when he formed ensembles and studio communities from album to album, from an array of musical and studio regulars and new guests. Sometimes, it's not about the project, it's about the people.

It was as though he was learning to work again, learning how to innovate, flying solo with company, with what were effectively a bunch of roommates, a social circle, skewed male, with him at the centre, but also sometimes moving from the centre, looking in, watching himself. He had decided he was at his best when he enlarged his mind to take in the positions and experiences of others, and this attitude rushes into *Black Tie White Noise*.

There's an appearance by his Spiders from Mars guitarist Mick Ronson, who would die the month the album was released, with Mike Garson, whose piano on *Aladdin Sane*, all its concentrated excitement, was still ringing down the years and echoing back and forwards. There's the reunion with his *Let's Dance* producer, Nile Rodgers, and abstract collaborations with Scott Walker (a Camus-quoting mentor, on a searing, grateful cover of 'Nite Flights'), with Morrissey (protégé, on a fastidiously overblown cover of 'I Know It's Going to Happen') and with Madonna (copyist, using Rodgers, Madonna collaborator, to reference her subversion of sexuality, race and gender, the evolution of her identity as she pulls herself apart and puts herself together again). House music, which had emerged from Kraftwerk, collides with Black underground club music – a fervid, inverted hybrid of the European canon and American groove Bowie had foreseen, and therefore a new angle on the traditional, troubled alliance between Black and white music.

The record even contains a loose partnership with a musician who 'shares' his name, the avant-fusion jazz trumpeter

Lester Bowie, co-founder of the politically and socially active Art Ensemble of Chicago. He was invited 10 per cent because of the name but 90 per cent because of his consistently daring style, because he grew up in the forties, when jazz was supreme and its traditions were leading to innovations, and Louis Armstrong was king. In the sixties, when rhythm and blues was flowing, Lester was playing with Albert King, Rufus Thomas, Jackie Wilson and Gene Chandler. His own music was full of funk and humour, poetry and personality. Bowie wanted to plug into that.

In interviews, Bowie wanted to make it clear the album was a response to his deep disappointment with the slow, painful walk in America towards any kind of real equality between Black and white. Any forward progress was almost at a standstill after four officers in the Los Angeles Police Department were acquitted after being caught on camera using excessive force in the arrest and vicious, 15-minute beating of activist Rodney King, while other cops stood by watching. King's injuries led to permanent brain damage. The police action was defended as a 'reasonable expression of police control toward a black motorist'. It led to six days of riots and unrest, 63 deaths, 7,000 arrests and an estimated $1 billion of damage, and a distrust between the police as an ideologically motivated controlling force and Black Americans that would only get worse.

Bowie was as stunned as anyone. During the great civil rights marches of the sixties, it seemed things would change, but it became evident over the next decades that white America would only accept equality if Black assimilated into white sameness, which soured the civil rights movement.

The Black and Hispanic communities were continually repressed and totally ignored. Bowie would say, we might edge towards a superficial equality but true integration will take an absurdly long time because there are so many forces against it. There is ultimately no great desire for it from the white world.

The album is an intimate gift for his new wife, a complex exploration of race relations and fusion music, a record about energy – creative, conceptual and cultural – and it recaptures the forward-looking energy that his 1980s engulfed. It didn't become, for the critics channelling to a wider world, a clear comeback, or a glowing relocation of cool, or a definitive new 'debut' – it couldn't quite produce the necessary, clarifying fusion of the cryptic, doubtful Berlin Bowie and the commercial, confident 'Let's Dance'. But the general view was that Bowie certainly had not run out of ideas, or forgotten that art begins with resistance and being well-organised in your individuality. And he was in love. It happens.

HOME AND AWAY

With Iman, his energy changed, he finally seemed to have come to an armistice with his deeper problems and he drew strength from her self-assurance. It was as though Iman had joined him so he could complete his work and manage a life inside his art.

If his first, free and frantic marriage to Angie was part of a conceptual transformation which took over his life, his second marriage to Iman separated homelife from the conceptual, from the drama. Whereas when Angie and Bowie were together, all doors seemed to lead in and out of their private life, 20 years later, there was now a private part of Bowie's life even beyond the private life he would disappear into before he met Iman, a refuge within a refuge – and around this private life, all doors were shut. If you ever saw inside his homes, as if this was any use to understanding or knowing him, it was only when he had moved on and they were no longer his.

He became a New Yorker, the man who lived all over the world, leaving every place. He would live there longer than anywhere else. He moved with Iman to New York in 1992, into a condominium apartment in the Art Deco Essex House on Central Park South, its original red neon sign on top of the building one of the city's great, pre-Trump touchstones, home over the years to soul singer Donny Hathaway – who would die there – Igor Stravinsky and Miles Davis.

It turned out he'd moved to New York for good – until he moved out in the most final of ways – 20 years after catching an early flight from London to New York after a Ziggy show and arriving at Madison Square Garden ten minutes after his birthday buddy Elvis Presley had started his show. He made his way more or less clad like Ziggy as Elvis roared through

'Proud Mary' to his very exposed free seat, supplied by RCA, the label they shared, for a show that only had another 40 minutes to go. For decades, America would still think of Bowie as this red-headed, weird interloper tottering down the aisle in his Space Age platform shoes.

On the first visits to New York, in his early twenties, starting in 1971, later accompanied by Angie and Tony Defries, late to the place he loved from afar at a time when it still seemed impossible to actually get to, he would make good use of the city that famously never slept, getting to bed at four or five in the morning. It was the beginning of the limo era, of acting like a star before he was a star, years spent navigating the haze and offering himself up for anyone to read a million things into.

By the time he started living there with Iman, the man who slept until midday had become an early riser, a blended-in local citizen, living the life after long-term addiction, making good use of the city as an urban walker's paradise. He loved getting out early and watching the city change shape in front of him as people poured in and out of buildings. After decades wandering the land of placelessness in a damaged goods costume, he'd found the space to settle down, especially necessary after his heart attack in 2004.

His hair natural, stripped of his make-up, of his representations of otherness and outsiderness, with no attention-grabbing entourage, Bowie could easily pass for no one in particular doing nothing much with his time. He could pass for David Jones if you only knew what he looked like.

The whole world could seem within a few minutes of his home from 1999 in SoHo, whether through the cultural history – 'emotional history' he called it – contained in Washington Park, the sights and sounds of any random ramble through the East Village, the books contained in the Strand bookshop – which had its own mysterious way of leading you to a book you had never heard of or thought you wanted but which would become another irreplaceable volume of ideas. Psychology, plays, science, philosophy, he'd take it all.

He could go to museums and movies in the middle of the day, and it seemed OK to do that in New York, where there were masterpieces everywhere. Glance at the Rothkos in MOMA, move on, check in at the Guggenheim, then a few minutes at the Met, strolling through the objects in the *Art and Love in Renaissance Italy* exhibition.

He'd slip into a diner on the way to an improvised art space in the Meat District, on the way to some fringe theatre, places he never knew existed until he came across them, never knowing if they still existed once he left them.

He'd be at some jazz club after midnight, watching Herbie Hancock play something deep with a melancholy tone, thinking something is missing, and then realise, there was no smoke in the club. It was too clear, to clean, too real for jazz. He stepped out into the night onto the naked sidewalk, still crooning something Hancock had played.

He was at home amidst all the delirious New York architecture, inside and out. Spiritual-seeming buildings, utopian fragments, classical landmarks, glimpses of an old New York; the sulphurous light against the pale towers and anomalous phenomena impressed their own stories upon the story of the city.

Only a few would notice he walked amongst them, tossing him a cheeky 'Oy, Bowie!' or a furtive glance, losing sight of him before it fully dawned on them who that had been. Or they might find themselves in a queue in front of their hero in a café – but what can you say to him? Where do you begin and what will he say to you, other than a quick quip, a smile that you swear was a little shy, but on the other hand filled with the mystery of the man who knew the effect he had on people. Look into his eyes and then look away quickly, as if they might turn you to jelly if not stone.

Millions who lived, worked and visited never caught a sight, not even those who knew him and lived only a few blocks away. He'd adopted a persona that blended into human society, always in rhythm, knowing all the shortcuts, going to work himself, always working on himself.

RETREAT AND REMAKE

In 2003, Iman and Bowie, now with their daughter Lexi, born in 2000, completing a family unit, followed by the inevitable, keeping-the-crowd-at-bay *Hello!* spread, found a 64-acre plot of land they couldn't resist in the Catskill Mountains in Ulster County along the Hudson River, not far from Woodstock in upstate New York, a hundred miles north of the city.

When he was younger, he found Woodstock 'too cute for words', congested with artists, musicians and twee-seeming artists colonies, stuck in time with its associations with the 1969 festival. 'All those old hippies,' he laughed when his bass player Gail Ann Dorsey told him where she lived. 'Why are you living with them?!'

She led him there, as well as becoming his final bass player in some of his most dynamic ensembles, inheriting some of the importance of Ronson, Alomar, Fripp and Eno. She stayed with him for two decades, having joined him in 1995, after he saw her play on television with a forceful, soulful power that was definitely not hippy and definitely city glamorous.

As his life and circumstances changed, Bowie slowly fell for Woodstock's discreet charms, especially after recording part of *Heathen* at Allaire Studios in the Shokan hamlet up in the mountains, where you felt apart from America, and dreams and thoughts and writing and reading books would come easily. *Heathen* was his post-Lexi album, deeply anxious about an aggressive, collapsing world, a fraught, unnerving and inward-looking America, a godless century he had just brought a child into. It is an album made in peace, looking for how and where peace might survive in the future.

After his 2004 heart attack, he would often visit the area, taking Lexi into local bookshops, a regular dad buying books for his daughter with his David Jones credit card. Using the Jones name had become a disguise and his final character. The person who had always been there as he played with other faces and points of view was now who he was, fading into the fabric of community life, nothing special and therefore completely special.

Released from the tight, busy Manhattan streets, decades after his limo era had ended, he would drive himself around the valley, where there were plenty of musicians he would use on *The Next Day*, including Gerry Leonard, who had a drum machine, something Bowie happened to need one day. Bowie drove in his rented car to Leonard's place, finding his way around the winding roads there better than he thought. They were soon working on new songs, a couple of which appeared on *The Next Day*.

The place Bowie found secluded in the mountains suited him more than the cutesy bohemian towns, with a wildness that seemed outside of time. The land he built his home on, recreating his late-1980s rock star, Indonesian-style villa on the Caribbean island of Mustique, was part of its own mountain, Little Tonshi, the vast windows of his new house taking in the endless views and the nearby Ashokan Reservoir.

Before he first revealed to Iman and Lexi the home he had built in the mountains, far above the world, designed to see the sunsets Bowie loved so much, on the drive there, he played them the German romantic composer, Richard Strauss. It was as though the music was a ticket that took you into a different dimension.

A final love letter to his wife, Strauss's 'Four Last Songs' were written in the late 1940s after the nightmare of Nazism was over. The Third Reich had thrown a desperate, hate-filled darkness over the world that could never be removed, with Germany itself reduced to rubble, its dying embers never fully extinguished, adding to the darkness. Atom bombs had been recently dropped on Hiroshima and Nagasaki. Musical landmarks and opera houses connected with his life's works lay in ruins. Used to retreating into music to fight pessimism, to look for joy, he initially felt helpless, overcome with grief, as though the world as he knew it was finished.

Strauss lived long enough to see one world end – was another one beginning to emerge, one that would bring back hope? His hedonistic world of musical pleasure seemed to have succumbed to the harsh, unforgiving and mostly unloved serialism of Schoenberg and the moody starkness of Hindemith. Still out of sight, just around the corner, there was rock and roll and electronic sounds and mass consumer culture. He was in a kind of limbo.

Re-reading the sublime German romantic poetry he loved as a young boy, the 84-year-old mustered up the strength to produce four orchestral songs that were given the title posthumously of *Vier letzte Lieder*, 'Four Last Songs', set to three poems by Hermann Hesse and one by Joseph von Eichendorff, named and ordered by his publisher. It was possibly not arranged or titled as Strauss intended, but it became the most gloriously serene and romantic way for a composer to complete their musical life, treating death not as something to heroically resist but to calmly accept – a natural transmigration of the soul. The songs were a farewell to pre-war life, to his kind of tonal splendour and the grand forces of the symphony, and occasional miraculous strange tones, and to nature and birdsong before mechanism and more intrusive, destabilising technology takes over.

Strauss began writing them in early 1947, about the same time Bowie was born. A fifth piece was left lingering in the air, eventually found but left outside the main four songs, leaving composers to perhaps imagine their own musical farewell, their own departure from earthly struggles and a rapidly, dangerously changing world, achingly nostalgic for their own time, their own concerns and fascinations, but with a certain confidence in eternity and immortality, in the lasting value of their music. Saying goodbye wistfully but not tragically. Not looking backwards or forwards but towards the sky, and therefore in all directions at once.

'Spring' dreams of trees, sky and birdsong. 'September' represents the poignant, final shuddering of summer and, as summer finally falls asleep, the singers hold onto the word *augen* – eyes – as if following the gentle drifting into unconsciousness and the closing of the eyes. 'When I Go to Sleep' accompanies the soul to heaven, following the transition into 'the magical circle of the night'.

In 'Im Abendrot' – evening-red – based on a poem about an old couple contemplating death together, he uses the orchestra to paint a sunset. Strauss elegantly appropriates his own tone poem 'Death and Transfiguration', that he had written nearly 60 years before, a hint of his early music answering the question 'Can this perhaps be death?' with a musical yes and no. An autobiographical requiem, the song fades away and the light dims.

(Strauss's late-nineteenth-century 'Also sprach Zarathustra' was originally subtitled 'Symphonic optimism in *fin de siècle form*, dedicated to the twentieth century' before he replaced that with a simpler nod to his direct inspiration, Nietzsche. It was a self-styled history of evolution up to Nietzsche's idea of the Übermensch, the superman. In his book *Thus Spoke Zarathustra*, in which he addressed a crisis of values and announced God was dead, Nietzsche had sent Zarathustra into the mountains to enjoy his solitude and commune with his thoughts. It was the piece of music inspired by this part of Nietzsche's book that Stanley Kubrick used to accompany his cosmic sunrise in *2001: A Space Odyssey*, as if knowing that Strauss had originally imagined it accompanying the mountaintop sunrise that opens Nietzsche's book.)

Bowie loved New York City but this treasure to the north was an extension of the city and an open, unfussy, golden place folding in on itself that became his last musical scene, his final point of contact with a musical community that helped him achieve his visions. His final thinking place, some say his final resting place.

Buddhists regard mountains as sacred sites, symbols of stability and higher perspectives, the perfect spaces for spiritual practices and meditation. At the top of a mountain, sages view life differently. Bowie had his place in the mountains, but he was still a New Yorker, embedded in the history of the city. Like his friends John Lennon and Yoko Ono, like Andy Warhol and Lou Reed, he was a New Yorker as much as he was part of the history of Berlin, where the pressure, the lament of 'Heroes' had helped bring down the Wall, sounding an advance.

In New York, you were surrounded by ghosts and the aftereffects of their adventures – those who were born there, those who came to live there, those who changed the city with their art, music, drama and writing, creating scene after scene, passing on secrets and whispers. When Bowie walked through the city – the invisible man, finding it hard to sit still, never one to take for granted this much freedom – he followed trails and routes established by legends and myths, leaving his own trails, his own presence. Residents or visitors who had died in the city, leaving behind traces and stories, an American melting pot, included: Malcolm X, Heath Ledger, Greta Garbo, Bix Beiderbecke, Leonard Bernstein, Billie Holiday, Milt Jackson, Stefan Wolpe, Allen Ginsberg, Tennessee Williams, Charlie Parker, Sid Vicious, Nancy Spungen, Lead Belly, Pete Seeger, Jim Carroll, Grant Green, Nikola Tesla, Ethel Merman, Klaus Nomi, Blossom Dearie, Lee Morgan, Jim Henson, Charles Ives, Lena Horne, Adam Goldstein, Gil Scott-Heron, Woody Guthrie, Igor Stravinsky, Ed Sullivan, Louis Armstrong, Ornette Coleman, Béla Bartók, Rudolph Valentino, Irving Berlin, Lionel Hampton, Kurt Vonnegut, Lester Young, Merce Cunningham, John Cage, Richard Rodgers, Lorenz Hart, Tito Puente, James Cagney, Arthur Russell, Joan Crawford, Frank

O'Hara, Norman Mailer, Mark Rothko, Tallulah Bankhead, Nicholas Ray, Tupac Shakur, King Curtis, Keith Haring, Jean-Michel Basquiat . . . and many more fellow travellers and soulmates, helping make New York New York, and the world The World.

Many more were in the shadows, less decorated and acknowledged, great lives reduced to ashes, but still thought plenty and brought plenty to New York, where they could easily reach the world.

The dead can't imagine us but we can imagine them.

GHOSTS AND ANGELS

The radical, deep-thinking, German post-expressionist artist Max Beckmann, who added to the Icarus mythology, took refuge in New York after the war, painting numerous works at speed between 1949 and 1950, driven by sheer need and something else he couldn't put his finger on.

Born in 1884, he had worked as a medical orderly on the Belgian front in the First World War, up close to its mind-pummelling physical and mental terrors. He was discharged after a mental breakdown, channelling the experience into his newer, harsher, more urgent paintings. By the 1920s, Beckmann was a successful artist transcending expressionism and capturing the queasy excitement and narcotic allure of the Weimar Republic.

He'd been working since the early 1900s, passionate about what he called the romance of everyday life. He was the product of a completely alien culture and time that by the 1960s and 70s seemed ancient and lost; just as by the 2020s, the 1950s and 60s seem as alien, as otherworldly, to those born in the twenty-first century.

Beckmann's themes and subjects became predominantly theatre, circus, cabaret, vaudeville and carnival, as well as masked balls, beaches and bars – wherever people tried on different personas and slipped outside themselves. He would paint himself in costumes, playing various roles from circus ringmaster and court fool to the Harlequin, with its visually fractured connection to Cubism, experimenting with the shapeshifting world of appearances, concealment and camouflage as a form of revelation, where things were unreal, but which reflected through a shattered looking glass a world of dreams and history.

His successive transformations, like Bowie's, were made to broaden his metaphysical experience, creating an objectified essence of his predicament as an artist, choosing the unsettled life of a bohemian entertainer of no fixed abode, who works wonders to earn a daily crust, struggling to draw an audience, continually having to flee a hostile city. He sings in the sun and dances under the stars without hope of being taken seriously by the Establishment, the grown-ups, who might one day find themselves outdated and outplayed.

In 1925, Beckmann met and married his second wife, an elegant Viennese violinist from a well-off family, Mathilde von Kaulbach, known as Quappi, and they became a kind of Weimar society couple. She immediately started appearing in his paintings that transformed reality into theatrical events, joining him in his *commedia dell'arte* world of wonder and alter egos, of outcasts, alienated creatures and unusual figures on the fringes of ordinary society, excluded from normal life, as fascinating off stage as on stage. In one of his carnival paintings, the title gives away his new status – 'The Artist and the Wife', painted within months of meeting her. His is a severe-faced harlequin, stoical and melancholy, poignant and pathetic, she a lonely, lovely smiling horsewoman. The costumed pair, the fantastic swindler and his enigmatic accomplice, are now joined at the hip.

As he became known internationally around 1930, the Weimar vitality and verve was beginning to crack and show early signs of a hurriedly built utopia tearing itself apart, its insolent spirit being sucked out of it, its dissidence squashed. Beckmann would talk of what he called 'political gangsterism', hoping it would soon pass, retreating in the face of it to 'an island of the soul'.

A portrait of Quappi as a quintessentially modern woman with a confident smile on her face was begun in 1932 and finished in 1934, with the smile fading into uncertainty. Beckmann then started work on a painting that combined all his loves: cabaret, vaudeville, jazz, performance and Quappi, in bright, alluring yellow, smiling and holding a banjo. He finished it three years later, when all the glamour and debauched, off-kilter night flair had ended, adding a menacing creature behind her, about to wreck the carefree joyousness and sweep all the magnificent misfits and dreamers off the stage and into the abyss.

With Hitler on the horizon, the Nazis turning from small, almost mocked party to dominant force, his painting needed to change to keep pace and not seem merely decorative, if only to satisfy his soul. His response to what he called the talentless madness of the times was to make increasingly intense, elemental work.

He was the prestigious, well-connected contemporary of other bitter, biting, post-expressionist New Objectivity social satirists like Otto Dix and Georg Scholz, conscious of their place in history, suddenly outed as being delusional delinquents. Their world turned upside down, and the separate world of a modern artist was made political when Hitler rose to power in 1933 and his brownshirts started to roam the streets targeting racial and ideological enemies. Beckmann was unsurprisingly designated by the Nazis during 1936 as a degenerate artist, a 'cultural Bolshevik', for his uneasy, distorted Weimar Republic era art. Over 20 of his artworks were included in an 'exhibition of shame' that visited a dozen German cities to denounce their degeneracy, then either confiscated, sold abroad or destroyed.

In Hitler's speech introducing the National Socialist approved version of Great Art in 1937, he raged against the modern artist's 'gruesome malfunctioning of the eyes'. Beckmann lost his job as art professor at the Frankfurt Städel art school and, under a total ban on modern art, his ability to sell his paintings, and be heard. He always knew there would be consequences to breaking taboos, to seeing so vividly how the barrier between dreams and normality was breaking down, but was stunned by the extent of the social trauma, the ferocity of the hatred.

He never tried to hide his disgust with Hitler's ruinous, abominable Germany, the nightmare made real, exemplified by 1938's sinister, tormented, comic and Bosch-like crowded furies of 'Bird's Hell', where grotesque feathered flesh – and newspaper – eating, knife-wielding bird-humans pay bloodthirsty homage to a multi-breasted fertility goddess, depicting a world being overrun by cruelty, brutality and inhumanity. Naked, fragile humans gather, hunted and haunting, forced to obediently raise their arms in a Nazi salute. Beckmann referred to himself as a 'teller of truths' that were difficult to put into words.

Leaving Germany the day after Hitler's diabolical, freedom-crushing, anti-art, anti-internationalism speech, Beckmann eventually made it to America, via a decade of precarious, self-imposed exile in occupied Holland, where there was cold, hunger, danger and desperation. Quappi, who had married him when he was a respected leading light in the arts community and wider society, was still by his side now that everything was lost, including a future. He would never see Germany again.

Finished in 1941, 'Double Portrait' with Quappi, his first double portrait of both of them for 16 years, when they had made it to Amsterdam after years on the run, is a dark, weighty picture of a different couple from the more playful one seen a decade and a half earlier – close, but with a little more distance between them, still clearly lovers but now in a different world. There are different pressures and an emotional isolation under the shadow of war and the unique mood it draped over all everyday life, which had once to him been so romantic and exciting. Beckmann is ahead of his wife, leading the way, needing some alone time. She holds a bunch of flowers and gently rests her hand on his shoulder, respecting his need to be with his own thoughts, his own secrets, the

20-year age difference much more obvious as he clings onto a walking stick.

He arrived in New York with Quappi when abstract expressionism was the energetic new wave, making his representative paintings seem, temporarily, a little pre-war, even conservative; his particular unsentimental rejection of romantic idealism, a hybrid of the medieval and modernist, of Bosch and Cézanne, appeared cautious next to the Pollocks and Rothkos. He hadn't been swayed by the arrival – and departure – of the Dadaists, so he wasn't going to be suddenly seduced by another cultural emergency – for him, merely one more distraction from his own passions, which couldn't be easily defined and labelled.

He was also a few decades older than the prowling, growling new art monsters, which threatened to create a different kind of exile. It was a time of youth and few artists forcibly displaced survived it with their talents intact, let alone able to extend them in their new, alien environment.

The extent of Beckmann's mythic imagination, what he referred to as his 'transcendental objectivity', was underestimated and he would influence the 1960s reaction to abstract expressionism, the redefining of the historic power of painting symbolised by the figurative, intensely humane, post-abstract neo-expressionism of Philip Guston.

Stimulated by the energy of New York, finding it a 'pre-war Berlin multiplied a hundredfold', he produced Picasso and Rembrandt-level numbers of intense, revelatory self-portraits, introspection and egotistical vanity bursting at the seams. One of his last works was 'Falling Man'. A chunky, flattened, semi-naked figure, as if carved from wood, was captured, painted from behind, plunging gracefully through the dislocated space of Manhattan, tearing through infinity, halted in life, kept above the Earth and toward the Earth.

Beckmann was obsessed by the space an artist must fill when making a painting, and the way a painting with depth and volume pressed into its two dimensions made him feel secure, faced with the infinity of space – 'the great void and uncertainty of the space I call God.' This compression of space was something Bowie would do in his own paintings, with his origins in the German expressionism that fired Beckmann into other dimensions. 'My aim,' Beckmann once said, 'is always to get hold of the magic of reality and to transfer reality into painting – to make the invisible visible through painting.' He found the experience of transforming three into two dimensions to itself be full of magic.

In 1950, 'Falling Man' was another episode in the eternal fall of the hubristic Icarus, falling from the sky again and again. There is nothing more he can do. It was his fate. But after 11 September 2001, a falling figure framed by two burning skyscrapers, smoke gathering around his feet, diving toward certain death, with a face we cannot see, final thoughts streaming through his mind, was to become a different kind of falling man, a different kind of legend.

One of Beckmann's New York self-portraits, 'Self Portrait in Blue Jacket', was shown as part of an exhibition at the Metropolitan Museum of Modern Art, *American Painting Today*. (A group of upset abstract expressionists including Pollock, de Kooning and Rothko forcibly complained in writing that they were not included, the punk painters wanting some Establishment love.) Beckmann's colours were bold and loud now that he lived in New York. He painted himself looking calm, bringing a lit cigarette to his mouth, looking to the side, lost in thought, deep inside his mind, which took in everything. He even looks, after all his effort during the crushingly worst moments of the twentieth century, a little lost in time.

A great self-portrait is ultimately a way of looking inside who you are from the outside, examining the exterior from within the interior. It can be an impression of your thoughts, and Beckmann would paint his with such forensic penetration it was like he was searching for the source of what he called, after his terrifying experience during the Great War, his 'soul wounds'.

Beckmann also used his self-portraits to create different characters and try on a variety of poses, painting himself as circus master, musician, Pierrot, acrobat, clown, aristocrat, dandy, existential loner, nightclub manager, Pontius Pilate or sailor, rarely without a cigarette. It is the kind of self-consciousness Bowie relished playing with, especially on *Blackstar*, circling at the end the great veiled mystery of the self, getting ready to not be himself, past pausing, falling through his life, caught between thought, reason, intellect and delirium, hallucination, madness, thinking unbearable thoughts of what might have been.

He'd always felt comfortable with having a conclusion in mind, as an endless would eventually take a turn for the worse, and Ziggy, let alone the fucking Thin White Duke, might always be with him, and how many more places can he really go to and see and enjoy without feeling he's got nothing left to feel.

He'd grown accustomed to how the pace of life increases as you grow older, as if there's a rush towards the end, the last few pages of your story flying by, characters saying their last words, making their final gestures. You used to soar through the air as if the ground would always be far below you, of no interest to you, and then suddenly, it was racing towards you, you were racing towards it, and a crashing final embrace. He found he could handle that, though. Songs and books and art had readied him; reading and listening was a form of freefall.

But that conclusion – not just yet, even if pleasure now came mostly through thinking, and loving and being loved, and dreams and ideas which seemed clearer and richer than ever.

On 27 December 1950, Beckmann was on his way to the museum to see his portrait as part of the exhibition, a significant moment for him, and as he walked from his nearby apartment, taking a route through Central Park, he had a fatal heart attack on the corner of 69th Street and Central Park West.

Three days before, on 24 December, he had finished his ninth triptych – his first, the devastating, end-of-reason sadness of 'Departure', issuing an urgent warning about a ferociously changing, increasingly chaotic Germany, was produced in the mid-1930s. He was still full of ideas for future work and still believed there was time left to work in his new home. He had been extremely productive and was at the height of his powers. He would probably have started a new painting on 28 December, moving on after the temporary satisfaction of seeing his eighty-third self-portrait hanging in the distinguished Metropolitan Museum, all that thirties shame eradicated. He'd worked hard on the triptych since April and he dedicated 'Argonauten' to the adventurous trip of Greek heroes on their quest for the golden fleece, on a ship called *Argo*.

Was the painter's life now complete, even though his death was unexpected? There were plenty of references in the triptych to his art and life, making it an evocative autobiographical allegory of the life of the artist as well as a wider allegorical representation of an artistic life, a saga of worldly tribulation and eternal reward.

Quappi, who would outlive her husband by 36 years, dedicated the rest of her life to his legacy. She would write that Beckmann saw his falling man as having been thrown from the cloud by angels; he was falling to Earth, where he would live amongst its horrors, but also its delights, until he was finally freed.

REALITY AND BEYOND

For a while, after the emergency heart surgery he underwent in 2004 to treat an acutely blocked artery, falling ill in the middle of a 62-date tour of Europe and North America, tumbling from the tightrope, caught seriously off guard, it seemed that *Reality*, released in 2003, would be the last David Bowie album ever made.

A fantasy follow-up to the never-made follow-up to *Scary Monsters*, it also proposes a possible final album title, a question as much as an answer. But before his illness, there were hints of further revelations and a looking forwards towards a final kind of settled down, sorted out, seriously revealing, ultimately fluctuating David Bowie debut, beyond reality and the empty spaces around it, where he could finally be himself.

Instead, the reality it led to was one of deep, unsettling and intriguing uncertainty. After years of hearing a knocking at the door at night, as if that was that the long-time death-fetishist might have to let in what DH Lawrence in his haunting 1914 poem about art and transcendence 'Song of a Man Who Has Come Through' called the three strange angels. (Lawrence was a favourite writer of Bowie's; his 1928 modernist, humanist but mostly scandalous, expletive-laden novel *Lady Chatterley's Lover*, which led to the freedoms of the 1960s and 1970s that Bowie revelled in, was on Bowie's list of 100 favourite books.)

The angels represent the difficult sometimes frightening elements of change and transformation, urging one to embrace a new stage of life, engage with the final complexities of existence and find hidden spaces to explore.

The messages of love and support after news of the heart attack were a rehearsal for the canonising outpouring of grief, gratitude and shock that would greet his death twelve years later. It was not time though, yet, for a last line. There was plenty of unfinished business.

Sometimes it seemed as though too much was expected of him, too much read into his songs and history, a responsibility he hadn't asked for. Or maybe he had, simply by persevering, and coming through, as David Bowie, with his understanding that poetry, performance, theatre and art are inextricably linked to healing and growth, and how we all have a fundamental if unconscious need for ritual, for enchantment and myth. He was a true inheritor of ancient traditions, believing in the mysterious, believing in DH Lawrence's three angels.

After a sudden, unexpected brush with fate, a vivid sighting of the final enigma, a blank screen, there was, after all, a lot of life left – if not to be lived exactly at the pace he was used to travelling at and possibly not involving another record. As he said from his hospital bed as he recovered, with some classic English keep-your-pecker-up fortitude, he wasn't going to write a song about what happened. He didn't want to write about the end, or even just past the end, until he'd fixed a few problems.

He'd float a few things out there, occasionally appear in public, make guest performances, piece together a life in ways yet to be determined, but at times he seemed to have become the faded, reclusive figure he'd only played before in films, metaphorically disappearing into the margins with Thomas Pynchon and Syd Barrett, becoming an expert at living in the here and now with nothing new to say, sighted now and then heading into the mountains.

His energy always impelled him to look forward, to feel now, at last, he was really beginning. The man who was interested in everything, finding a way to put that into the next song, the next set of songs, had reached a real turning point, that needed a significant change in attitude and appearance.

Illness and frailty sent him into exile where mystique built around his name alone and the silences that grew between appearances, messages, displays and diminishing musical output. Any rebirth and renewal in his final few years came in different forms and with a different sense of himself as a project, treating his life as a work of art that would only be completed by a death that suddenly raced towards him.

Reality, as the latest example of late-period Bowie, was released to a mild, typical tussle amongst critics about where it fitted inside Bowie's history – the best since when, then, or the other, another 'nothing much to see here', perhaps a positive sign Bowie could yet catch up with himself or simply keep being himself. It still seemed to be too early to be considering it a potential last album, but if it had ended up being the last one he ever made, it would have meant that the last track on the last David Bowie album would have been 'Bring Me the Disco King'. Which suggests, at least to Bowie – he didn't know about you – that it was never too early to start planning.

The song had been through many incarnations, beginning as part of the *Black Tie White Noise* sessions sounding glib and obvious, not implausible enough, too much like its title, disco as disco, and not enough like something with a sting in its tail. He said he considered it for *Earthling*, but where was the derangement, the strange atmosphere, something that would suit the sly, confrontational shows he was playing at the time, stark in their no-nonsense drive?

Something about the Disco King's evocative glimpses of his life and twentieth-century trajectory could have easily appeared on *Hours* and *Heathen*, part of that memory trilogy with *Earthling*, as he set the stage for the next few years. This was about the time his new addiction – following the records, the books, the recording studio, the sex, the drugs, Eno, the fame, the travel, the collecting, Iman, all those things that helped him adjust to the world, was the internet, the ultimate tool of pleasure and self-transformation, which he could see coming, and see where it was going, before most – and where it was taking humanity, algorithms and bots pushing everyone this way and that, more connected than ever, lonelier than ever.

But he was saving the song, tinkering with it, letting it build up in his mind so that when he sang it, you'd get the feeling he could hear his own heart and see the future getting nearer and blacker.

In the end, it was Mike Garson, who'd decorated *Aladdin Sane* with derangement, a springing into life, and here swept up some grievous bodily swing and tangled swagger, and Tony Visconti, on the way to becoming his producer to the end, who helped Bowie work it out. Not as disco, or a processed disco, but traces of lived experience and raw experience.

It's the theatre of Bowie, remembering a time, but somehow not looking back, when it seemed that pop music – or rock music – could define a new, free time. The song is a series of fragments, loops, declarations, motifs and moments, situating it in various spaces against a backdrop of disconnection, lingering in the groove and then not. It can sound like the last two records he heard before getting to finishing off the song were by 'Hold On' by Tom Waits and 'Transmission' by Joy Division.

It starts as though it's definitely the end of something, possibly the world, possibly of some sort of series he only had in his head, or a road trip, a fever dream, a life that contained some of his own, the life of a fantasist inside the life of a loner, expressing a little regret about all that excess and all that self-absorption.

Two or three of the verses and some of the lines, cut up with a relish that would make Luis Buñuel smile knowingly and Lou Reed roar with rare laughter, come straight out of *Diamond Dogs*, of *Scary Monsters*, and can be heard shadowed in the last songs and dark fairy tales of *Blackstar*. He keeps catching sight of his own reflection, making connections between unrelated things, with the mindset of a Parisian *flâneur* wandering through the Paris arcades.

Maybe as he was making it, he intended *Reality* to be his last album, as in one of those that records that continued the sequence he'd begun 36 years before, a grand exit breathing through the years somewhere between 'My Way' and 'Exit Music for a Film'. He's giving up the old-fashioned constant record release and accompanying punishing world tour schedule – which would eventually bite back – but though still bristling with energy, he suggests that soon there will be nothing left to release. It's the end of the line; the end of all that continuity.

WHERE AND WHEN

He'll be back, but never again as the maker of albums, as the star of big business tours that take up so much time and keep him away from his family. There'll be songs, but released in bursts of activity, if and when, as the modern equivalent of extended plays, or even as plays themselves, as theatrical pieces and autobiographical films, new forms that replace the album.

'Disco King' was one of his longer tracks and the last track on what could have been his final album, so the extreme fan of albums would have taken it seriously. Even as the idea of the album was becoming more nostalgic than utopian, the idea of a last track, on the increasingly illusory idea of a record's side two, was something to be treated with respect. On compilations or playlists of Bowie songs that consist only of songs that end his albums, a scattering blast of last words, last messages, last thoughts, recollections and reminders, 'Bring Me the Disco King' could be the last track amongst last tracks. A possible last instruction on how to live in a fragmented world of ever-multiplying identities.

On a Bowie playlist that could be called the Impossibility of Conclusions, a selection of some of those great ways he found again and again to bring an album to a close, 'Bring Me the Disco King' would come after 'Rock and Roll Suicide' from *Ziggy Stardust*, 'Subterraneans' from *Low*, 'The Bewlay Brothers' from *Hunky Dory*, 'The Supermen' from *The Man Who Sold the World*, 'Memory of a Free Festival' from *Space Oddity*, 'Lady Grinning Soul' from *Aladdin Sane*, 'The Secret Life of Arabia' from *Heroes*, 'Red Money' from *Lodger*, 'It's No Game (Pt 2)' from *Scary Monsters (and Super Creeps)*, 'The Wedding Song' from *Black Tie White Noise*, 'Underground' from the soundtrack to *Labyrinth*, 'The Dreamers' from *Hours*, 'A Better Future' from *Heathen* . . .

'Bring Me the Disco King' wouldn't be the last song he ever wrote, or the last song he ever sang live – the last song he sang on the *Reality* tour, his last performance before he fell ill, crawling through the pain, was 'Heroes' – but for a few years it would be the last song fixed in place on a studio album made as a purposeful selection of original songs that was deliberately structured to end the record the way it did. For a few years, it would be the end of something. In the end, it was the beginning of one long pause, where there were no clear conclusions about where it all would all lead, and why should there be?

'Heat' was the perfectly strange, slow-burning, sombrely exciting last song on *The Next Day*, his penultimate album, coming down from the mountains after an 11-year pause, when it was very definitely time for Bowie to start bending reality because there was only so much time left. It would be another candidate for the very last song on a compilation of last songs that represent the obsessional finesse and delicate power of Bowie, haunted and hounded by disintegration and fragmentation, staggering under a black cloud.

It's based on his impressions of the gravity-defying Japanese novelist Yukio Mishima's majestic and gorgeously tragic novel, *Spring Snow*, the first of his Sea of Fertility tetralogy, so he's wearing the mask of its writer – another blending of his life with another, in this case with a writer whose major theme was masks, who wrote about stars and their masks, and the public role all humans are destined to play out. Bowie is compressing into four minutes his love for Japan, for Buddhism, for Yukio Mishima – who lived a life of unending self-invention and used another name to cover his real self – for beautiful prose, for romance, for mountain views, for aphoristic statements, for mystery, for the sheer commitment of an artist to his art and life.

In November 1970, Mishima, aged 45, Japan's most famous writer, committed *seppuku*, the ritual suicide of the samurai, traditionally involving final decapitation by an apprentice, on the day that he delivered the novels that made up his tetralogy and wrote the words: 'Human life is limited but I would like to live forever.'

The spectacular way he left life defined his life as much as anything he achieved as a novelist, essayist, poet, actor, director; he is famous for dying as much as writing. He regarded suicide as a work of art and turned out to mean it.

He wrote a short story called 'Star' in 1960 about the trials and tribulations of an adored, exalted 23-year-old film actor who is falling apart physically and psychologically. His fans would kill for a moment with him. He loves it, mostly, but then starts to wonder – is there ever a way we can escape how others see us? A tragic conflict ensues if you can't find a self, or if you aren't sure you want to because it scares you.

When the camera rolls and someone shouts action, Bowie immediately becomes someone else: a Nietzschean Buddhist, an alien rock and roll star, a witness to an American nightmare, a fascistic coke addict, a young, nervy dad, a blind prophet, king of the goblins, a blonde bombshell, a professional celebrity, the playful and daring, melancholy and sensitive Pierrot, the governor of Judea who condemned Jesus to death, the smartest man in the world, a crooner with a never-ending yearning for a piece of meaning, for an inspiration point, and then, when he comes out of character, he crashes back into his own obsessions and anxieties, his own volatility and uncertainty.

After he has spent days switching back and forward in time filming scenes out of sequence, going from night to day, business meeting to sex scene, eating to sleeping in a matter of minutes, he finds the strict chronological order of life boring and disappointing.

In the cathartic, naturally cryptic last song from *Blackstar*, Bowie's last studio album, 'I Can't Give Everything Away', recorded when he knew something was very wrong, he can't help feeling low, but he can't help but try to blow some more minds. He's letting us in on a tragedy, shapeshifting before our eyes, building up to a climax that's like no climax at all as everything turns upside down and everything emerges helter skelter from the pools of memory. And some things have to remain private, even as he seems to give everything away.

At the end of his final album, a Bowie song with a glorious, desperate saxophone solo, a fantastic, desperate guitar solo, a 'low' voice that challenges the mind. It's a celebration of being light, of being high, of dancing, of almost levitating. He's completing the formidable task of sublimating his warring inner personalities into a single creative character. Here is an entertainer hero admitting, one way or another, there's no limit to how far a dream can take you. The silence at the end – at the end of side two of an album – becomes part of the song, and part of what happens next, the stillness of death that is the one certain and common thing to all of us in the future. A little bit of a downer, some would say, thinking that maybe by the first decades of the twenty-first century, the pursuit of grace and beauty is a little obsolete.

Even as he falls, half in the real world and half in a haunted landscape, he's still charting the movements of a mind towards greater understanding, exerting control while at the mercy of the gods. He can't help himself. The self is a blindfold; one looks but one begins to understand he cannot see. At the end, the veil is both lifted and restored. He doesn't seem to flinch as he makes another album that could seem like his first, something he had never made before, but which wouldn't have existed without everything that had come before.

EVER AND EVER

Another candidate for a last song amongst last songs might have come much earlier. Around *Station to Station*, when for a time every day and night sent him spinning close to a near-death experience, closer and closer to the edge of all things, might have been the first time he seriously thought that the last track on side two of his new album might be his goodbye, and what to make of that.

Station to Station closes with Dimitri Tiomkin and Ned Washington's extraordinary, exquisite 'Wild Is the Wind', a fragile, fearful reaction to the fragile, fearful Nina Simone version of a song originally sung by Johnny Mathis as the theme for a 1957 western with the same title. The Mathis original was weighed down by bitter, shrill strings and the rushed, boyish balladeering blankness of Mathis, like he just didn't have the experience and insight to know what he was dealing with, what problems to solve. But Simone found the air, the ice, the patient, battle-weary grandeur, the modern tragedy, the sadness. She turns it into a story connecting her with uncounted and uncountable ancestors.

Bowie transforms it but sticks to her rules, the temple she built from a precise kind of loneliness, the complexity of being adrift and alone, the truth she was demanding, in a world where telling the truth was increasingly a revolutionary act. It had been passed from one icon to another, from one act of reverence to another, one intelligent, delving mind straining for meaning to another.

It can also be seen as a tribute to Tiomkin, for bringing us the scores to films *Duel in the Sun*, *High Noon*, *Giant*, *It's a Wonderful Life*, *Rio Bravo*, *Shadow of a Doubt*, *Red River*, *The Unforgiven*, *The Thing From Another World* and *Lost Horizon*. And

Ned Washington, for finding the words to such standards as 'My Foolish Heart', 'Stella by Starlight', 'On Green Dolphin Street', 'The Ballad of High Noon', 'Town Without Pity', 'I Don't Stand a Ghost of a Chance with You' and 'I'm Getting Sentimental Over You', and 'I've Got No Strings' and 'When You Wish Upon a Star' from Disney's *Pinocchio*. Where did all that come from? Life's full of moments, full of surprises, one way or another, and a lot of despairing frivolity. There would be plenty he would miss if his time was up.

'Wild Is the Wind' is a song that sounded like it already existed, like it was in the air even before it was structured and drawn into reality by the writers, like something by Bach, Beethoven or Satie, waiting to be discovered. Bowie made it exist again in a different way through his interpretation, encapsulating his understanding of the transitory things in life, for those things made more beautiful because they can't last. Like love, like life, like language itself, a cherished instrument for passing what's precious from one age to another. Like a voice like Nina Simone's, a voice like David Bowie's, abandoned and enlightened, social and isolated, forever and ever.

There's a kind of gratitude expressed by interpreting the song at a time when he was made, however painfully, to see life up close and feel it may be slipping away from him. A gratitude that such a song exists, that such a singer as Nina Simone exists and that, thanks to others, the listeners and the listened to, he has found a voice. How astonishing it is to be a human being – that's there in the song, falling into a whisper, dissolving into nothing, reminding us of our scale in time and space, and the immensity of our surroundings.

We're all of us falling, that's for sure. But how we do it is up to us. Let everyone find their own inner peace, their own inner space. There, at the end, even if it's just a song sung by a twentieth-century pop star who knew a few tricks, maybe thinking it was the last song he would ever sing, David Bowie is lifting himself up and providing some gentle advice, explaining how he made it through the confusing maelstrom of life. How he made sense of it all. Explaining how to sort through the chaos of data to find your own meaning, guidance and path, come to your own conclusions about the nature of reality. How did he survive the struggles of living? By being authentic and creative, and understanding in his final years that the end of life can be an enhancement of life.

Look . . . somewhere on YouTube, where he's settling into his new position, throwing new shapes, still in lively, life loving motion, still sharing his views, helping people get used to the fact that he's no longer living, that he's in a place where he doesn't have a yesterday or a day after tomorrow, but he's beginning a new chapter in the drama of the self. He's amiably talking to some interviewer who took him seriously enough to wonder if he meant it when he said he didn't believe in an afterlife . . . He didn't say he didn't believe in an afterlife, he replies.

I believe in a continuation, a kind of dream-state without the dreams. Oh, I don't know. I'll come back and tell you what I think when I'm gone. I might be coming back and telling you now.

Thanks and Noted

Thanks to David Bowie, for living out loud, and always deepening the mystery.

This is the second book I have written about David Bowie. I have also written essays, articles and other pieces for various publications and organisations, because there is always something new to write about Bowie. The more you think you know the more you discover how much the stories and myths and even the facts of David Bowie keep changing shape. Maybe there's a third book I could write about Bowie, to complete a trilogy, always an attractive idea.

Thanks to Iain McGregor who commissioned my first David Bowie book in 2016, *The Age of Bowie*, and also commissioned this one, encouraging me to write more about Bowie and see where it might take me.

Absolute love and golden thanks to Elizabeth Levy, with me at every stage of the writing; checking, suggesting, patiently listening to my rants, and rescuing me more than a few times. Her commitment to the book made it immeasurably better and as collaborator, adviser and partner, she is my Alomar, Coco, Duffy, Eno, Iman and Visconti.

Many thanks to Zoë Blanc at Headline for taking over the book after Iain changed flights, and helping make the transition so smooth, giving me the time and space to write with just the right level of deadline-reminding hustle. Thanks to Liz Marvin for the initial copy edit, Raiyah Butt at Headline for her diligence and Rose Cook for coordinating the audiobook.

Thanks to those I had conversations with at various stages over the last ten years that led to thinking about ways to write the second part of a possible trilogy; Jonathan Barnbrook, Sean Purdy, Madeleine Morley, Carol Morley, Chris Duffy, Sandie

Goodman, Jane Pollard, Iain Forsyth, Jim Wilson and David Le Page.

Thanks to my agent David Godwin at DGA for his continuing support; 25 years and counting.

Thanks to Mat Maitland for the 'far above' cover.

Thanks to Max Dax for permission to use the quotes on pages 32 and 338 from his interview with David Bowie that took place on 5 June 1997 in the Hamburg Atlantic Hotel and was originally published in his book *Thirty Conversations*.

The third part of any trilogy could include a version of 'Sense of Doubt' from *Heroes* performed by the Art of This, an off shoot of the Art of Noise featuring AoN original members JJ Jeczalik, Gary Langan and myself with Ian Peel. Hear it wherever you go to hear things.

PICTURE CREDITS

page 1 *top*, Cyrus Andrews/Michael Ochs Archives/Getty Images; *bottom*, Pictorial Press Ltd/Alamy
    2 *top*, Roger Bamber/Alamy; *bottom*, Trinity Mirror/Mirrorpix/Alamy
    3 *top*, ZUMA Press, INC/Alamy; *bottom*, Jack Kay/Daily Express/Hulton Archive/Getty Images
    4 *top*, CBS via Getty Images; *bottom*, Steve Schapiro/Corbis via Getty Images
    5 *top*, Kent Gavin/Mirrorpix/Getty Images; *bottom*, Images/Getty Images
    6 *top*, Denis O'Regan/Getty Images; *bottom*, Dave Hogan/Getty Images
    7 Anton Corbijn/Contour by Getty Images
    8 *top*, Lester Cohen/Getty Images; *bottom*, Retro Ad Archives/Alamy

Look and Now

A YOUTUBE BOWIE PLAYLIST

'Drive in Saturday' live at the Elysée, Montmartre, Paris, 14 October 1999

David Bowie and Iggy Pop interviewed on *The Dinah Shore Show*, 15 April 1976

'Stay' and 'Five Years' live on *The Dinah Shore Show*, 1 March 1976

'Time' live at the Hammersmith Odeon, London, July 1973

'Quicksand' live at Capitol Theatre, Port Chester, 14 October 1997

'Hallo Spaceboy' with Nine Inch Nails, from the *Outside* Tour 1995

'Bewlay Brothers' live at the Hammersmith Apollo, London, 2 October 2002

'Valentine's Day' video, July 2013

'Life on Mars' and 'Ashes to Ashes' live on *The Tonight Show Starring Johnny Carson*, 9 May 1980

'Survive' live on *Top of the Pops*, November 1999

Index

Abbey Road Studios 98
'Absolute Beginners' 74
AC/DC 291
'Across the Universe' 189, 190
Advision Studios 103
Akron, OH 134
'Aladdin Sane' 192
Aladdin Sane 157-8, 195, 224, 241, 299, 310, 333, 345, 369, 371
Alamo, Battle of the 83
Albuquerque, NM 224
Ali, Mohammed 168
'All The Young Dudes' 165
Allaire Studios 352
Allen, Daevid 141
Allen, Lee 67
'Alley Oop' 152
Alomar, Carlos 110, 180-94, 248, 260, 265, 272, 326-7, 352
Alomar, Robin 183
Amadeus, Kristina 57-8
America First 27-8
American Painting Today exhibition 363
Amsterdam, Holland 361
Andersen, Hans Christian 56
Anka, Paul 151, 152
Antolin, Teddy 339
Apollo 11 mission 124, 130-2
Apollo Theatre 64, 65, 182-3
Apple Records 129
'April in Paris' 340
Arlen, Harold 42
Armstrong, Louis 221, 356
Art and Love in Renaissance Italy exhibition 350
Art Ensemble of Chicago 291, 346
Arts Lab 109, 141
'Ashes to Ashes' 57, 121, 194, 241, 273, 314-15, 317, 319, 320, 330, 336

Astronettes 233
Atomic Age 14
Auden, WH 278
Ayers, Roy 185
Aznavour, Charles 149

Baal 324-5
Bach, Johann Sebastian 150, 309
Bacharach, Burt 177
Bacon, Francis 220, 285
Bailey, David 241
Baker, Ginger 68
Bankhead, Tallulah 357
Barrett, Syd 134-5, 141, 367
Bartók, Béla 356
Basie, Count 97
Basquiat, Jean-Michel 357
Batman: The Dark Knight Returns 170
Baudelaire, Charles 90, 163
BBC 38, 42, 104, 131, 149, 221, 240, 324
'Be My Wife' 336
Beatles 17, 37, 62, 66-7, 76, 79, 97, 103, 105, 116, 124, 127, 128, 129, 146, 162, 164, 189, 205, 206-7
Beckenham, UK 109, 141, 212, 235
Beckett, Samuel 230
Beckmann, Max 358-65
Bee Gees 127, 263
Beefheart, Captain 133
Beethoven, Ludwig van 117
Beggars Opera 273
Beiderbecke, Bix 356
Belasco Theatre 193
Belew, Adrian 110
Bell, Edward 317-18
Bell, Thom 177
Benjamin, Walter 251
Berkeley, George 230
'Berlin' 291

Berlin, Germany 237, 266, 274-8, 284, 286, 342, 356, 362
Berlin, Irving 356
Berlin Trilogy 116, 117, 176, 186, 194, 261, 262, 286, 311, 324, 335
Berlin Wall 13, 287, 321, 356
Bernstein, Leonard 356
Berry, Chuck 98, 180
'A Better Future' 372
'The Bewlay Brothers' 371
B-52s 291
Billboard 100 133, 175, 198, 200
Black, Cilla 107
Black Sabbath 150
Black Tie White Noise 337, 344-5, 368, 371
Black Trinity 240-1, 285
'Blackstar' 120, 273
Blackstar 95-6, 110, 113, 116, 118, 121-2, 145, 320, 364, 369, 373-4
Blair, Lionel 74
Blake, Peter 292
Blake, William 296, 309
Bland, Bobby 80
Blitz Club 311-13, 314, 319
Blondie 291
Blue Notes 177, 184
Boards of Canada 114
Bobby Gregg and His Friends 65
Bolan, Marc 41, 78, 99, 101-3, 106, 111, 127, 135, 142-3, 147, 233, 312
Bond, Graham 68
Bono 37
Bono, Sonny 96, 162, 166, 199-200, 202
Bosch, Hieronymus 284, 292, 361, 362

Boshier, Derek 292, 293-4, 295, 296, 298, 300, 302-4, 306-10
Boty, Pauline 292
Bowie, Angie (wife) 142, 143, 212, 215, 217, 233, 290, 348, 349
Bowie, Jim 83
Bowie, Rezin 83
Boyd, Joe 101
Boyd, Patti 241
'Boys Keep Swinging' 290, 300, 315
Branca, Glenn 141
Brando, Marlon 168, 229
Brecht, Bertolt 278, 323, 324-5, 342
Brel, Jacques 92, 157
Breton, André 161, 248
Bricusse, Leslie 99
The Bridge movement 238
'Bring Me the Disco King' 368, 371, 372
British Empire 44
Britten, Benjamin 176
Brixton, London 54-5
Broadway 56, 103, 110, 193, 303, 324
Bromley Court Hotel 68
Bromley Summer Scout Camp 76
Bromley Technical High School for Boys 62
Bromley, UK 54-5, 58, 61-3, 66, 70, 72, 73, 82, 102, 182, 187, 342
Bronx, NY 180
Brooker, Gary 150
Brooklyn 56, 96, 97
Brown, James 62, 64-5, 141, 173, 178, 180, 182-3, 185, 191, 208, 326
Bruce, Jack 68, 146
Bruegel, Pieter 297
Bryars, Gavin 254
Bubbles, Barney 293
Buchanan, Ray 65-6
Buckmaster, Paul 127-8, 130-2
Budd, Harold 254
Buddha of Suburbia 337
Buddhism 30, 92, 100, 106, 145, 271, 356, 373

Buffalo Springfield 201
Bulgakov, Mikhail 163
Buñuel, Luis 248, 249, 369
Burns, Terry (half-brother) 42, 60, 135, 145, 344-5
Burretti, Freddie 240
Burroughs, William S 89, 146, 147, 168, 279-81, 330-1, 342
Butler, Artie 97
Buzz 83, 88, 92, 159
Buzzcocks 291

Cabaret 278
Cage, John 16-17, 254, 257, 271, 281, 356
Cagney, James 356
Cale, John 90, 257
Cameron, Barrie 67
Cammell, Donald 163
Campbell, Glen 206
Camus, Albert 52, 345
Can 15
Carlisle House, Soho 308
Carnaby Street, London 78
Carroll, Jim 356
Carroll, Lewis 280
Casanova, Giacomo 163, 308
Castaneda, Carlos 211
Castle, Philip 242
Caulfield, Patrick 292
Cavett, Dick 168-70, 172-3, 179, 189, 198-9
Central College of Art and Design 292
Cézanne, Paul 362
Chagall, Marc 296-7
Chandler, Gene 346
'Changes' 137, 149, 225, 293, 336
Chantels 206
Chaplin, Charlie 10
Charles, Ray 43, 71, 174, 177
Château d'Hérouville 262, 275
Chelsea School of Art 317
Cher 96, 162, 166, 198-208
Chic 183, 291, 323, 326, 328-9
Chicago, IL 134, 291, 328, 346
Child, June 143
Chime Rinpoche, Lama 106
Chippendale, Thomas 309
Chopin, Frédéric 262

Christie, Julie 222
Clark, Candy 226
Clark, Petula 78
Clark, Robin 181
Clark Terry Big Band 185
Clarke, Alan 324
Clash 291, 292, 302
Clavet, Antony 298
Clearmountain, Bob 329
Clinton, George 191, 208
Cluster 15, 258
Coasters 207
Cochran, Eddie 64-5, 98
Cocker, Joe 99
Coleman, Ornette 70, 90, 356
Collins, Phil 334
Coltrane 185
Conn, Leslie 78-9, 82
Conrad, Tony 257
Cooper, Alice 220
Cordell, Denny 96-7, 100-1, 103, 104-5, 140
Cornelys, Theresa 'the Empress' 308-10, 313
Costello, Elvis 37, 291
Covent Garden, London 294, 317
Covid-19 7, 13
Cox, Terry 129
Cracked Actor 221, 223
Crawford, Joan 356
Cream 68, 146
Crew-Cuts 96
Crooked Billet pub 55
Crosby, Bing 207
Crowley, Aleister 34-5, 144, 146-7, 212-14, 217
Croydon 73, 74
Croydon School of Art 73
Crumb, George 141
Crystals 205
Cunningham, Merce 356
Cure 291
Currie, Billy 319
Curry, Tim 193
Curtis, King 357
Curtis, Tony 90
Czukay, Holger 291

Dalí, Salvador 248, 249
Daltrey, Roger 84

INDEX « 383 »

DAM Trio 185-6, 186, 208, 260, 261-2, 265, 272, 273, 287, 311, 339
Danes, Claire 21
Dankworth, Johnny 70
Dante, Alighieri 102, 296
Dark Enlightenment 146
Dartford 66
Dave's Reds and Blues 77
David Bowie & the Buzz 83, 88, 92, 159
David Bowie Centre 2
David Bowie Is (exhibition) 2, 118, 133, 239, 242
'David Bowie, Jack Kerouac and David Bowie' (painting) 307
David Bowie (1967 album) 85, 103, 106, 108, 117
David Bowie (1969 album) 111-12, 115
'David Bowie Twice' (painting) 306-7
David Jones and the Lower Third 82, 83
David Live 67
Davie Jones and the King Bees 77-8
Davies, Ray 81, 99
Davis, Dennis 185-6, 208
Davis, Miles 68, 107, 136, 177, 257, 260, 262, 265, 272
Day, Doris 78, 164, 180
De Bono, Edward 271
de Kooning, Willem 363
De Niro, Robert 229
Dean, James 90, 167
Dearie, Blossom 356
Decca Records 77, 78, 79
Defries, Tony 181, 212, 216-17, 290, 325, 349
DeGeneres, Ellen 29-30
Delfonics 177
Delyanoff, Sophia (character) 166
Denmark 24, 106
Denmark Street, London 106
Deram Records 99, 103, 106, 108
Detroit Symphony Orchestra (DSO) 175, 177

Diamond Dogs 67, 110, 117, 168, 179, 182, 194, 195-6, 237, 250, 251, 279, 333, 369
Diamond, Neil 205
The Dick Cavett Show 168-70, 172-3, 179, 189, 198-9
Dick, Philip K 255
Dickens, Charles 99, 181
Diddley, Bo 66, 181
Dietrich, Marlene 164, 278
Disney 55-6, 175, 376
'Distant Early Warning' 271
Dix, Otto 359
Dizzy Gillespie Quintet 43
'D.J.' 290
Döblin, Alfred 278
Dr Barnado's 82
Dogme 95 20-2, 24-5
Domino, Fats 57-8, 67
Donatello 340, 342
Doncaster 36
Donegan, Lonnie 76, 98
Donny McCaslin Quartet 113
Donovan 108
Donovan, Terence 241
Don't Look Now 222
Doors 323
Doré, Gustave 102
Dorsey, Gail Ann 352
Dos Passos, John 280
Double Trouble 326
Dowland, John 174
DownBeat 181
'The Dreamers' 372
'Drive In Saturday' 137, 336
Drury Lane Arts Club 109
Dudgeon, Gus 126-8, 130, 131
Duffy, Brian 240-4, 292, 293, 298-300, 317-18
Dvořák, Antonín 105
Dyer, George 285
Dylan, Bob 66, 88, 89, 90, 98, 99, 109, 124, 140, 141, 164, 260, 291

Earth, Wind and Fire 291
Earthling 337, 368
Edwards, Bernard 183
Egan, Rusty 311, 319
Eichendorff, Joseph von 354
Electric Avenue 54

Electric Ladyland 189
The Elephant Man 303-5, 324
Elgar, Edward 44
Eliot, TS 18, 95, 280
Ellington, Duke 83, 97
EMI Records 101, 325
EMI Studios 98, 129
Eno, Brian 15, 17-18, 25, 29, 116, 253-60, 261, 266-72, 281, 284-7, 291, 298, 337, 352, 368
Epstein, Brian 66-7
Essex Music 98
Eurovision Song Contest (ESC) 150
Evans, Bill 106
Evans, Gil 74
Everly Brothers 66, 102
'Everything's Alright' 162
Extras 42

The Face 318-19
The Factory 312
Fairport Convention 101
Faith, Adam 78
Faithfull, Marianne 162, 165-6, 203, 291
Fall 136, 291
'Fame' 179, 182, 183, 185, 189-92, 198, 237, 269, 313, 336
Fame, Georgie 78, 97, 107
Fantasia 175
Farlowe, Chris 108
Farrow, Mia 229
Farthingale, Hermione 92
'Fascination' 191-2
'Fashion' 313, 336
Fassbinder, Rainer 278
Feathers 92, 126
Feld, Mark 78, 99
Feldman, Morton 257
5th Dimension 206
Film 230
Finnigan, Mary 141
Fisher, Matthew 150
Fitzgerald, F Scott 78
'Five Years' 39, 157
Flares 179
Floor Show (1980) 159, 161-2, 166, 202, 233
Florence, Italy 340-1, 342

Flowers, Herbie 129
Flux Fiddlers 177
Flying Lizards 291
Folk Club 109
Frampton, Owen 62-3, 73
Frampton, Peter 62
France 52
François, Claude 150
Franklin, Aretha 177
Freed, Alan 57
Fripp, Robert 110, 183, 254-6, 260, 261, 287, 291, 313, 327, 352
Froese, Edgar 208
The Fugitive 225
Fugs 90, 106, 107, 141
'Funky Music (Is a Part of Me)' 191
Fury, Billy 66

Gabrels, Reeves 110
Gabriel, Peter 259
Gamble, Kenny 174-5
Gang of Four 291
Garbo, Greta 356
Garcia, Jerry 229
Gardiner, Ricky 110, 273
Garland, Judy 42, 169
Garson, Mike 191-2, 369
Gauguin, Paul 18
Gaye, Marvin 181
Genesis 259
Genet, Jean 52
Gentle Giant 102
George and the Dragons 76
Gervais, Ricky 42
Getz, Stan 136
Gillespie, Dizzy 43, 70
Ginsberg, Allen 60, 89, 356
Glass, Philip 17, 44, 209, 291
Goblin King (character) 48
'Golden Years' 336
Goldstein, Adam 356
Gong 262, 263
Gordon, Bob 42
Gorky, Maxim 41
Gorma, Paul 306
Goya, Francisco de 307
Grass, Günter 278
Grateful Dead 229, 262
Great Migration 176

Green, Al 174
Green, Grant 356
Gregg, Bobby 65-6
Guevara, Che 300
Guggenheim Museum 350
Guiliana, Mark 113
Guston, Philip 362
Guthrie, Woody 356
Guys and Dolls 56
Gysin, Brion 280, 281

Haig, Al 43
Haight Ashbury 229
'Hallo Spaceboy' 320
Halloween Jack (character) 48, 168, 216, 307
Hamilton, Richard 292
Hampton, Lionel 356
Hansa Tonstudio 284, 325
Harburg, Yip 42-3
Hardin, Tim 140
Haring, Keith 357
Harmonia 258
Harold Melvin and the Blue Notes 177, 184
Harriott, Joe 68
Harris, Lady Frieda 213
Harris, Sir Percy 213
Harrison, George 162
Hart, Lorenz 356
Havens, Richie 140
Hayes, Tubby 68
Hayward Gallery 293
Heathen 21, 24, 27, 117, 136, 338, 352, 368, 372
'The Heavenly Music Corporation I' 255-6
Heckel, Erich 237-8
Heckstall-Smith, Dick 68
Hendrix, Jimi 85, 105, 168, 255, 326
Henry Cow 291
Henson, Jim 356
'Heroes' 237, 256, 261, 286-9, 314, 336, 356, 372
Heroes 16, 21, 116, 186, 238-9, 262, 266, 270, 273, 281, 285, 287, 290, 292, 324, 328, 371
Hesse, Hermann 354
Hindemith, Paul 354
Hiroshima, Japan 353

Hockney, David 292
Hoffman, Dustin 229
Holiday, Billie 356
Holliday, Billie 136
Holly, Buddy 98, 135, 206, 293
'Hollywood Party' 207
Holmes, Alan 'Boots' 67
Hooker Brothers 77
Hooker, John Lee 44, 62, 77, 141
Horne, Lena 356
Horton, Ralph 82, 83
Hours 338, 368, 372
Hudson, Keith 291
Huff, Leon 174-5
Human League 291
Humperdinck, Engelbert 98
Hunky Dory 38-9, 102, 116, 124, 144, 147, 148, 148-9, 196, 224, 309, 371
Hunter, Ian 165
Hutchison, John 'Hutch' 92, 126
Huxley, Aldous 211

'I Can't Give Everything Away' 373-4
'I Got You Babe' 162, 165, 202
'I Know It's Going to Happen' 345
'I Pity the Fool' 80
Icarus exhibition 295
The Idiot 21, 236, 253, 264-5, 266, 273-4, 327
'I'm Waiting for the Man' 87-8
Imagine 177
Iman (wife) 306-7, 339-40, 342-3, 344, 348, 352, 368
'Inchworm' 56-7
Incredible String Band 141
Isherwood, Christopher 41, 278
Island Records 108, 150
Isolar/World Tour (1976) 248-50, 251
Isolar II/Thin White Duke Tour (1978) 186
'It's All Too Much' 162
'It's No Game (Pt 2)' 371
Ives, Charles 356
Ivor Novello Awards 132

Jackson 5 207
Jackson, Michael 16, 43, 207, 291, 304, 329
Jackson, Milt 43, 356
Jagger, Mick 67, 84, 103, 162–3, 211, 222
James, Elmore 62
Jane (shop assistant) 63–4, 65
Jay, Peter 77
Jaywalkers 77
'The Jean Genie' 137, 269
Jethro Tull 262–3
Jimmy and Charles (shop assistants) 62, 71
John, Dr 67
John, Elton 151, 263
'John, I'm Only Dancing' 137
Johnny Kidd and the Pirates 76
John's Children 101
Johnson, Linton Kwesi 141, 291
Johnson, Robert 44, 62
Jones, Allen 242, 292
Jones, Davy 82, 162
Jones, Duncan (Zowie) (Joe) (son) 176, 276, 342
Jones, Elvin 185
Jones, Haywood (father) 36, 57, 59, 70, 82, 304
Jones, Lexi (daughter) 29, 30, 352, 352–3, 353
Jones, Margaret 'Peggy' (mother) 36, 342
Jones, Quincy 16, 43
Jones, Rickie Lee 291
Jones, Steve 251
Joplin, Janis 168, 229
Joy Division 291, 369
Joyce, James 279
'Jumpin' Jack Flash' 163
Junior's Eyes 128–9

Kabbalah 213
Kafka, Franz 195
'Karma Man' 107
Kaulbach, Mathilde von, *see* Quappi
Kaye, Danny vii, 56–7, 87, 99, 126
Keaton, Buster 10, 230, 248

Kemp, Lindsay 41–2, 233, 268, 309
Kennedy, John F 64, 149, 151, 163, 278
Kentish Wall of Sound 66
Kerouac, Jack 60, 167, 183, 197, 307–8
Khrushchev, Chairman Nikita 64
Kidd, Johnny 76
King, Albert 62, 326, 346
King, BB 37
King, Ben E 180
King Crimson 254
King, Dr Martin Luther, Jr 229
King, Rodney 346
King, Stephen 30
Kink Records 64
Kinks 17, 37, 62, 77, 79–80, 107, 124
Kirk, Roland 71
Kiss 220
Knight, Gladys 174
Konrads 76, 77
Korner, Alexis 68
Korniloff, Natasha 316
Kraftwerk 208, 248, 251, 311, 328
Kraftwerk 15–16
Kretzmer, Herbert 149–51
Kubrick, Stanley 125, 355

La Roche, Pierre 194, 242
Labyrinth 372
'Lady Grinning Soul' 371
LaFaro, Scott 106
Laing, RD 211
Lang, Fritz 196
Larger Than Life exhibition 317
Las Vegas, NV 204
Lateral Thinking 271
'Laughing Gnome' 126
Lausanne, Switzerland 340, 342
Lawrence, DH 366, 367
'Lazarus' 273
Lead Belly 356
Led Zeppelin 81, 217
Ledger, Heath 356
Legendary Stardust Cowboy 133, 134–6, 140–1

Leger, Hervé 343
Leiber, Jerry 207
Lennon, John 52, 98, 146, 177, 179, 189–90, 192, 207, 323, 356
Leonard, Gerry 353
'Let Me Sleep Beside You' 107, 108
'Let's Dance' 323, 327–8, 329, 332, 334, 336, 337, 347
Let's Dance 302, 332, 333, 337, 345
Lewis, Jerry Lee 83
Life 229
'Life on Mars' 121, 137, 149, 152–3, 225, 248, 269, 336
'Like a Rolling Stone' 66
Lindner, Jason 113
Listen My Brother 180
Live at the Apollo 64, 65, 182
'Lives' 302
Lives exhibition 293
'Liza Jane' 78
Lodger 116, 239, 241, 262, 266, 281, 285, 290, 291, 298, 300, 302, 304, 311, 315, 324, 371
Loesser, Frank 56
Logan, Nick 318
London, UK 2, 41, 52, 54–5, 74, 79, 83, 87, 90–2, 96, 100, 109, 159–60, 313
'Look Back in Anger' 315
Loren, Sophia 149
Los Angeles, CA 79, 137, 167, 172, 196–7, 205, 208–16, 218–20, 227, 230, 236, 245–7, 253, 259, 263, 268, 275–6, 295, 302, 339, 344
Love 107
Low 16, 19, 116, 186, 224, 253, 261, 262, 265, 266–7, 269, 270, 272, 273, 281, 284, 285, 290, 292, 324, 327, 328, 333, 371
Lower Third 82, 83, 159
Lubbock, TX 135
Lulu 164, 180
Lust For Life 273–4
Lynch, David 304
McCartney, Paul 98, 129
McCaslin, Donny 113–14
MacCormack, Geoff 187

McCormack, Geoff 64
MC5 71
MacInnes, Colin 74
McLaughlin, John 107
McLuhan, Marshall 271, 292
McTell, Ralph 99
Madison Square Garden 348
Madonna 329, 345
Magazin 291, 319
Magne, Michel 262
Mahler, Gustav 175
Mailer, Norman 168, 357
Main Ingredient 184
Major Tom (character) 141, 315, 320
Mallet, David 315, 316
A Man of Words/A Man of Music 111, 115
The Man Who Fell to Earth 48, 218, 224, 225, 243
'The Man Who Sold the World' 162, 164, 180
The Man Who Sold the World 115, 117, 124, 133, 144, 146, 148, 309, 371
Mancini, Henry 177
Manfred Mann 78, 83
Manhattan, NY 189
Manish Boys 79, 80-2, 159
Manson, Charles 210
Mantegna, Andrea 300
Marceau, Marcel 231, 295
Marquee Club 159-61
Marriott, Steve 84
Martin, George 96, 98, 103, 105, 127
Martin, Millicent 149
Martyn, John 101
Marx, Karl 161, 309
Maslin, Henry 189
Matching Mole 254-5
Mathis, Johnny 375
Mayersberg, Paul 225
Mayfield, Curtis 174
Meatloaf 193
Medhursts 61-3, 65, 70, 71, 76
Melvin, Harold 177, 184
'Memory of a Free Festival' 336, 371
Mendelssohn, Felix 105
Mercer, Johnny 136

Mercury Records 108, 125-7, 128, 133, 135
Merman, Ethel 260, 356
Merrick, Joseph 303-5
Merry Christmas, Mr. Lawrence 15
Merseybeat 162
Metropolitan Museum of Modern Art (Met) 363, 365
MFSB (Mother Father Sister Brother) 174-5, 177
Michael, George 332
Michaelangelo 341
Midnight Cowboy 229
The Midnight Special 159-60, 180
Mike Garson Band 191-2
Miller, Frank 170, 173
Milton, John 102
Mingus, Charles 68, 70, 71-2, 97, 106, 141
Mishima, Yukio 372-3
Mitchell, Joni 291
Modern Jazz Quartet 42-3
'Modern Love' 336
Mojos 162
MOMA 350
Monder, Ben 110, 113
Monk, Thelonious 97, 181
Monkees 82, 97
Monroe, Marilyn 146, 284
Montreux Jazz Festival 43, 326
Moody Blues 99, 128, 159
'Moonage Daydream' 137
Morgan, Lee 356
Morofer, Giorgio 311
Morrison, Jim 52
Morrissey 345
Mothership Connection 191
Motown 175, 177, 182, 183, 206
Mott the Hoople 102, 165
Move 99, 105, 108
'Move On' 285
Mr Fish 'man dress' 133
MTV 37-8, 41, 313, 323, 330
Mugler, Thierry 343
Mulaney, John 9
Mulligan, Gerry 68
Murray, George 185-6, 260, 265, 272

My People Were Fair . . . 103

Nabokov, Vladimir 285
Nagasaki, Japan 353
NBC 159
Neal Street Gallery in 317
Nelson, Adm. Horatio 293
Neu! 15
Never Let Me Down 332
Nevin D. Hurst 73
New Music Night and Day 265
Newley, Anthony 84-5, 87, 88-9, 91, 99, 151, 337-8
Newman, Tony 67
Newton, Thomas (character) 218, 220-1, 224, 225-6, 229, 243, 250
The Next Day 21, 116, 118, 238-9, 353, 372
Nico 87, 89, 90, 92, 164
Nietzsche, Friedrich vii, 30, 144-7, 210, 355, 373
'Nightclubbing' 165
Nilsson, Harry 205
Nine Inch Nails 338
'The 1980 Floor Show' 159, 161-2, 166, 202, 233
'Nite Flights' 345
Nitzsche, Jack 206
NME 318
Nomi, Klaus 198, 356
Nyman, Michael 254
Nyro, Laura 206

Oblique Strategies 270-1, 307
O'Brien, Richard 193
Obscure Records 254, 259
Odam, Norman Carl 134-6, 140-1
'Oh You Pretty Things' 39
O'Hara, Frank 356-7
Ohio Players 184
O'Jays 177, 184
The Old Grey Whistle Test (OGWT) 38, 39
On Stage Bowie (1976) 248, 248-50, 251
100 Club, London 251
Ono, Yoko 177, 356
Ormandy, Eugene 175-6
Orwell, George 5, 52, 195-6
Orwell, Sonia 195

Osborne, John 166
Osterberg, James 264
O'Toole, Peter 222
Outside 116, 337

Pablo, Augustus 291
Page, Jimmy 80, 107, 217
Parker, Charlie 'Bird' 43, 70, 356
Parlophone 79
Partners, Vendice (character) 74
'The Passenger' 273
A Patriot for Me 166
Paul, Billy 177
Peebles, Ann 174
Peel, John 101, 128
Penn, Sean 21
Pentangle 129
People 229
'People Are Turning to Gold' 315
Performance 163, 222, 223
Pet Shop Boys 320
Philadelphia International Records (PIR) 174–5, 177, 198
Philadelphia Orchestra 175, 176, 177
Philadelphia Sound 175–8
Philips Records 108, 133
Phillips, Esther 181
Philly Dogs Revue 194
Philly Dogs tour 179, 191
Phoenix, Joaquin 21
Piaf, Edith 157
Picasso, Pablo 362
Pickett, Wilson 174, 180
Pierrot (character) 48, 306, 317, 318, 330, 364
Pin Ups 160–2, 196, 263, 344
Pine, Courtney 42–3
Pink Floyd 85, 124, 135
Pitt, Ken 83–4, 87, 108, 127, 151
Pixies 44, 136
Platters 58, 207
Platz, David 98–101, 103–4, 106, 124–7, 140, 149–51
Poitier, Sidney 180
Pollock, Jackson 362
Pomus, Doc 207
Pop Group 291

Pop, Iggy 37, 107, 124, 165, 236–7, 253, 260, 263–5, 273–4, 275, 291, 333
Popeye the Sailor Man 63
Popol Vuh 291
Porter, Cole 72
Powell, Bud 70
Presley, Elvis 58, 59, 136, 152, 156, 167, 204, 207, 348–9
Pretenders 291
'Prettiest Star' 142
Pretty Things 37
Primark 61
Prince 291
Procol Harum 96, 149, 150
Prokofiev, Sergei 176
'Proud Mary' 349
Public Image Ltd 291
Puente, Tito 356
Pye Records 79
Pynchon, Thomas 367

Quant, Mary 160
Quappi 358–61, 365
Quarrymen 76
'Queen Bitch' 39

Radio Caroline 104
Radio City Hall 235
Radio London 104
Radio 1 (BBC) 104
Radio 2 (BBC) 42
Rainbow Theatre, London 233–4, 258
Raincoats 291
Ralph, May 224
Raposo, Joe 180
Rat Pack 151–2, 153
Ravel, Maurice 52
RCA Records 57, 184, 323–5, 328
Reality 118, 366, 368–70, 372
'Rebel Rebel' 29, 137, 168, 336
'Red Money' 371
Redding, Otis 62
Redford, Robert 229
Reed, Lou 37, 69, 88–91, 129, 134, 165, 183, 324, 356, 369
Regal Zonophone 101, 128, 140
Reich, Steve 17, 141, 209, 254
Reid, Keith 150–1

Rembrandt 362
Renaissance 175, 213, 300, 337, 340, 342, 350
'Repetition' 336
Revaux, Jacques 150
Rich, Buddy 72
Richard, Cliff 66
Richard, Little 43, 44, 54, 58–9, 61, 62, 64, 66, 67, 69, 89, 141, 183, 273, 328
Riefenstahl, Leni 278
Riley, Terry 17, 257
Rimbaud, Arthur 90, 220
The Rise and Fall of Ziggy Stardust and the Spiders from Mars 38–9, 65, 71, 102, 115, 123, 124, 154, 157–8, 196, 309, 333, 371
Roach, Max 43, 70, 185
'Rock 'n' roll Suicide' 157, 336, 371
Rodgers, Nile 183, 323, 326–9, 333, 337, 345
Rodgers, Richard 356
Roeg, Nic 163, 221–3, 225
Rolling Stones 37, 62, 67, 68, 79, 80, 82, 97, 98, 124, 159, 163, 201, 202, 329
Rollins, Henry 303
Rollins, Sonny 114
Ronnie Scott's 68
Ronson, Mick 69, 115, 129, 146, 154, 160, 234, 352
Ross, Ronnie 68–9
Rother, Michael 291
Rothko, Mark 224, 285, 350, 357, 362, 363
Rotten, Johnny 251
Roxy Music 17, 183, 194, 233, 254, 271, 311, 329
Royal College of Art (RCA) 292, 296
Royal College of Music (RCM) 128
Rubens, Peter Paul 284, 285
Russell, Arthur 356
Russell, Curley 43
Russell, Ken 292
Russell, Leon 206
Sade 74
Sakamoto, Ryuichi 15–16, 18–19, 29

Sane, Aladdin (character) 48, 157–8, 160–1, 168, 170, 192, 194, 216, 235–6, 241, 242, 291
Sassoon, Vidal 160, 235
Satie, Erik 257
Saturday Night Live (SNL) 198, 199
Scary Monsters (and Super Creeps) 116–17, 178, 186, 285, 313, 317, 327, 366, 369
Schapiro, Steve 224, 229, 231
Schmidt, Peter 270, 271
Schneider, Alan 230
Schoenberg, Arnold 16, 175
Scholz, Georg 359
Schwab, Coco 219, 275, 298, 300, 314
Schwartz, Delmore 89
Scott-Heron, Gil 356
Scott, Ken 147
Seeger, Pete 356
Selby, Hubert 89
Sellers, Peter 149
Serious Moonlight Tour 327
Sesame Street 180, 183, 192
Sex Pistols 251
Sgt. Pepper's Lonely Hearts Club Band 85, 97, 103, 105, 114, 117, 146, 150
Shadows 76, 78
Shakur, Tupac 357
Shankar, Ravi 229
Shaw, Sandie 150
Shepp, Archie 114
Shipp, Matthew 43
Shirelles 206
Shostakovich, Dmitri 117
Sigma Studios 174, 179
Simon and Garfunkel 126
Simone, Nina 78, 99, 376
'The Simoniac Pope' illustration 296
Sinatra, Frank 83, 136, 151–2
Siouxsie and the Banshees 291
Sister Sledge 326, 328–9
Slick, Earl 110, 183
Slits 291
Sly and the Family Stone 184, 185, 260

Small Faves 37, 72, 77, 107
Smash Hits 318
Soho, London 68, 73, 106, 159, 309–10, 312
SoHo, NY 54, 349
Sonny and Cher 96, 162, 202
'Sorrow' 162
'Sound and Vision' 272
Sound + Vision Tour 335
Sounds Incorporated 66, 67
'Space Oddity' 92, 121, 124–32, 136, 137–8, 141, 143, 170, 225, 248, 269, 273, 293, 309, 320, 333, 336
Space Oddity 111–12, 115, 371
Specials 291
Spector, Phil 96, 97, 206
'Speed of Life' 285, 336
Spiders from Mars 38–9, 65, 71, 102, 115, 160, 182, 185, 234
Spotify 120, 121, 205
Springsteen, Bruce 329
Spungen, Nancy 356
Squarepusher 114
Städelschule 360
Staples, Mavis 174
Stardust, Ziggy (character) 38–40, 48, 71, 94, 135, 149, 156–8, 160–2, 165, 168, 186, 194, 195–6, 202, 212, 216, 220, 224, 227, 229, 233–7, 240–2, 248, 251, 264, 266, 275, 307, 310, 314, 335, 348, 364
'Starman' 42, 137, 154, 170, 171, 240, 269, 315, 335, 336
Starr, Edwin 184
'Station to Station' 121, 249
Station to Station 137, 185–6, 193, 194, 205–8, 211, 213, 218, 237, 246–54, 260, 261, 326, 328, 333, 375
Stax Records 183, 198
'Stay' 336
Steele, Tommy 66, 103
Stein, Gertrude 280
Stevens, Cat 84, 99, 108, 140
Stevens, Guy 150
Stokowski, Leopold 175
Stoller, Mike 207

Stooges 107, 124, 263–4
Strange, Steve 311, 314, 315–16, 319
Stratford, London 2
Strauss, Richard 353, 354
Stravinsky, Igor 44, 141, 175, 356
Strawbs 129
Strummer, Joe 292
Stylophone 127, 128, 130, 131, 142
'Subterraneans' 336, 371
'Suffragette City' 71, 309, 336
Sukita, Masayoshi 233–7
Sullivan, Big Jim 80, 107
Sullivan, Ed 356
Summer of Love (1967) 149
'The Supermen' 371
Supremes 206
Sutherland, Donald 222
Swell Maps 291
Sylvester, Tony 184

T. Rex (Tyrannosaurus Rex) 99, 100–3, 110, 111, 147, 233
Takahashi, Yasuko 'Yacco' 235
'Take My Tip' 79
Talking Heads 259, 291
Talmy, Shel 79–81, 107
Tangerine Dream 208
Taupin, Bernie 151
Taylor, James 129
Temple, Julien 74
Temptations 175
Terry, Clark 97, 106, 185
Tesla, Nikola 356
Tevis, Walter 225
That Was the Week That Was 149
Thatcher, Margaret 74, 251, 319
Thibault, Laurent 263
Thibaut, Gilles 150–1
Thin White Duke (character) 48, 94, 164, 170, 186, 187, 209–10, 214, 216–17, 218, 224, 227–8, 230, 236, 241, 246, 249, 250, 251, 275, 364
This Heat 291
Thomas, Rufus 346
Three Degrees 175

Three Dog Night 205
Throbbing Gristle 291
Tim, Tiny 133
'Time' 336
Tin Machine 333-4, 339, 344, 345
Tin Pan Alley 78, 106
Tiomkin, Dimitri 375
Took, Steven Peregrine 101
Toots and the Maytals 141
Top of the Pops (*TOTP*) 38, 39, 131, 240, 315
Torn, David 110
Townshend, Pete 80, 81, 99
Trident Studios 129, 140, 309
Truth Social 10
Turner, JMW 309
Turquoise 92
'TVC15' 336
Twiggy 160-1
Tyler, Alvin 67
Tzara, Tristan 280-1

Ultravox 319
'Underground' 371
Understanding Media (McLuhan) 271
Underwood, George 71, 76, 77, 102-3
Ure, Midge 319
U2 259

V&A 2, 242
Valentino, Rudolph 356
Van Heusen, Jimmy 136
Vandross, Luther 183-4, 191-2
Vaughan, Frankie 78
Vaughan, Stevie Ray 110, 326-7
Velvet Underground 44, 87-9, 91-2, 107, 111, 124, 127, 141, 254

Vic (shopkeeper) 71
Vicious, Sid 152, 356
Vinterberg, Thomas 20-2, 24, 26, 29
Visage 315, 319
Visconti, Siegrid 96
Visconti, Tony 24, 96-7, 100-20, 124-6, 128, 131, 136, 137, 139, 140, 142, 146-7, 260, 261, 266, 272, 287, 298, 311, 327
Vocalion Records 78
von Trier, Lars 20-1
Vonnegut, Kurt 356

Waits, Tom 369
Wakeman, Rick 128-9, 152
Walker, Scott 44, 345
Walkers Brothers 107
Wall of Sound 206
Warhol, Andy 69, 87, 167, 284, 299, 312, 356
Washington, Dinah 136
Washington, Ned 375, 376
Waters, Muddy 71, 79
Watts, Charlie 68
Wayne, Mick 129
Weather Report 114
Webb, Jimmy 200
'The Wedding Song' 344, 371
Weill, Kurt 323, 325
Welles, Orson 168
Wells, H. G. 61, 63
Wells, Joseph 61
Wesley, Fred 178
West, Mae 146
West, 'Major' Griff 67
White Light Tour (1976) 248-50, 251
Who 17, 62, 77, 80, 85, 99, 107, 124, 157, 159, 162

'Wild Eyed Boy From Freecloud' 132
Williams, Tennessee 356
Williams, Vaughan 44
Williams, William Carlos 297
Wilson, Jackie 174, 346
Wilson, Nancy 182
Wire 291
Withers, Bill 207
Wodehouse, PG 60
Wolpe, Stefan 356
Woodmansey, Woody (Mick) 115
Woodstock 352
Wyatt, Robert 141, 254

X, Malcolm 356
XTC 291
xylophone 101, 127

Yacco Maricard 237
Yamamoto, Kansai 235-6, 310
Yardbirds 44, 81, 159
Yellow Magic Orchestra (YMO) 16, 291, 311
'Young Americans' 170, 172, 183, 198, 204-5
Young Americans 167, 174, 178, 182, 185, 190, 192, 193, 194, 196, 198, 208, 224, 259, 326, 333
'Young Blood' 207
Young, La Monte 17, 257
Young, Lester 356
Young, Neil 136, 201, 202, 291

Zappa, Frank 18, 106
Ziggy (album), *see The Rise and Fall of Ziggy Stardust*
Zimmerman, Tucker 140-1